ANALYTICAL TECHNIQUES IN CHEMICAL AND BIOLOGICAL SCIENCES

ENV BOOKS SERIES

ANALYTICAL TECHNIQUES IN CHEMICAL AND BIOLOGICAL SCIENCES

Editors

Dr. Deep Mala
Inorganic and Physical Chemistry
Indian Institute of Science, Bengaluru
(India)

Dr. Pawan Kumar 'Bharti'
Society for Environment, Health
Awareness of Nutrition & Toxicology (SEHAT)
B-225/5D, Top Floor, Subhash Gali, Road No. 7, Block B
Ashok Nagar, Shahdara
Delhi - 110 093
(India)

Associate Editor

Mr. Prasann Kumar
Assistant Professor
Department of Agronomy, School of Agriculture
Lovely Professional University, Jalandhar - 144 411
Punjab (India)

DPH

DISCOVERY PUBLISHING HOUSE PVT. LTD.
INDIA

Published by:
Namit Wasan
DISCOVERY PUBLISHING HOUSE PVT. LTD.
4383/4B, Ansari Road, Darya Ganj
New Delhi-110 002 (India)
Phone : +91-11-23279245, 43596064-65
Fax : +91-11-23253475
E-mail : discoverypublishinghouse@gmail.com
namitwasan9@gmail.com
sales@discoverypublishinggroup.com
web : www.discoverypublishinggroup.com

***First Edition:* 2018**

ISBN: 978-93-86841-59-9

Analytical Techniques in Chemical and Biological Sciences

Printed at:
Infinity Imaging Systems
Delhi

ENV Books Series, India

Calls descriptive and error free chapters for upcoming volumes of books on various environmental issues. Send your manuscripts to envbooks@gmail.com

Founding Editor (Editor-in-Chief)

Dr. Pawan Kumar 'Bharti'
Society for Environment, Health, Awareness of Nutrition & Toxicology (SEHAT-India)
1775, Sohanganj, Near Clock Tower, Delhi-7, (India)
E-mail:*gurupawanbharti@rediffmail.com*

Other Important Titles by Editor-in-Chief:

1. **Advances in Biotechnology and Ecological Sciences**
   Bharti, P.K., Chauhan, A. and Ray, J. (eds.)
   (ISBN: 978-93-5056-358-8).
2. **Advances in Agriculture and Ecology**
   Bharti, P.K.; Chauhan, A. and Ezeaku Peter Ikemefuna (eds.)
   (ISBN: 978-93-5056-362-5).
3. **Agriculture and Environmental Biotechnology**
   Bharti, P.K. and Chauhan, A. (eds.)
   (ISBN: 978-93-5056-479-0).
4. **Agriculture Crops and Food Security**
   Bharti, P.K., and Chauhan, A. (eds.)
   (ISBN: 978-93-5056-881-1)
5. **Agriculture Development and Sustainable Environment**
   Ray, J. and Bharti, P.K. (eds.)
   (ISBN: 978-93-5056-759-3).
6. **Agriculture Ecology and Environment**
   Bharti, P.K. and Olubukola O. Babalola (eds.)
   (ISBN: 978-93-5056-480-6).
7. **Agriculture Ecology, Sustainable Development and Agribusiness Management**
   Mehta Piyush; Sharma Pankaj; and 'Bharti' P.K. (eds.)
   (ISBN: 978-93-5056-851-4).
8. **Agriculture, Environment and Nano-science**
   Bharti, Pawan K. (ed.)
   (ISBN: 978-93-5056-760-5).
9. **Agriculture Production and Climate Change**
   Khalid, Monowar Alam; Bharti, P.K. and Chauhan, Alka (eds.)
   (ISBN: 978-93-86841-54-4).

10. **Agricultural Practices and Crop Disease Control**
Chauhan Alka and Sharma Anubhuti (eds.)
(ISBN: 978-93-5056-859-0).

11. **Agro-biodiversity:** ***Conservation and Sustainable Development***
Sharma, Pankaj; Singh, Narayan; and Bharti, P.K. (eds.)
(ISBN: 978-93-505-782-1).

12. **Agro-forestry and Climate Change**
Bharti, Pawan K. and Singh, Narayan (eds.)
(ISBN: 978-93-5056-514-8).

13. **Agro-forestry and Sustainable Agriculture**
Sharma, Pankaj; Bharti, P.K. (eds.)
(ISBN: 978-93-5056-786-9).

14. **Air Pollution and Ecosystem Health**
Swami Abhishek and Bharti, P.K. (eds.)
(ISBN: 978-93-5056-877-4).

15. **Aquaculture and Fisheries Environment**
Gupta, S.K. and Pawan K. Bharti (eds.)
(ISBN: 978-93-5056-408-0).

16. **Aquatic Biodiversity and Pollution**
Bharti, P.K.; Chauhan, A. and Kaoud, H.A.H. (eds.)
(ISBN: 978-93-5056-359-5).

17. **Aquatic Ecology and Biotechnology**
Bharti, P.K. and Zaki, M.S.A. (eds.)
(ISBN: 978-93-5056-451-6).

18. **Aquatic Environment and Toxicology**
Bharti, Pawan K. (ed.)
(ISBN: 978-93-5056-236-9).

19. **Biodiversity, Biotechnology and Environmental Conservation**
Bharti, P.K. and Bhandari, G. (eds.)
(ISBN: 978-93-5056-750-0).

20. **Biodiversity, Biotechnology & Pollution Control**
Bharti, P.K., and Chauhan, A. (eds.)
(ISBN: 978-93-5056-887-3)

21. **Biodiversity of Aquatic Ecosystem:** ***Significance, Threat and Conservation***
Bharti, P.K. and Kaoud, H.A.H. (eds.)
(ISBN: 978-93-5056-297-0).

22. **Biological Diversity and Ecology**
Arya, M.K.; Bharti, P.K. and Ritesh Joshi (eds.)
(ISBN: 978-93-5056-785-2).

23. **Bioremediation and Microbial Biotechnology**
Gupta, Sandeep; and Bharti, P.K. (eds.)
(ISBN: 978-93-5056-783-8).

24. **Biotechnological Approaches and Water Ecosystem**
Zaki, M.S.A.; and Bharti, P.K. (eds.)
(ISBN: 978-93-5056-779-1).
25. **Biotechnology, Agro-ecology and Environment**
Chauhan, Avnish and Bharti, P.K. (eds.)
(ISBN: 978-93-5056-757-9).
26. **Biotechnology and Environmental Management**
Arya Arun; Maheswari Raaz K., & Bharti, P.K (eds.)
(ISBN: 978-93-5056-862-0).
27. **Clean Technologies and Environmental Protection**
Chauhan, A.; Sharma, S. and Bharti, P.K. (eds.)
(ISBN: 978-93-5056-731-9).
28. **Climate Change and Agriculture**
Bharti, P.K. and Chauhan, Avnish (eds.)
(ISBN: 978-93-5056-148-5).
29. **Climate Change and Biodiversity**
Bharti, P.K. and Chauhan, Avnish (eds.)
(ISBN: 978-93-5056-360-1).
30. **Climate Change, Disaster Management and Environment**
Chauhan, Alka; Bharti, P.K. (eds.)
(ISBN: 978-93-5056-784-5).
31. **Conservation and Cultivation of Medicinal Plants**
Bharti, P.K. and Singh Narayan (eds.)
(ISBN: 978-93-5056-740-1).
32. **Crop Irrigation and Farming System**
Chauhan, Alka and P.K. Bharti (eds.)
(ISBN: 978-93-86841-40-7).
33. **Crop Productivity and Plant Disease Management**
Chauhan, Alka; Bharti, P.K. and Sadana, Deepti (eds.)
(ISBN: 978-93-5056-791-3).
34. **Eco-tourism, Environmental Problems and Sustainable Development**
Singh, Soubam Premchandra; Rathoure, Ashok Kr. and Bharti, P.K. (eds.)
(ISBN: 978-93-86841-57-5)
35. **Eco-toxicology and Eco-technology**
'Bharti', P.K. and Zaki, M. (eds.)
(ISBN: 978-93-5056-313-7).
36. **Energy Technologies for Clean Environment**
Bharti, Chhavi Kumar and 'Bharti', P.K. (Eds.)
(ISBN: 978-93-86841-22-3).
37. **Environmental Biotechnology and Application**
Bharti, P.K. and Chauhan, Avnish (eds.)
(ISBN: 978-93-5056-262-8).

38. **Environmental Conservation and Biotechnology**
Chauhan, A. and P.K. Bharti (eds.)
(ISBN: 978-93-5056-512-4).

39. **Environmental Economics and Sustainability**
José G. Vargas-Hernández; Khalid Alam Monowar and Bharti, P.K. (eds.)
(ISBN: 978-93-86841-37-7).

40. **Environmental Health and Problems**
Bharti, P.K. and Gajananda, Kh. (eds.)
(ISBN: 978-93-5056-263-5).

41. **Environmental Pollution and Biodiversity**
Bharti, P.K.; Chauhan, Avnish and Kumar, P. (eds.)
(ISBN: 978-93-5056-149-2).

42. **E-waste and Environmental Issues**
Bhalla, R., and Bharti, P.K. (eds.)
(ISBN: 978-93-5056-886-6)

43. **Experiments on Enhancement of Agricultural Yield**
Chauhan, Alka and P.K. Bharti (eds.)
(ISBN: 978-93-86841-50-6).

44. **Farming Techniques and Crop Production**
Chauhan Alka; Sharma Anubhuti; Ray Jaswant and 'Bharti' P.K. (eds.)
(ISBN: 978-93-5056-855-2).

45. **Faunal Biodiversity and Biotechnology**
Sethi, V. Kumar; Bharti, P.K. (eds.)
(ISBN: 978-93-86841-44-5).

46. **Fisheries and Toxicology**
Zaki, M.S.A.; Bharti, P.K. and Chauhan, A. (eds.)
(ISBN: 978-93-5056-452-3).

47. **Fish Habitat and Aquaculture**
Bharti, P.K.; Gupta Kr. Sanjay (eds.)
(ISBN: 978-93-5056-744-9).

48. **Forest and Biodiversity Conservation**
Chauhan Alka; Bharti, P.K. (eds.)
(ISBN: 978-93-5056-873-6).

49. **Food Processing, Management and Nanotechnology**
Chauhan, Avnish; Bharti, P.K. (eds.)
(ISBN: 978-93-5056-796-8).

50. **Food Technology and Research Advancement**
Chauhan, Avnish; Bharti, P.K. (eds.)
(ISBN: 978-93-86841-49-0).

51. **Freshwater Ecosystem and Xenobiotics**
Bharti, P.K.; Zaki, M. and Chauhan, A. (eds.)
(ISBN: 978-93-5056-299-4).

52. **Geospatial Technology and Ecosystem Assessment**
'Bharti' Chhavi Kumar; Chauhan, Alka & Bharti, P.K. (eds.)
(ISBN: 978-93-86841-36-0).

53. **Geospatial Technology and Water Management**
Chauhan, Alka; Bharti, P.K. (eds.)
(ISBN: 978-93-5056-885-9).

54. **Heavy Metals and Metalloids in Biosphere:** ***Impacts & Assessment***
Chauhan, Avnish, Gupta, Sandeep; and Bharti, P.K. (eds.)
(ISBN: 978-93-5056-860-6).

55. **Heavy Metals and Pesticides in Environment**
'Bharti', P.K.; Bhalla, Resham; Chauhan, Abhishek & Mala, Deep (eds.)
(ISBN: 978-93-86841-60-5).

56. **Land Reclamation, Soil Quality and Agriculture**
Bharti, P.K., and Chauhan, A. (ed.)
(ISBN: 978-93-5056-882-8).

57. **Limnology and Aquatic Science**
Sharma, S., and Bharti, P.K. (eds.)
(ISBN: 978-93-5056-735-7).

58. **Medicinal and Nutritional Values of Plants**
Chauhan, Alka; Bharti, P.K. (eds.)
(ISBN: 978-93-5056-883-5).

59. **Medicinal Plants:** ***Distribution, Utilization and Significance***
Sharma, P.; Bharti, P.K. and Narayan Singh (eds.)
(ISBN: 978-93-5056-734-0).

60. **Microbial Applications and Environment**
Bharti, Pawan K. (ed.)
(ISBN: 978-93-5056-515-5).

61. **Microbial Ecology and Habitat**
'Bharti', Pawan K. (ed.)
(ISBN: 978-93-5056-514-8).

62. **Microbial Environment and Bioremediation**
Chauhan Alka; K. Ashok Rathoure; and K Maheshwari Raaz (eds.)
(ISBN: 978-93-5056-856-9).

63. **Microbiological and Pharmacological Aspects of Biodiversity**
Sharma, P., Sharma, N.G.; Sharma, P., and Bharti, P.K. (ed.)
(ISBN: 978-93-5056-878-1).

64. **Natural Ecosystem and Climate Change**
Bharti, P.K., and Kh. Gajananda (ed.)
(ISBN: 978-93-5056-745-6).

65. **Nutraceuticals and Pharmaceuticals from Medicinal Plants**
Bharti, P.K., Khan, M.M. Abid Ali and Rathoure, Ashok Kumar (ed.)
(ISBN: 978-93-86841-55-1).

66. **Organic Farming and Bio-fertilizers**
Sethi, Vinaya Kumar; and Bharti, P.K. (eds.)
(ISBN: 978-93-86841-23-0).

67. **Pest Management and Agro-Techniques**
Biswas, Asim; Bharti, P.K., Chauhan, Avnish (eds.)
(ISBN: 978-93-5056-794-4).

68. **Physical and Chemical Analysis of Environment**
Mala, Deep; Bharti', P.K. & Bhalla, Resham (eds.)
(ISBN: 978-93-86841-61-2).

69. **Plant Biomass and Energy Solutions**
'Bharti', P.K.; 'Bharti' Chhavi Kumar; Rastogi, Amit and
Chauhan, Alka (eds.)
(ISBN: 978-93-86841-62-9)

70. **Plant Biotechnology and Industrial Applications**
Chauhan, A., and Bharti, P.K. (ed.)
(ISBN: 978-93-5056-884-2).

71. **Plant Disease Management:** ***Control & Elimination Strategies***
Chauhan, A., and Bharti, P.K. (ed.)
(ISBN: 978-93-86841-41-4).

72. **Plant Response to Environmental Stress**
Chauhan, Alka; 'Bharti', P.K. and Chauhan, Avnish (eds.)
(ISBN: 978-93-86841-58-2).

73. **Pollution, Plant Health and Biotechnology**
'Bharti', P.K.; Rathoure, Ashok Kumar; Tripathi, Rashmi (eds.)
(ISBN: 978-93-86841-63-6).

74. **Prakriti me Aushadhi (*in Hindi*)**
Singh, J.R.; Bharti, P.K. and Bharti, B.
(ISBN: 978-93-5056-200-0).

75. **Production of Fruits and Vegetables:** *Technologies and Challenges*
Chauhan, Avnish; Bharti, P.K. and Chauhan, Alka (ed.)
(ISBN: 978-93-86841-25-4).

76. **Seed Technology, Plant Growth and Cropping System**
Tyagi, P.K. and Bharti, P.K. (eds.)
(ISBN: 978-93-5056-738-8).

77. **Seed Treatment, Plant Health and Agro-technology**
Chauhan, A. and Bharti, P.K. (eds.)
(ISBN: 978-93-5056-810-1).

78. **Soil Characteristics and Agro-ecology**
Avnish Chauhan and Bharti, P.K. (eds.)
(ISBN: 978-93-5056-758-6).

79. **Soil Contamination and Conservation**
Ezeaku, P.I. and Bharti, P.K. (eds.)
(ISBN: 978-93-5056-737-1).

80. **Soil Quality and Contamination**
Bharti, P.K. and Chauhan, Avnish (eds.)
(ISBN: 978-93-5056-361-8).

81. **Stress Tolerance and Plant Productivity**
Kumar, Prasann; 'Bharti', P.K (eds.)
(ISBN: 978-93-86841-56-8).

82. **Sustainable Aquaculture Management**
Gupta, S.K.; Bharti, P.K (eds.)
(ISBN: 978-93-5056-797-5).

83. **Waste Disposal and Management**
Bharti, P.K.; Tabassum, B. and Bajaj, P. (eds.)
(ISBN: 978-93-5056-729-6).

84. **Waste Generation and Utilization**
Bajaj Priya; Tabassum, B., and Bharti, P.K. (eds.)
(ISBN: 978-93-5056-792-0).

85. **Waste Management and Environmental Health**
Tabassum, B., Bajaj Priya, and Bharti, P.K. (eds.)
(ISBN: 978-93-5056-777-7).

86. **Water Resources:** ***Mapping Monitoring and Management***
Tyagi, P.K., Chauhan, Avnish and Bharti, P.K. (eds.)
(ISBN: 978-93-5056-861-3).

87. **Water Resources and Agriculture**
Bharti, P.K. and Ezeaku Peter Ikemefuna (eds.)
(ISBN: 978-93-5056-481-3).

88. **Waste Resources Management:** ***Monitoring and Assessment***
Gupta, Sandeep and Bharti, P.K. (eds.)
(ISBN: 978-93-5056-799-9).

Preface

There is an increasing need for analysts to understand and be able to quantify the performance of analytical instruments. This book links together an understanding of performance characteristics with an appreciation of the limitations imposed by instrument design, leading to the interplay of the validation and qualification processes within quality assurance systems.

This book will appeal to a broad range of professional chemists, biologists, technicians and students, whether with reference to specific analytical techniques, or within a general course of study in chemical and biological sciences.

The book provides coverage of all of the major analytical techniques and their application in the most important areas of physical, life science and materials science. Each text is presented in an open learning/distance learning style, in which the learning objectives are clearly identified. The reader's understanding of the material to be constantly evaluated by the use of self-assessment and based on feed back.

Thanks are due to publisher and contributors from various institutions and universities.

The book will be helpful for the researchers, academia working in the field of physical, chemical and biological analysis including various environmental components.

Editors
(envbooks@gmail.com)

Contents

Analytical Techniques in Chemical and Biological Sciences
Edited by: Dr. Deep Mala and Dr. Pawan Kumar 'Bharti'
ISBN: 978-93-86841-59-9
Edition: 2018
Published by: Discovery Publishing House Pvt. Ltd., New Delhi (India)

1 Introduction

Analytical chemistry studies and uses instruments and methods used to separate, identify, and quantify matter. In practice separation, identification or quantification may constitute the entire analysis or be combined with another method. Separation isolates analytes. Qualitative analysis identifies analytes, while quantitative analysis determines the numerical amount or concentration.

Analytical chemistry consists of classical, wet chemical methods and modern, instrumental methods. Classical qualitative methods use separations such as precipitation, extraction, and distillation. Identification may be based on differences in color, odor, melting point, boiling point, radioactivity or reactivity. Classical quantitative analysis uses mass or volume changes to quantify amount. Instrumental methods may be used to separate samples using chromatography, electrophoresis or field flow fractionation. Then qualitative and quantitative analysis can be performed, often with the same instrument and may use light interaction, heat interaction, electric fields or magnetic fields . Often the same instrument can separate, identify and quantify an analyte.

Analytical chemistry is also focused on improvements in experimental design, chemometrics, and the creation of new measurement tools. Analytical chemistry has broad applications to forensics, medicine, science and engineering.

Analytical chemistry has been important since the early days of chemistry, providing methods for determining which elements and chemicals are present in the object in question. During this period significant contributions to analytical chemistry include the development of systematic elemental analysis by Justus von Liebig and systematized organic analysis based on the specific reactions of functional groups. The first instrumental analysis was flame emissive spectrometry developed by Robert Bunsen and Gustav Kirchhoff who discovered rubidium (Rb) and caesium (Cs) in 1860.

Most of the major developments in analytical chemistry take place after 1900. During this period instrumental analysis becomes progressively dominant in the field. In particular many of the basic spectroscopic and spectrometric techniques were discovered in the early 20th century and refined in the late 20th century.

Major analytical techniques in chemical sciences are given below:

1. Classical methods
2. Qualitative analysis
3. Chemical tests
4. Flame test
5. Quantitative analysis
6. Gravimetric analysis
7. Volumetric analysis
8. Instrumental methods
9. Spectroscopy
10. Mass spectrometry
11. Electrochemical analysis
12. Thermal analysis
13. Separation
14. Hybrid techniques
15. Microscopy

Analytical chemistry is the science of obtaining, processing, and communicating information about the composition and structure of matter. In other words, it is the art and science of determining what matter is and how much of it exists.

Analytical chemists use their knowledge of chemistry, instrumentation, computers, and statistics to solve problems in almost all areas of chemistry and for all kinds of industries. For example, their measurements are used to assure the safety and quality of food, pharmaceuticals, and water; to assure compliance with environmental and other regulations; to support the legal process; to help physicians diagnose diseases; and to provide measurements and documentation essential to trade and commerce. Analytical chemists often work in service-related jobs and are employed in industry, academia, and government. They conduct basic laboratory research; perform process and product development; design instruments used in analytical analysis; teach; and work in marketing and law. Analytical chemistry can be a challenging profession that makes significant contributions to many fields of science.

Automation has decreased the demand for analytical chemists to conduct repeated routine analysis—robots can prepare and analyze many samples, while advances in computer power allow the development of increasingly sophisticated algorithms to analyze and interpret analytical results. Though high-volume routine instrumental analyses using well-defined procedures are automated, knowledge of the organic, inorganic, and physical chemistry of the sample and the measurement is valuable, particularly when troubleshooting.

These increasingly sophisticated analytical methods and instrumentation as well as increasing regulatory requirements have opened new opportunities for analytical chemists in a variety of areas. For example, quality assurance specialists help to guarantee that analytical laboratories follow documented and approved procedures, and chemists with solid technical and computer skills are needed to develop and use complex analytical techniques. Government agencies need analytical chemists to verify compliance with regulatory requirements. Finally, corporate downsizings and outsourcing have provided the impetus for many entrepreneurial analytical chemists to start their own businesses, specializing in particular kinds of analyses or classes of compounds.

Analytical chemists are generally involved with making measurements by using sophisticated state-of-the-art computer controlled instrumentation in government laboratories and laboratories in all areas of the chemical, pharmaceutical, biotechnology, and food industries. They may also be involved in developing techniques within these laboratories as well as in the laboratories of instrumentation vendors. Analytical chemists are also suited for positions as quality assurance specialists to guarantee that procedures and protocols are followed and in quality control where they ensure the quality of products being produced.

Biological Sciences is an exciting and rapidly developing subject area. The study of living things has undergone tremendous expansion in recent years, and topics such as cell biology, neuroscience, evolutionary biology and ecology are advancing rapidly. This expansion has been accompanied by a blurring of the distinctions between disciplines: a biologist with an interest in tropical plants may well use many of the tools and techniques that are indispensable to a molecular geneticist.

Biologists address a wide variety of topics but we all use a similar method. We use observations and experiments to generate data and statistical analysis to draw conclusions from these measurements. The ability to critique the methods used in biological studies, make inferences from biological data and optimize experimental approaches will benefit scholars taking a wide range of research and project based units, as well as interpreting and evaluating studies from the scientific literature.

REFERENCE

http://pubs.acs.org/doi/pdf/10.1021/ac00007a600

https://www.omicsonline.org/the-importance-of-analytical-chemistry-in-quantitative-pharmaceutical-sciences-2153-2435.1000e142.php?aid=10657

https://en.wikipedia.org/wiki/Analytical_chemistry

http://www.sciencedirect.com/science/bookseries/01679244

https://www.acs.org/content/acs/en/careers/college-to-career/areas-of-chemistry/analytical-chemistry.html

http://onlinelibrary.wiley.com/bookseries/10.1002/SERIES8247

http://onlinelibrary.wiley.com/book/10.1002/9780470511282

https://www.monash.edu/science/schools/biological-sciences/units/bio2060

https://searchworks.stanford.edu/view/9171877

https://www.ox.ac.uk/admissions/undergraduate/courses-listing/biological-sciences?wssl=1

Analytical Techniques in Chemical and Biological Sciences
Edited by: Dr. Deep Mala and Dr. Pawan Kumar 'Bharti'
ISBN: 978-93-86841-59-9
Edition: 2018
Published by: Discovery Publishing House Pvt. Ltd., New Delhi (India)

2

Heavy Metals Analysis in Sediment and Water of Phrinkaruh River in East Khasi Hills, Meghalaya, India

Pawan K. Bharti[1] and Vijender Singh[2]

ABSTRACT

Anthropogenic factors mainly local people's activities and catchments runoff may influence the index of nutrients in river water and may alter the physico-chemical characteristics and also the whole water quality. Physico-chemical parameters play an important role into system restoration maintenance and self-regulation of water quality. Location variation in Heavy Metals concentration of the river was studied with special reference to physico-chemical parameters in the river water and sediment.

The present study deals with the preliminary physico-chemical characteristics and Heavy Metals of the river water and exhibits the status of natural quality of water with minimum anthropogenic activities, which contribute in pollution load of an aquatic system. Heavy Metals were found almost nil or in very low concentrations at selected site.

Key words: Water Quality, Pollution status, Transfer factor, Heavy Metals, river sediment.

INTRODUCTION

Water quality characteristic of aquatic environment arise from a multitude of physical, biological and chemical interactions (Dezuane, 1979). The water bodies, lakes, rivers, dams and estuaries are continuously subject to a dynamic state of change with respect to the geological age and geochemical characteristics. This is demonstrated by continuous circulation, transformation and accumulation of energy and matter through the medium of living thing and their activities (Adefemi, 2007). The present study deals with the characteristics the water nutrient chemistry, influenced by anthropogenic activity & quarrying of the geologically sediment environments and to determine the nature and degree of anthropogenic impacts on qualitative and quantitative variations occurred

[1] Shriram Institute for Industrial Research, Delhi-7, India
[2] Green Environmental Consultancy and Services, 3263, Urban Estate, Safido Bypass, Jind (Haryana), India

in nutrients in relation to physico-chemical parameters and Heavy Metals of river water and sediment.

Adequate understanding of the North-East regional streams is extremely important for the development of a realistic program for utilizing the potential of water that exist in the form of hidden water resource in the area. The impact of anthropogenic pollution from industrial, agricultural, sources, quarrying and tourists activity on water quality has concerned environmentalists and scientists for the past three decades. Ecological, geo-chemical and hydrological research has been carried out in various ecosystems to understand the factors controlling the chemistry of natural water (Baron & Bricker, 1990; Malik and Bharti, 2005a). Many of such studies have been under taken during the last two decades to understand the processes that control the hydrochemistry of alpine and sub-alpine systems of North America and Europe (William *et al.* 1993 and Psenner, 1989).

The present study reveals to characteristics the water nutrient chemistry, influenced by anthropogenic activity & quarrying of the geologically sediment environments and to determine the nature and degree of anthropogenic impacts on qualitative and quantitative variations occurred in Heavy Metals in relation to physico-chemical parameters of river water and sediment.

Study Area

The Meghalaya has been surrounded by the natural beauties with lovely trees and cool climate, which is not only a pleasant place to live in but relaxing for holiday also. This is not only a popular state but also valuable or important place for tourism. Shillong is the capital of Meghalaya state. Mowlong Cherra Cement Ltd and Lafarge Umaim Mining Ltd are the major industries of the region. The all seven states of North East India are quite famous as Seven Sisters. Meghalaya is very well known for the record of rainfall, the state consists of the two places namely Cherrepunjee and Mawsinram for maximum rainfall throughout the year. So, the maximum water resources are depending chiefly on total precipitations of the region.

Population of the region is completely depending upon the river water for drinking, bathing, and other activities. *Meteorologically,* region has a cool & pleasant climate. *Geologically,* North-east hills are enriched with various minerals and the hills near Bangladesh are rich in limestone. *Geographically,* the study area is situated in the globe on a Latitude 25° 11′ 5.8″ N & Longitude 91° 37′ 26.1″ E for Upstream site and Latitude 25° 10′ 51.9″ N & Longitude 91° 37′ 22.5″ E for Downstream site.

MATERIALS AND METHODS

The water samples were collected from Phrinkaruh River upstream (U/S sampling site A) near Phrinkaruh Village and downstream (D/S sampling site B) near Bangladesh border according to the analytical requirement in morning period 9:00 Hrs. to 10:00 Hrs. along with the water samples, sediment samples was also collected from the river bed with the help of Eckmen Dredge sediment sampler.

Table 2.1: Physical Characteristics of Phrinkaruh River Water

S.No.	Para-meters	Unit	Phrinkaruh Upstream			Phrinkaruh Downstream			Desirable Limit
			Winter	Summer	Monsoon	Winter	Summer	Monsoon	
1.	Tempe-rature	°C	12	16	15	12	17	16	-
2.	Colour	-	Clear	Clear	Clear	Clear	Clear	Clear	-
3.	Odour	-	Nil	Nil	Nil	Nil	Nil	Nil	-
4.	Turbidity	NTU	1	4	7	1	5	8	5
5.	Velocity	m/s	0.3	0.3	0.4	0.2	0.3	0.4	-
6.	TDS	Mg/l	120	118	148	125	120	155	500

The water samples for physico-chemical parameters and Heavy Metals were collected by using rinsed Borosil glassware, and analyzed with the help of the procedure described by APHA (1995) and Trivedi and Goel (1984). Colour, odour, turbidity, velocity, temperature and Dissolved oxygen were analyzed on sampling sites. Samples were collected from selected sites and immediately preserved in ice boxes, and transfer to the lab for further analysis. Water and sediment samples were digested and Heavy Metals were detected using Atomic absorption spectrophotometer. Transfer Factor (TF) was calculated according to Bharti (2007) to assess the status of Heavy Metals transfer from river water to river sediment of Phrinkaruh river. Geo-accumulation factor (I_{geo}) and Enrichment factor (EF) were calculated according to Bharti (2007).

RESULTS & DISCUSSION

Phrinkaruh river is flowing throughout a valley of North-east hills chain near the Bangladesh Border, enriched with limestone and lignite rocks, which affect the water quality of river according to the locations. Nutrients concentration, Heavy Metals and related physico-chemical parameters from selected sites are depicted in tables.

Table 2.2: Chemical Characteristics of Phrinkaruh River Water

S.No.	Parameters	Unit	Phrinkaruh Upstream			Phrinkaruh Downstream			Desirable Limit
			Winter	Summer	Mon-soon	Winter	Summer	Mon-soon	
1.	pH	-	7.6	8.4	7.6	7.7	8.3	7.5	6.5-8.5
2.	Alkalinity	Mg/l	92	81	133	96	85	130	200
3.	Total Hardness	Mg/l	107	97	128	109	101	128	300

4.	Calcium	Mg/l	38	34	48	26	34	38	75
5.	Magnesium	Mg/l	3	7	12	4	11	14	30
6.	Chlorides	Mg/l	5	2	5	6	4	5	250
7.	DO	Mg/l	9.6	9.8	8.1	8.6	9.0	8.6	-
8.	BOD	Mg/l	Nil	1	Nil	Nil	Nil	Nil	-
9.	COD	Mg/l	6	8	5	5	6	6	-

Phrinkaruh river has the spatial variations of water temperature, which plays a significant role in all physico-biochemical reactions and self-purification power of aquatic system (Badola & Singh, 1981). Higher value of temperature was found 17-°C in summer at downstream and minimum 12 °C in winter season at upstream. Turbidity is striking characteristic of the physical status of the water bodies. Although in Phrinkaruh river water is clear because there is no more pollution, siltation was the main source of turbidity in tributaries. Detritus and other non-organic material being added to water mass due to rainfall and anthropogenic activities (Camron, 1996). Maximum turbidity was recorded 8 NTU during rainy season at downstream and minimum 1 NTU in summer season at upstream. The maximum depth of photic zone provides the better biological production for all aquatic organisms (Malik and Bharti, 2005b).

Total dissolved solids were found in the range of 118 mg/l in summer to 148 mg/l in monsoon season, due to the gradual increases in velocity of river which favoured effective sedimentation (Subramanian, 1979). Chemical oxygen demand was found 5 mg/l to 8 mg/l during the study period. Chemical oxygen demand represents chemically oxidizable organic matter load in water, while biochemical oxygen demand is only biodegradable materials (Malik and Bharti, 2005c). In the present study the values observed during monsoon months may be attributed maximum biological activities and high temperature, stimulate the growth of microorganisms (William *et al.*, 1993).

The pH of natural water was controlled in a great extent by the interaction of hydroxyl ions arising from the hydrolysis of bicarbonate (Sharma, 1986). The pH of Phrinkaruh river was recorded alkaline (7.5-8.4). Total hardness is mainly due to percentage of calcium and magnesium salts of bicarbonates, carbonates, sulphates and chlorides, while the value of alkalinity occured due to presence of bicarbonates. The concentration of hardness was analyzed 97-128 mg/l during the study. Alkalinity was also found 81-133 mg/l with a small fluctuation. A positive relationship between hardness and alkalinity was recorded in river Ganga at Rishikesh (Chopra and Patric, 1994). Maximum chloride concentration was recorded maximum (6 mg/l) in winter and minimum in summer (2 mg/l). Chloride and hardness showed a positive relationship to one another (Chopra and Patric, 1994). Chloride was found in the form of chloride ion, and one of the major inorganic anion present in natural water (Malik and Bharti, 2009).

Table 2.3: Heavy Metals in Phrinkaruh River Water and Sediment

S.No.	Parameters	Unit	Phrinkaruh Upstream			Phrinkaruh Downstream			Phalankaruh Sediment mg/kg
			Winter	Summer	Monsoon	Winter	Summer	Monsoon	
1.	Cadmium	Mg/l	BDL	BDL	BDL	BDL	BDL	BDL	BDL
2.	Copper	Mg/l	BDL	BDL	BDL	BDL	BDL	BDL	20
3.	Iron	Mg/l	0.06	0.02	BDL	0.03	0.06	0.04	2800
4.	Lead	Mg/l	0.01	BDL	BDL	BDL	BDL	BDL	30
5.	Manganese	Mg/l	BDL	BDL	BDL	BDL	BDL	BDL	370
6.	Zinc	Mg/l	BDL	0.02	BDL	BDL	0.02	0.02	114

BDL = Below Detection Limit

Calcium and magnesium the dominant cations, and these represent the main weathering products, but significant hydro-chemical differences between the two sampling sites associated with the bedrock geology exist (Jenkins *et al.*, 1995). Calcium is one of the essential nutrients, which plays an important role in biological system. Maximum calcium concentration was recorded (48 mg/l) in monsoon and minimum in winter (26 mg/l). Positive relationship between, calcium and temperature was also reported by Khanna and Singh (2000) in river Suswa, Dehradun. Magnesium is also an essential element but it is toxic at higher concentration. The concentration of magnesium in Phrinkaruh river was found maximum (14 mg/l) and minimum (3 mg/l) and it was very low in comparison to Hill-streams of Uttarakhand (Bharti, 2004). During the summer season nutrients concentration in rivers and hill-streams became more. Miller *et al.* (1997) described the nutrients availability in selected environmental settings of the Potomac River and Cameron (1996) showed the similar type of fluctuation in Fraser river of British Columbia. Bond (1979) described similar nutrients concentration pattern in a stream draining a mountain ecosystem in Utah. The concentrations of Calcium were observed in similar range in Phrinkaruh river water at upstream as well as downstream in comparison to rivers and hill-streams of North India, while magnesium was found in low range. Dissolved oxygen was found 8.1 to 9.8 mg/l at upstream and downstream during the study period. Heavy Metals were found almost nil or in very low concentrations at both selected site.

Heavy Metals like Cadmium, copper, iron, manganese, lead and zinc were not found in high concentration at both sites during any season. Cadmium, copper and manganese were absolutely absent in all seasons, while Lead, Zinz and Iron concentrations were also found below detection limit in maximum samples. The concentration of iron was maximum observed 0.06 mg/l during winter season. Lead was found 0.01 mg/l in winter season at upstream site and

Zinc concentration was 0.02 mg/l in summer and monsoon season. Malik *et al.*, (2009) described the role of Heavy Metals in the surface water of north India. The results of Bharti *et al.*, (2010) were also indicated the relation of Heavy Metals and phytoplankton in a north Indian water body.

The physico-chemical characteristics of Phrinkaruh river sediment were found quite natural. It was found in silty sand category with 74% sand and 25% silt. Moisture, Ca, Mg and chlorides were found 6.1, 5.2, 0.6 and 0.3 % by mass respectively, while conductivity was observed 89 µmho/cm. Physico-chemical parameters of river sediments are also depicted in Table 2.4.

Table 2.4: Physico-chemical Characteristics of Phrinkaruh River Sediment

S.No.	Parameters	Unit	Phrinkaruh Sediment	Method
1.	Texture	—	Silty sand	IS: 2720 p-4
2.	Grain size analysiss and Silt Clay	% by mass	74251	IS: 2720 p-17
3.	Moisture Content	% by mass	6.1	IS: 2720 p-2
4.	pH	—	5.4	IS: 2720 p-26
5.	Conductivity	µmho/cm	89	Conductivity meter
6.	Calcium	% by mass	5.2	APHA (1998)
7.	Magnesium	% by mass	0.6	APHA (1998)
8.	Chlorides	% by mass	0.3	Volhard's method

Transfer factors from river water to sediment for all metals were found quite irregular. Transfer factor for cadmium was found 0, while it was found constant for copper in all seasons. It was found 93333.3, 46666.7 and 70000 in winter, summer and monsoon seasons respectively for Iron. Transfer factor was calculated 74000 in winter, summer and monsoon seasons for manganese. For Lead, transfer factor was calculated constant 6000. For zinc, transfer factor was calculated from 5700 to 22800. All results of transfer factors are depicted in Table 2.5.

Table 2.5: Transfer Factor of Heavy Metals from Phrinkaruh River Water to Sediment

S.No.	Heavy Metals	Transfer factor		
		Winter	Summer	Monsoon
1.	Cadmium	0.0	0.0	0.0
2.	Copper	4000.0	4000.0	4000.0
3.	Iron	93333.3	46666.7	70000.0
4.	Lead	6000.0	6000.0	6000.0
5.	Manganese	74000.0	74000.0	74000.0
6.	Zinc	22800.0	5700.0	5700.0

Values for Igeo and EF for river sediment are given in Table 2.6. The geo-accumulation index rating was not found positive for almost all metals. Igeo rating for lead was found 0.0, while rating was found with negative value. Besides Igeo index rating, metal value was not found more than 1.0. Enrichment factor was observed 0.0, 7.1, 1000, 10.7, 132.1 and 40.7 for Cd, Cu, Fe, Pb, Mn and Zn respectively.

Table 2.6: Geo-accumulation Index and Enrichment Factor for Heavy Metals

S.No.	Heavy Metals	Geo-accumulation Index		Enrichment factor
		Value	Igeo	-
1.	Cadmium	0.01	-6.49	0.0
2.	Copper	0.30	–1.75	7.1
3.	Iron	0.04	–4.66	1000.0
4.	Lead	1.00	0.00	10.7
5.	Manganese	0.29	–1.78	132.1
6.	Zinc	0.80	–0.32	40.7

The present results conclude that significant differences in river water nutrient concentrations exist among different environmental settings within the two subunits. Absence or low concentration of Heavy Metals shows that the water is still industrial pollution free. However, the Indian standards are not so strict (Bharti, 2007b), but Heavy Metals never cross the limits during the study period. On the basis of physico-chemical parameters and Heavy Metals, the water may be considered for drinking and other purposes.

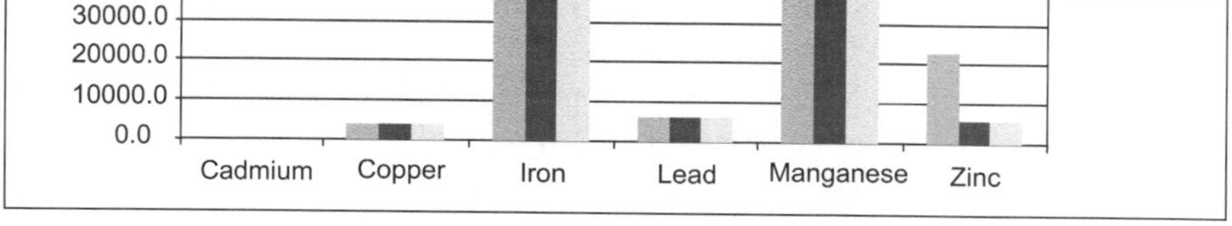

Fig. 2.1: Showing the Transfer factor for Heavy Metals in Phrinkaruh river water to sediment

REFERENCE

APHA (1995): Standard Methods for Examination of Water and Waste Water. *American Public Health Association, 19th edition. Inc, New York.* pp. 1970.

Adefemi, O.S.; Asaolu, S.S. and Olaofe, O. (2007): Assessment of the Physico-Chemical Status of Water Samples from Major Dams in Ekiti State, Nigeria, *Pakistan Journal of Nutrition*, 6 (6): 657-659,

Badola, S.P. and Singh, H.R. (1981) Hydrobiology of the River Alaknanda of Garhwal Himalaya. *Indian J. Ecol.*, 8(2): 269-276.

Baron, J. & Bricker, O.P. (1990) Hydrological and Chemical Flux in Loch Vale Watershed, Rocky Mountain National Park. In: Biogeochemistry of Major Rivers. SCOPE 42. Wiley and Sons, New York, USA.

Bharti, P.K. (2004): Limnobiological Study of Sahastradhara Hill-stream at Dehradun, *M.Sc. Dissertation*, Submitted to Gurukula Kangri University, Hardwar, pp. 102.

Bharti, P.K. (2007): Effect of Textile Industrial Effluents on Ground Water and Soil Quality in Panipat Region (Haryana), *Ph.D. Thesis*, Submitted to Gurukula Kangri University, Hardwar, pp. 191.

Bharti, P.K. (2007b): Why Indian Standards are not so Strict? *Current Science*, 93(9): 1202.

Bharti, P.K., Malik, D.S. and Rashmi Yadav (2010): Influence of Heavy Metals on Abundance of Cyanophyceae Members in Three Spring-fed Lake in Kempty, Dehradun, In: 'Advances in Aquatic Ecology, Vol. III' ed. by V.B. Sakhare, *Daya Publishing House, New Delhi*, pp. 107-111.

Bond, H. B. (1979): Nutrient Concentrations Patterns in a Stream Draining a Montane Ecosystem in Utah. *Ecology*. 60(6): 1184-1196.

Cameron, E. M. (1996): Hydrogeo-chemistry of the Fraser River British Columbia: Seasonal Variation in Major and Minor Components. *J. Hydrol.* 182(1-4): 209-255.

Chopra, A. K. and Patrick, N. J. (1994): Effect of Domestic Sewage on Self-purification of Ganga Water at Rishikesh. *A. Bio. Science.* 13(11): 75-82.

Dezuane, J. (1979): Handbook of Drinking Water Quality. Indiana University Press, pp. 3-17.

Jenkins, A., Sloan W.T. & Cosby, B.J. (1995) Stream Chemistry is the Middle Hills and High Mountain of the Himalaya, Nepal. *Journal of Hydrology*. Vol-166, No-1-4: 61-79.

Khanna, D.R and Singh. R.K. (2000). Seasonal Fluctuations in the Plankton of Suswa River at Raiwala Dehradun. *Env. Conservations J.* 1(2 & 3): 89-92.

Malik, D. S. and Bharti, Pawan K. (2005a): Nutrient Dynamics in Rhithron Zone of Shivalik Himalayan Stream Sahastradhara, Dehradun (Uttaranchal), *Env. Cons. J.* 6 (2): 63-68.

Malik, D. S. and Bharti, P. K. (2005b): Fluctuation in Planktonic Population of Sahastradhara Hill-Stream at Dehradun (Uttaranchal), *Aquacult.* 6 (2): 191-198.

Malik, D. S. and Bharti, P. K. (2005c): Primary Production Efficiency of Sahstradhara hill-Stream, Dehradun, *Env. Cons. J.* 6 (3): 117-121.

Malik, D. S. and Bharti, P. K. (2009): Ecology of Sahastradhara Hill-stream at Dehradun (Uttaranchal), In: 'Advances in Aquatic Ecology, Vol-I' ed. by V.B. Sakhare, *Daya Publishing House, New Delhi*, pp: 1-11.

Malik, D. S. and Bharti, P. K., Negi, K.S. and Rashmi Yadav (2009): Distribution of Metals in Water of an Artificial Lake at Mussoorie, Uttarakhand, In: 'Aquatic Biology and Aquaculture' edited by V.B. Sakhare, Ambajoagi, MS, *Manglam Publication, New Delhi*, pp. 77-95.

Miller, C. V.; Denis, J. M.; Ator, S. W. and Brakebill, J. W. (1997): Nutrients in Stream During Baseflow in Selected Environmental Settings of the Potomac River Basin. *J. American Wat. Resources Association*. 33(6): 1155-1171.

Psenner, R. (1989). Chemistry of High Mountain Lakes in Siliceous Catchments of Central Alps. *Aquatic Sci.* 51: 108-128.

Shrama, R.C. (1986). Effect of Physico-chemical Factors on Benthic Fauna of Bhagirathi River Garhwal Himalaya. *Indian. J.Ecol.* 13(1): 133-137.

Subramanian, V. (1979) Chemical and Suspended Sediment Characteristics of River of India. *J. Hydrol.*, 44: 37-55.

Trivedi, R. K. and Goel, P. K. (1984): Chemical and Biological Methods for Water Pollution Studies. Karad. Environmental Publication, pp. 1-298.

William, M.W., Brown, A. & Melack, J.M. (1993). Geochemical and Hydrologic Controls on the Composition of Surface Water in the High Elevation Basin, *Sierra Navada. Limnol. Oceanogr*, 38: 775-797.

Xue, H.B. and Schooner, J.L. (1994) Acid Deposition and Lake Chemistry in Southwest China. *Wat. Air, Soil Pollut.* 75: 61-78.

Analytical Techniques in Chemical and Biological Sciences **Page: 14-41**
Edited by: Dr. Deep Mala and Dr. Pawan Kumar 'Bharti'
ISBN: 978-93-86841-59-9
Edition: 2018
Published by: Discovery Publishing House Pvt. Ltd., New Delhi (India)

3 Catalysis and Inhibition of SO_2 in Atmospheric Environment

A Perspective of Acid Rain Chemistry

Dr. Arun Kumar Sharma[1], Dr. D.S.N. Prasad[1], Dr. Rashmi Sharma[2]

ABSTRACT

Today acid rain problem is one of serious global problem to environment in which pH of the rain water decreases cause harmful effect to nature, buildings, monuments, vegetation and human being also. This reaction is catalyzed by various metals and their oxide (in present study Ag(I)) so it is very important to find out such compounds which inhibit this reaction in atmosphere. In our study we report that organics are best inhibitorsfor control the rain water acidity, (Studied Isopropyl and Isoamyl alcohols, sodium benzoate, Benzamide, aniline, Formic acid) and observed particularly alcohols having greater inhibition power compared to others and these all are control the rain water acidity and save our environment. In our study kinetics of reaction have been done by calculating rate constants, rate law, mechanism, activation energy etc in acidic medium.Organics are able to inhibit the oxidation of SO_2 so by using it in the atmosphere Hence rain water acidity can be controlled.

By change at one can increase the life span of SO_2 so that vegetation, national buildings, monuments, fishes and other aquatic life of water bodies and human being are not adversely affected by rain water acidity.

INTRODUCTION

1. Air Pollution: The study of air pollution has only been of major interest to the scientific community since the end of World War II. The earliest perceived problems were those related to theincomplete combustion of coal, soot and ash abounded in the major industrial cities of the world. Air pollutants are divided into two general categories: (Dentener *et al.*, 1994)[1]

1. *Primary:* Those emitted directly into the atmosphere, and
2. *Secondary:* Those formed by subsequent reactions of primary pollutants. The first category includes soot, carbon dioxide, carbon monoxide, sulphur oxides, nitrogen oxides and hydrocarbons. The latter includes

[1] Department of Chemistry, Govt. P.G. College, Jhalawar-326001 (Raj) India
[2] S.P.C. Govt. College, Ajmer-305001 (Raj) India

sulphuric and nitric acids, ozone and oxygenated organic compounds. It is the intent of this research to study how two primarypollutants, soot and sulphur dioxide, interact to form sulphuric acid.

2. Acid Rain Precursors: A large number of organic and inorganic chemical species are released into the atmosphere by anthropogenic and natural sources. The subsequent photochemical and thermal reactions of1 these species in gas and aqueous phase form the backbone of the atmospheric chemistry. The atmospheric reactions of SO_2 and NO_x etc. are major acid rain precursors and are responsible for acidification of various forms of atmospheric water. Studies in India and abroad have shown that anthropogenic sources in the atmosphere are the major contributors of SO_2 and NO_x which are transformed in to acids such as HNO_2, HNO_3, H_2SO_3 and H_2SO_4. Several reports on acid rain have shown the contribution of nitric acid and sulphuric acid to decrease the pH of rain water. (Acker *et al.,* 2001[2] 2005[3]; Brimblecombe1996[4]).

A large number of laboratory and field studies on acid rain chemistry have been carried out globally. Turning to our own country, field studies on rain water acidity have been carried out by several workers notably, kulshreshtha (1995, 1996, 2003), Banerjee *et al.,* (2008), Saxena *et al.,* (1991), khemani *et al.,* (1989, 1994) and Gupta *et al.,* (2000).

Types of Acid Precipitation: There are two types of acid precipitation

Wet depositions: These include various forms of atmospheric water such as rain, fog, mist, dew and snow. Rain water in atmosphere is buffered by the dissolution of atmospheric CO_2.

$$CO_2 + H_2O\ H^+ + HCO_3 \qquad ...(1)$$

The calculation using equation (1) predicts that in an unpolluted and dust free atmosphere, the background pH of rain water should be 5.5 – 7.5. However natural pH of a region may be quite different than this value due to the presence of suspended particulate matter (SPM). If the SPM loaded heavily by alkaline material, as in Rajasthan (India) the pH of the rain water will be high and often exceed 8.0 on the other hand, if the soil is acidic in nature, the rain water pH shall be low. It is rightly indicated that the trace constituents, depending upon the location can significantly change this pH value. Other sulphur compounds like H_2S and CH_3SCH_3 also contribute to acid rain by their prior oxidation in to SO_2[15]NO_x is formed by biomass burning, lightening, soils, and high temperature fuel combustion.

Dry acid precipitation: It refers to the deposition of acidic gases such as NO_x SO_2 etc. and particles like nitrate, sulphate, chloride etc. in dry atmosphere.

4. Atmospheric Sulphur-Sources and Health Aspects: Sulphur as a pollutant exists mainly in three forms, reduced as hydrogen sulphide (H_2S) and oxidized as sulphur dioxide (SO_2) and sulphur trioxide (SO_3) The two oxidized forms, which are species of the oxidation states S(IV) and S(VI), also exist as ionic species; bisulphite (HSO_3^{-1}), sulphite (SO_3^{-2}), bisulphate(HSO_4^{-1}) and sulphate(SO_4^{-2}). These sulphur containing species have many sources. They can come from man's burning of fossil fuels as well as from the decomposition and combustion of organic materials, sea salts and volcanoes. Man has little, if any, control over these natural sources of pollutant sulphur, which can contribute as much as 50 percent of the globally emitted sulphur each year. It is the remaining 50 percent which is of major interest in the development of air pollution control strategies.The sulphurdioxides contribute to the formation of acid rain and directly to deleterious health effects. Respiratory and cardiopulmonary problems have been shown to be caused by sulphur dioxide, as well as asthmatic attacks and eye irritations. The concentrations needed to cause serious health effects, however, are rarely achieved though. The formation of acid rain is a source of major interest and concern these days. Acid rain is caused by nitric and sulphuric acids which are formed by the oxidation of nitrogen oxides (NO_x) and sulphur dioxide. The increased acidity of the precipitation (down to pH about 3.0 has had many deleterious effects. Many lakes have become too acidicto sustain aquatic life, most fish not being able to live with a pH below 4.5. The acidity also affects the plant life, both byattacking the leaves and branches of the vegetation and by leachingmany of the nutrients in the soil into the runoff.

Its effects on buildings and statues as many older structures, especially those constructed of sandstone or marble, are literally dissolving. Knowledge of a problem is existence is not always the same asunderstanding its cause or how to prevent it. Simplistically, sulphuricacid is formed by the oxidation and dissolution of SO_2 But the concentration of sulphate present in the atmosphere is muchgreater than that which can be accounted for by the precedingreaction[1]. Clearly, additional mechanisms for the oxidation of SO_2 must play an important role in the atmosphere.

$$SO_2 + H_2O + 0.5O_2\ H_2SO_4 \quad ...(2)$$

SO_2 Oxidation Pathways: The atmospheric oxidation of acid precursors in both gas and aqueous phases occurs though the following pathways.

Gas Phase Oxidation: The oxidation of SO_2 is brought about by hydroxyl and other radicals and compounds formed by photochemical reaction. The chemistry of formation of OH radicals is as follows:

$$NO_2 + h\nu\ (\lambda < 430\ nm) \rightarrow O\ (^3P) + NO \quad ...(3)$$

$$O\ (^3P) + O_2\ (^+M) \rightarrow O_3\ (^+M) \quad ...(4)$$

$$O_3 + NO \rightarrow O_2 + NO_2 \quad ...(5)$$

$$O_3 + h\nu\ (\lambda < 290 - 306\ nm) \rightarrow O\ (^1D) + O_2 \quad ...(6)$$

$$O\ (^1D) + H_2O \rightarrow 2OH \quad ...(7)$$

The atmospheric concentrations of OH radicals is estimated to be $(6 \pm 3) \times 10^6$ molecule/cm^{-3} (Brandt and van Eldik 1995 calvert and stockwell 1984).

The reaction of OH radical with SO_2 is believed to proceed as follows:

$$NO_2 + h\nu\ (\lambda < 430\ nm) \rightarrow O\ (^3P) + NO \quad ...(7)$$

$$SO_2 + OH\ (^+M) \rightarrow HOSO_2\ (^+M) \quad ...(8)$$

$$HSO_2 + O_2 \rightarrow SO_3 + HO_2 \quad ...(9)$$

$$HO_2 + NO \rightarrow OH + NO_2 \quad ...(10)$$

The overall reaction can, therefore be written as follows:

$$OH + SO_2\ (^+M{+}O_2{+}H_2O) \rightarrow H_2SO_4 + HO_2\ (^+M) \quad ...(11)$$

Aqueous Phase Oxidation of S (IV) by H_2O_2 and O_3: In atmosphere, hydrogen peroxide is formed as a result of photochemical free radical reactions

$$HO + CO \rightarrow H + CO_2 \quad ...(12)$$

$$H + O_2\ (^+M) \rightarrow HO_2\ (^+M) \quad ...(13)$$

$$2HO_2 \rightarrow H_2O_2 + O_2 \quad ...(14)$$

$$HO_2 + H_2O \rightarrow H_2O.HO_2 \quad ...(15)$$

$$H_2O.HO_2 + HO_2 \rightarrow H_2O_2 + O_2 + H_2O \quad ...(16)$$

Due to very high value of Henary constant (7×10^4 mol L^{-1} atm^{-1} @ 25 °C) the concentrations of H_2O_2 in aqueous phase is relatively high. The oxidation of S (IV) is catalysed by hydrogen ions and hence with the increase in the pH, the rate decreases. The following gross mechanism has been proposed (Hoffmanand Edwards 1975[19] Halperin and Taube 1952[20]).

$$HO_2 + H_2O \rightarrow H_2O.HO_2 \quad ...(15)$$

$$HSO_3^- + \rightarrow H_2O_2^-O_2SOOH + H_2O \quad ...(17)$$

$$^-O_2SOOH + HA \rightarrow H_2SO_4 + A^- \quad ...(18)$$

Where HA is H^+ or other acid.

In troposphere ozone is usually found in 30-60 ppb range and formed as results of photolytic results of NO_2. Its solubity in water is much lower than that of H_2O_2 due to the low value of Henary Constant (1×10^{-2} mol L^{-1} atm^{-1}). A simplified mechanism for the reaction is as follows. (Halperin and taube 1952, Penkett *et al.,* 1979, Penkett 1972, Larson et al 1978, Martin 1984 etc.)

$$O_3 + HSO_3^{-1} + H_2O \rightarrow \text{INTERMEDIATE } SO_4^{-2} + H^+ + O_2 \quad ...(19)$$

The rate of reaction increases, when pH is increased.

Aqueous Phase Speciation of SO_2

The atmospheric oxidation of SO_2 by O_2 in aqueous media has been the subject of numerous studies, and the subject matter of several reviews, monographs and papers, notably by Kuo et al (2006), Clemitshaw (2006), Brandt and Van eldik, (1995), Calvert and Stockwell,(1984), Gupta (2002), Huie and Peterson, (1983), Hoffmann and Boyce (1983), Hoffmann and Jacob(1984), Hermann,(2000), Manoj *et al.,* (2000), Rani *et al.,* (1992), Manoj et al (1999), Prasad *et al.,* (1991), Martin (1984), Kraft and van Eldik(1989) etc.

$$S(IV) + 0.5 \rightarrow O_2S\ (VI) \quad ...(20)$$

The oxidation of SO_2 (aq.) by O_2 is slow but is strongly catalyzed by homogenous and heterogeneous catalysts (Prasad *et al.*, 1991, 1992, 1994, 2003, Rani *et al.*, 1991, 1992, Bhargava *et al.*, 1992, 1993, Gupta *et al.*, 1999, 2000, 2001, 2002, 2004, Manoj *et al.*, 1999, 2000, Martin 1984, Hoffmann and Jacob, 1984, Hoffmann and Boyce, 1983, Kraft and van Eldik, 1989, Brandt and van Eldik, 1995, Kuo *et al.*, 2006). The uncatalysed aqueous SO_2 oxidation is believed to be catalysed by trace metal ions and has been shown to be seized by addition of EDTA. This has been adduced as an evidence for the involvement of trace metal ions viz. iron(III) and Mn(II). EDTA renders these inactive by forming a strong complex.

Although the SO_2 oxidation by O_2 has been the subject of many studies, the mechanism of the reaction is far for settled. Both non radical and radical mechanism have been proposed. It is interesting to point out that reaction is strongly inhibited by alcohol, benzene, and other compounds., pointing to the participation of radical intermediates (Huss *et al.*, 1978, 1982a, 1982b, 1982c, Kuo *et al.*, 2006, Huie and Peterson, 1983, Huie and Neta, 1984). In aqueous solution SO_2 is present in four forms $SO_2.H_2O$, HSO_3^{-1}, SO_3^{-2}, $S_2O_5^{-2}$, governed by the following equations:

$$SO_{2(g)} + H_2O \underset{}{\overset{K_h}{\rightleftharpoons}} SO_2.H_2O_{(aq)} \quad ...(21)$$

$$SO_2.H_2O_{(aq)} \overset{K_2}{\rightleftharpoons} HSO_3^{-1} + H^+ \quad ...(22)$$

$$HSO_3^{-1} \overset{K_2}{\rightleftharpoons} SO_3^{-2} + H^+ \quad ...(23)$$

$$2HSO_3^{-1} \overset{K_3}{\rightleftharpoons} S_2O_5^{-2} + H_2O \quad ...(24)$$

K_h is Henry's constant and K_1, K_2 are acid dissociation constant. K_3 is the format ion constant for $S_2O_5^{-2}$at 25°C the values are K_h = 1.23 mol L^{-1} atm^{-1}, K_1= 1.4 × 10^{-2}, K_2 = 6.24 × 10^{-8}, and K_3 is 7.6 × 10^{-2}. The total concentration of dissolved sulphur dioxide [S(IV)] is governed by equilibria (21-24) and is given by equation (25)

$$[S\ (IV)] = (1 + k_1\ [H^+]^{-1} + k_1k_2\ [H^+]^{-2})\ [SO_2.H_2O] \quad ...(25)$$

The equation shows that the solubility of SO_2 in water increases with increase in pH and it is clear that nature of species of S(IV) depends on pH. For example in pH range 4.0 – 5.6 major species is HSO_3^{-1} and above pH 7.0 SO_3^{-2} is dominant species.

Kinetics of Homogenous Metal Ion Catalysed Autoxidation Reactions

In the atmosphere, the anthropogenic sources and soils are the major contributor of trace metal iron ion (II)/(III), copper ((II), cobalt(II), and nickel (II). The most important metal ions from atmospheric view are iron and manganese (Penkett et al 1979, Grgic *et al.*, 1991,Martin 1984 and to extent some copper).

The major studies on iron (III), manganese (II), copper (II), and cobalt (II) catalysed autoxidation of SO_2 in aqueous solution are collected below:

Fe (III) Catalysis: Manoj *et al.*, 2008, Martin 1984, Fuzzi, 1978, Brimblecombe and speeding 1974 and Hoffmann 1988[33] Huss *et al.*, 1982.

Mn (II) Catalysis: Wilkosz and Mainka 2008 Grigic *et al.*, 2007 Manoj *et al.*, 2000 Connick and Zhang 1996 Berglund et al 1993 podkrajsek *et al.*, 2004 Huss *et al.*, 1982.

Cu (II) Catalysis: Lunak *et al.*, 1978 Fuller and Crist 1941 Grigic *et al.*, 1991.

Co(II) Catalysis: Hobson *et al.*, 1986 Srivastava et al 1968.

Ag (I) Catalysis: Gupta *et al.*, 1999 2001.

Os (VIII) Catalysis: Gupta *et al.*, 2004.

Ni (II) catalysis: Linn Jr *et al.*, 1990.

Se Catalysis: Bronikowaski *et al.*, 2000.

Kinetics of Heterogenous Particle Surface Catalysed Autoxidation Reactions

The surface area of particles also plays a prominent role in the autoxidation of S(IV). The catalytical particulate materials, which are atmospheric importance include suspended particulate materials free fall atmospheric dust, SiO_2, Mg, CdO, CuO, CoO, MnO_2, Ni_2O_3, Cu_2O, Co_2O_3, CdS, flyash, Carbonaceous particles, minerals and rocks.

Catalysis by Suspened Particulate Matter (Spm)–Free Fall Atmospheric Dust

Dust is a heterogeneous mixture of several compounds. Its role in catalysing the autoxidation of aqueous sulphur di oxide was studied by Rani *et al.* The kinetics results were in agreement with rate law.

$$R_{obs} = k_6[S(IV)]\,[H^+]^{-1.3} + k_7[dust]^{0.42}\,[S(IV)]^2\,[H^+]^{-1.36} \qquad ...(26)$$

At pH 5.06 (Acetate buffer) the reaction was slow in the beginning for about 2.5 min and there after it attained the maximum rate. The initial slow reaction was due to surficial catalysis, which is subsequently overtaken by leached metal ion catalysis. EDTA reduces the rate of suspension catalysed reaction by about 80% by arresting the leachate reaction due to the complexing the metal ions. An increase in the particle size did not affect the rate but led to an increase in the induction period which probably the time taken by metal ions to leach in the solution.

Catalysis By Non–transition Metal Oxide and Other Compounds

The important features of catalytic autoxidation of non-transition metal oxide such as CdO, MgO, Silica and some other materials like rocks and minerals, glass and flyash, in their aqueous suspensions are as follows:

1. CdO, MgO and limestone are very efficient catalyst and there appears to be a linear relationship between rate of autoxidation and pH. Obviously, higher is the surface pH, greater is the catalytic activity of oxide.
2. In most of the cases a kinetic order of more than one in S (IV) has been found.

Catalysis by Carbonaceous Particles

Activated carbon and combustion produced soot particles have been studied for their catalytic effect on the oxidation of aqueous S(IV) species by brodzinsky et al 1980. These particles are found to be effective catalysts for the reaction. Combustion produced soots were tested for their catalytic behavior and found to be similar to the activated carbons. The reaction rate was found to be linearly dependent on the concentration of carbon particles in the solution. The rate was found to follow a Langmuir adsorption isotherm for its dependence on oxygen and the product of two adsorption isotherms for S(IV). The reaction is independent of the pH of the solution when the pH is below 7.6 The reaction does not occur when the pH is above 7.6 The three aqueous S(IV) species are catalyzed in their oxidation by the carbon particles in a similar manner. The pH cut-off is suggested as being a function of the catalytically active sites on the carbon surface. Activation energies for the reactions on the different carbons are all about 8.5 kcal/mole. A possible four-step reaction mechanism is proposed. It consists of the adsorption of a dissolved oxygen molecule onto the carbon surface, followed by the adsorption of two S(IV) molecules or ions. These are oxidized on the surface to sulphate, which desorbs from the surface, regenerating the catalytically active site. Saxena (1993) studied the autoxidation of S(IV) in the acetate suspension of exhaust carbon particles (Automobile dust) The following rate law was given by eq. (27)

$$R_{obs} = k_4[\text{dust}]^{0.5}\ [S(IV)\ [H^+]^{-0.8} \quad ...(27)$$

The addition of buffer enhance the rate of reaction by leaching the metal ion in to aqueous phase and these metal ions act as a catalyst.

Catalysis by Cds

Manoj *et al.,* (2000) studied the kinetics of autoxidation of S(IV) catalysed byCdS which obeys the rate law (28)

$$-d[S(IV)]/dt = k_3[S(IV)]^2\ [H^+]^{-2} + k_4[CdS]\ [S(IV)]^2\ [H^+]^{-1} \quad ...(28)$$

Where k_3= 1.17 × 10^{-12} mol $L^{-1}s^{-1}$and k_4 = 4.5 × 10^{-7} L^2 $mol^{-2}g^{-1}s^{-1}$ at 30 °C in acetate buffered medium. The addition of EDTA [(1–3) × 10^{-4} mol L^{-1}] reduced the rate only slightly as has been noted by Connick *et al*. The addition of ethanol of oxysulphur radicals pointing to the operation of free radical mechanism.

Catalysis by Transition Metal Oxides

The transition metals are an integral part of suspended particulate matter (SPM) Since the combustion process release the metals in the atmosphere in the form of their oxides, which are known to be heterogeneous catalysts for several liquid phase reaction of CoO, Co_2O_3, Ni_2O_3, CuO and MnO_2 as catalyst. In each case, the autoxidation led to the formation of sulphate ion as in (29)

$$HSO_3^- + 0.5 \rightarrow O_2SO_4^{-2} + H^+ \qquad ...(29)$$

The possibity of the catalytic activity of metal oxide suspensions being due to leached metal ions was ruled out by the fact that rates of autoxidation in leachate and blank reaction were found to be almost the same in case of the catalysis by CuO, which dissolves significantly to produce Cu(II) ions, it was shown that the homogenous catalysis due to leached Cu(II) ions was insignificant. This conclusion was reinforced by the fact that addition of EDTA did not have significant effect on reaction rates.

In acetate buffered suspensions, the following kinetics rate law was obeyed.

$$-d[S(IV)]/dt = R_{obs} = (k_1 + k_2[H^+]^{-1}) [Catalyst] [S(IV)] \qquad ...(30)$$

The proposed mechanism suggest the formation of surficial complex between metal oxide, S(IV) and dioxygen.

A comparison of the rate constant shows the reactivity order $MnO_2 > CuO > Co_2O_3 > CoO > Ni_2O_3$.Incidently all these oxides, except MnO_2 fails to oxidize S(IV) directly in the absence of oxygen. In the case of MnO_2 which shows the highest catalytic activity, a slow but perceptile oxidation of S(IV) does occur.

In case of CoO and NiO_3catalysed reaction in acetatebuffered acidic medium, the O_2 dependence of the reaction rate was also studied. This way in agreement with the rate law (31)

$$-d[S(IV)]/dt = (k_3 + k_4/[H^+]) [M_xO_y] [S(IV)][O_2] \qquad ...(31)$$

The values of k_1 and k_2 for different catalysts are given in Table 3.1.

Table 3.1: Values of k_1 and k_2 for Different Catalytic Autoxidation of S(IV)

Catalyst	Temp.° C	10^4 k_1 L $g^{-1}s^{-1}$	10^9 $k_2$mol $g^{-1}s^{-1}$	Ref.
CoO	30	2.7	2.8	27
CO_2O_3	30	11.3	16.4	31
CuO	30	16.6	37	24
Ni_2O_3	30	0.95	3.87	29
MnO_2	30	155	286	28

A study of the kinetics in unbuffered suspensions of CoO, CuO, CO_2O_3, and NiO_3 showed the reaction profiles to be biphasic in certain pH ranges, the first stage of the reaction being fast and the second being slower step, the general rate law (32) was observed.

$$R_{obs} = k_0\,[S(IV)] + k_2\,[M_xY_x]\,[S(IV)] \qquad (32)$$

The extensive studies with transition metal oxides suggest that the particle surface to be major cause of catalysis, which is in agreement with previous indication of Berresheim and Jaeschke and recent suggestion of Prasad *et al.*, that the wetted particles may absorb SO_2 and aid in its subsequent oxidation.

A study of effect of ethanol revealed the surface-catalysed reactions to fall in two categories. Firs categories included the reactions catalysed by MgO, CdO, SiO_2 etc. which were completely inhibited by addition of 0.17 mol L^{-1} ethanol and no reaction was observed for a period of one hour. The second category comprised the reactions catalysed by CdS, Cu_2O, MnO_2, CoO, Ni_2O_3 and CuO in which only a slight retardation in rate was observed.

SO_2 Oxidation Mechanisms

The proposed mechanisms for the oxidation of SO_2 in the atmosphere can be divided into two general categories; gas phase reactions and heterogeneous aqueous mechanisms. The aqueous mechanisms have traditionally been divided into catalyzed and uncatalyzedreactions. The uncatalyzed reactions can be the reaction of aquated SO_2 and dissolved O_2 in either the presence or absence of ammonia. The catalyzed reactions have usually been regarded as those involving the ionic species of transition metals, in particular Fe^{3+} and Mn^{2+}[5-13]. Aqueous ozone can also oxidize the SO_2. The gas phase reactions can be divided into homogeneous reactions, photochemical reactions (including free radical mechanisms) and gas surface reactions.

Non-radical Mechanism

A Non-radical Mechanism generally operates in the catalysis by transition metal oxide and by iron (III) when pH is low. As an example of non-radical mechanism of CuO –catalysed reaction is given below:

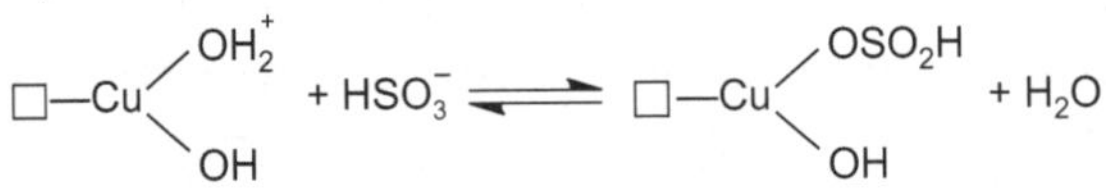

...(33)

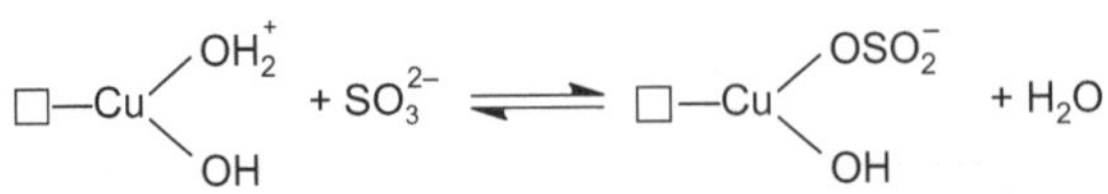

...(34)

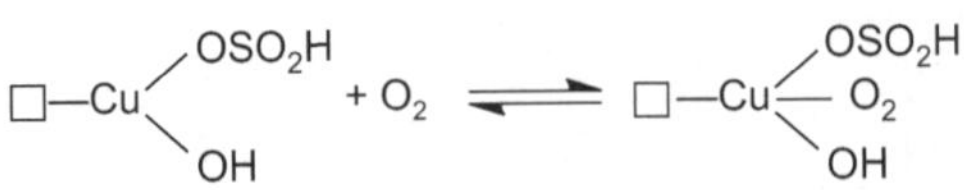

...(35)

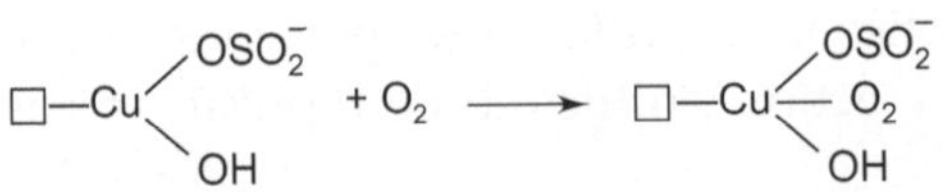

...(36)

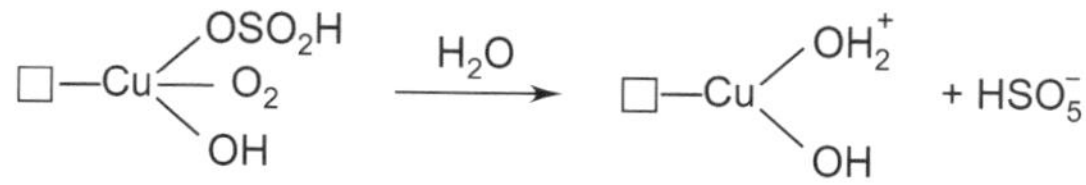 ...(37)

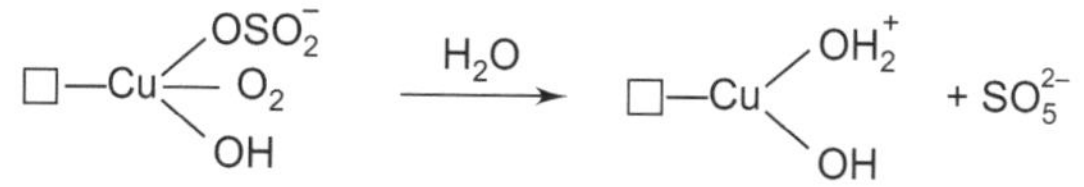 ...(38)

$$SO_5^{2+} + H^+ \rightarrow HSO_5^- \text{ (rapid)} \quad ...(39)$$

$$HSO_5^- + S(IV) \rightarrow 2S(VI) \text{ (rapid)} \quad ...(40)$$

The reactivity order for the different transition metal oxide has been found to be $MnO_2 > CuO > CO_2O_3 > CoO > Ni_2O_3$. In the autoxidation mechanism, the adsorbed S (IV) transfer its electrons to matrix M (where M = Cu, Mn, Ni, Co) and S (IV) so formed interact with adjacently adsorbed O_2, takes back an electron from matrix M and leave off as SO_5^{-2}.

Radical Mechanism

When the sulphur S (IV) autoxidation is inhibited by alcohol and other inhibitors, the reaction operates through oxysulphur radical intermediates (Huss *et al.*, 1978[69] 1982[34], 1982[71] 1982[70] Kuo *et al.*, 2006[28] Huie and Peterson 1983[72], Huei and Neta 1984[73] was first to propose a free radical mechanism.)

In aqueous solutions even in the absence of any added metal ions, the autoxidation is believed to be catalysed by trace metal ions M^{n+} present as impurities. The transition metal ions which are always present in atmospheric water in trace concentrations undergo one electron change and in general the catalysis proceeds though radical mechanism. The radical mechanism initial proposed by Backstrom has been modified subsequently by inclusion of sulphate ion radical SO_4^{-2} (Hayon 1972)[75] as presented below :

Initiation

$$M^{n+} + SO_3^{2-} \rightarrow M^{(n-1)+} + SO_3 \quad ...(41)$$

$$SO_3 + O_2 \rightarrow SO_5^- \quad ...(42)$$

Propagation

$$SO_5 + SO_3^{2-} \rightarrow HSO_5^- + SO_3 \quad ...(43)$$

$$SO_5 + SO_3^{2-} \rightarrow SO_4 + SO_4^{2-} \quad ...(44)$$

$$SO_4 + SO_3^{2-} \rightarrow SO_4^{2-} + SO_3 \quad ...(45)$$

Oxidation

$$HSO_5^- + SO_3^{2-} \rightarrow 2SO_4^{2-} + H^+ \quad ...(46)$$

Termination

$$2SO_3 \rightarrow S_2O_6^{2-} \quad ...(47)$$

$$SO_3 + SO_5 \rightarrow S_2O_6^{2-} + O_2 \quad ...(48)$$

$$SO_5 + SO_5 \rightarrow S_2O_8^{2-} + O_2 \quad ...(49)$$

Inhibitory effect was explained through scavenging of radicals as in equations (50-51).

$$RCH_2OH + SO_5 \rightarrow RCHO + SO_4 + H_2O \qquad ...(50)$$

$$SO_5 + RCH_2OH \rightarrow RCHO + SO_4^{2-} + H_2O \qquad ...(51)$$

Various other rate expressions having different values of the kinetic orders in the reactants can be obtained if a different termination steps is assumed.

$$-d\,[SO_3^{-2}]/dt \;=\; k\,[M^{n+}]^a\,[SO_3^{-2}]^b\,[O_2]^c \qquad ...(52)$$

The values of coefficients a, b, c depends on the choice of termination steps. Most of the studies support the experimental laws (52) (Martin, 1984 Gupta *et al.*, 2000).

Role of Inhibitors

Bigelow (1898) was the first to observe the inhibiting effect of alcohols such as methanol, ethanol, propanol, butanol on the rate of the reaction between sodium sulfite and oxygen. The inhibiting effect of alcohols was investigated subsequently by Alyea and Backstrom (1929). The other inhibitors studied are phenols (Altiwicker, 1980), alcohols (J. Ziajka 2003) organic acids (Lee and Rochelle, 1987, Grgic *et al.*, 1998, 2007 podkrajsek *et al.*, 2006 wilkosz al 2008 Wolf *et al.*, 2000), benzene (Ziajka *et al.*, 1994), toluene, naphthalene, paraffin oil (Pasuik Bronikowska *et al.*, 1997), alpha-pinene, cis-verbenol (Ziajka and Pasuik – Brobikowska, 1999), sobrerol (Pasuik – Bronikowska *et al.*, 1998, 1999), myrtenol (Pasuik – Bronikowska, *et al.*, 2000) and others (Rudzinski and Pasiuk – Bronikowska, 2001, 2003). The effect of ammonia has been studied on catalysed S (IV) autoxidation (Manoj *et al.*, 1999, Mudgal *et al.*, 2007).

Hayon *et al.*, (1972) proposed a radical mechanism involving SO_3, SO_4, SO_5 radicals to explain the inhibitory effect through scavenging of radicals as in equation (53).

$$RCH_2OH + SO_5 \rightarrow RCHO + SO_4 + H_2O \qquad (53)$$

The effect of alcohols has been studied on several catalysedS(IV) autoxidation by Gupta *et al.*, (2008). Gupta *et al.*, (2000) studied the effect of Ag (I) catalyzed autoxidation of S(IV) in acetate buffer medium. To explain the observed kinetics and inhibition effect of organic compounds, the following general radical mechanism involving SO_3, SO_4 and SO_5 radicals was proposed (Backstrom, 1934). Further experiments were conducted for finding reactivity of oxysulphur radicals with organics, which proved that these compounds react with SO_4 (Ashmore, 1963 Gilvert *et al.*, 1988 Dogliotti and Hayon, 1967; Clifton and Huie, 1989). The reactions with SO_3 and SO_5 appeared to be quite slow and hence unimportant (Hayon *et al.*, 1972). These studies have shown the reaction of SO_4 to bevery fast. Therefore, to explain the inhibiting effect, the following step has been proposed.

$$SO_4 + C_2H_5OH \rightarrow \text{non chain product} \qquad ...(54)$$

From the above discussion, it is this apparent that to understand the mechanism of SO_2 oxidation it is necessary to study the effect of inhibitors. There are some reactions for which mechanisms involving complex formation alone or combined with radicals may be operating depending up on the reaction conditions in particular pH. For example iron(III)-catalysed reaction in the pH range(1-3) is without any effect of free radical scavengers but is strongly inhibited when pH > 5 (Martin, 1984). In addition, aqueous phase concentration of methanol and ethanol were found 1.8×10^{-6} mol dm^{-3} and 3.1×10^{-7} mol dm^{-3} respectively in urban atmosphere (Herrmann *et al.,* 2000). The Concentration of benzene reported to be 1.7 ppb in the atmosphere (Bravo, 2002).

Experimental studies on the kinetics and products of sulphate radicals-alcohols (Clifton and Huie 1989 wine *et al.,* 1989 Ziajka *et al.,* 1996, 2001, Ziakjka and Pasiuk-Bronokowska 1998, 2000, 2003) have also been carried out.The methanol inhibition of the uncatalysed autoxidation of HSO_3^- was investigated by Connick *et al.,* (1995). The inhibition by methanol in the Manganese (II) catalysed S (IV) autoxidation has been studied by Connick and Zhang (1996).

Recently Gupta *et al.,* 2008 studied the inhibiting effect of ethanol on CoO,CO_2O_3 and Ni_2O_3 catalysed autoxidation of S (IV) in alkaline medium and based on the result a radical mechanism for CoO and CO_2O_3 catalysis in alkaline medium, and non –radical mechanism for Ni_2O_3 in both alkaline and acidic media and for CoO in acidic media proposed. Similarly Sameena, Faiyaz and Prasad el al studied on kinetics of formic acid inhibited uncatalysed and Co_2O_3catalysed autoxidation of S(IV) in alkaline medium and free radical mechanism proposed. (2013). In the same series the influence of VOCs on the oxidation of S(IV) by oxygen and role of some organic inhibitors on the oxidation of S(IV) by oxygen in rain water medium studied by DhayalChandel and Gupta *et al.,* (2014).

Purpose and Scope of the Proposedwork

Based on the literature survey and studies carried out so far, it is well established that the organic inhibitors have played a key role in the chemistry of acid rain. Further, it is fully realized that the role of inhibitors owing to their radical scavenging ability is a major diagnostic tool for the reaction mechanisms. Although the role of different moieties, ammonia and ammonia based derivatives are well studied. Among the inhibitors, the role of Formic acid, Aniline, Benzamide,Isoamyl alcohol, sodium benzoate, Isopropyl alcohol has not been studied so far in S(IV) autoxidation reaction. In view of the fact that inhibitor help in delineating the mechanism of autoxidation, whether radical or non- radical, it has been decided to study the effect of Formic acid, Aniline, Benzamide,Isoamyl alcohol, sodium benzoate, Isopropyl alcohol on the autoxidation rates of S(IV). This study will be beneficial to understand the related mechanism.

Importance of Proposed Research Work

This study is important in understanding the mechanism of the atmospheric oxidation of S(IV) by O_2 and the role of organic compounds which acts as inhibitors, many of which are found in atmosphere in trace amounts.It is useful to understanding rain water acidity and atmospheric chemistry. The main goal of this work is to determine rate constants for effect of organic compounds on sulphate radicals in order to shed some light on these reactions.

MATERIALS AND METHODS

Chemicals

Sodium Sulphite

In aqueous solution, SO_2 exists as $SO_2.H_2O$, HSO_3^-, SO_3^{-2} and $S_2O_5^{-2}$ and all these forms collectively referred to as S(IV). In order to obtain aqueous solution of S(IV), sodium sulphite Na_2SO_3(E. Merck) was used as such without any purification. Its solution was prepared in doubly distilled water. It was standardized iodometrically, every time before use. The solution was kept in refrigerator to prevent the autoxidation S(IV), which is considerably slow at low temperature.

Iodine

Iodine(E. Merck) of (99.9%)purity was used. To prepare 0.1 mol L^{-1} solution of iodine at first 40.0 g iodate free potassium iodide (E. Merck 99%) was dissolved in 50 cm^3 of doubly distilled water, to which 25.5 g iodine was added. When iodine was fully dissolved the solution was made up to 1.0 liter. The stock solution was kept in cool and dark place.The dilute solutions of desired strength were prepared by diluting this stock solution.

Potassium Iodide

Iodate free potassium iodide (E. Merck, 99%) was used.

Silver Nitrate

Silver nitrate was prepared in chloride free doubly distilled water. It was E. Merck make (99.90%).

Sodium Thiosulphate

Sodium thiosulphate (Hypo) was E. Merck make and 99.90% purity. Its stock solution was prepared by dissolving the weighed amount in freshly boiled doubly distilled water. The dilute solutions of desired strength were prepared by diluting this stock solution. The solution was standardized against iodine solution of known strength following the standard procedure (Jeffery *et al.*, 1989). A few drops of chloroform were added to the stock solution to prevent its slow decomposition.

Acetic Acid

For preparing 1.0 mol L^{-1} stock solution, 58 ml acetic acid (Merck 100%) was diluted with doubly distilled water. It was standardized by titrating against standard sodium hydroxide solution using phenolphthalein as an indicator.

Starch

For preparing indicator solution, starch (soluble) was used of Qualigens make.

Other Chemicals

The other chemicals used were of the following makes. Their solutions were prepared in doubly distilled water.

Table 3.2: Qualities of Some Chemicals Used

Chemicals	Make
Sodium Hydroxide (NaOH)	E.Merck (99.7%)
Sodium Acetate (CH_3COONa)	E.Merck (99.9%)
Copper Sulphate ($CuSO_4$)	E.Merck (99.9%)
Aniline($C_6H_5NH_2$)	E.Merck (99.9%)
Formic acid (HCOOH)	E.Merck (99.9%)
Sodium benzoate(C_6H_5COONa)	E.Merck (99.9%)
Benzamide($C_6H_5CONH_2$)	E.Merck (99.9%)
Isopropyl alcohol (C_3H_8O)	E.Merck (99.9%)
Isoamyl alcohol ($C_5H_{12}O$)	E.Merck (99.9%)

As the oxidation reactions of S (IV) are sensitive to the quality and source of chemicals, same reagents were used throughout the course of particular piece of work.

STANDARDIZATION METHODS

Iodine Solution

Iodine solution was standardized by taking its known volume in a flask, making it slightly acidic and titrating it against hypo solution using starch as indicator.

Sodium Thiosulphate (Hypo) Solution

It was standardized as follows. A known volume of standard copper sulphate was taken and to it potassium iodide was added. The liberated iodine was titrated against hypo using starch as indicator.

Sodium Sulphite Solution

A predetermined quantity of iodine which was always in excess over the sulphite to the estimated was taken in a conical flask and to it was added sodium sulphite solution to be standardized. Solution was made slightly acidic by adding acetic acid. The unreached iodine was titrated against hypo solution using starch as indicator.

Acetic acid Solution

It was standardized by titrating it against standard sodium hydroxide solution using phenolphthalein as an indicator.

EQUIPMENT

Reaction Vessel

The reactions were conducted in 0.15 L Erlenmeyer flask open to air and room light. The reaction vessel was placed in 0.5 L beaker provided with an outlet at the top and inlet at the bottom for circulating thermostatic water for maintaining the desired temperature of the reaction mixture (+1°C). The assembly was mounted on a magnetic stirrer.

pH meter

The digital pH meter (Systronics – pH system 361) was used for measuring the pH of the reaction mixture.

Magnetic Stirrer

The reaction vessel was mounted on a magnetic stirrer and the reaction mixture was continuously stirred magnetically at a speed of 1600 + 100 rpm for ensuring the rapid diffusion of oxygen in to reaction mixture and to keep the catalyst in solutions. The magnetic stirrer was calibrated with the help of Tachometer.

Kinetics Procedure

The experimental procedure was exactly the same as described earlier by Brodzinsky *et al.,* (1980) Mudgal *et al.,* (2008) and Gupta *et al.,* (2008) and is briefly given here. The all chemicals were used as reagent grade and solution were prepared in double distilled water. The reaction were conducted in 0.15 L Erlenmeyer flask, open to air and follow to passage of atmosphere oxygen. The flask was placed in a beaker which had an inlet at a lower part and an outlet at a outer part for circulating thermostatic water for maintaining the desired temperature 30 + 1 °C. The reaction was initiated by adding the desired volume of Na_2SO_3 solution to the reaction mixture containing other additive such as buffer and catalyst. The selection of suitable stirring speed is necessary to save the reaction from becoming oxygen mass transfer controlled. For this reason, the rate of reaction were studied at different stirring speeds measured with the help of a tachometer (Mudgal *et al.,* 2008). This led us to select a stirring speed of

1600 + 10 rpm for stirring the reaction mixture continuously and magnetically to allow the passage of atmospheric oxygen and to save the reaction from becoming oxygen mass transfer controlled.

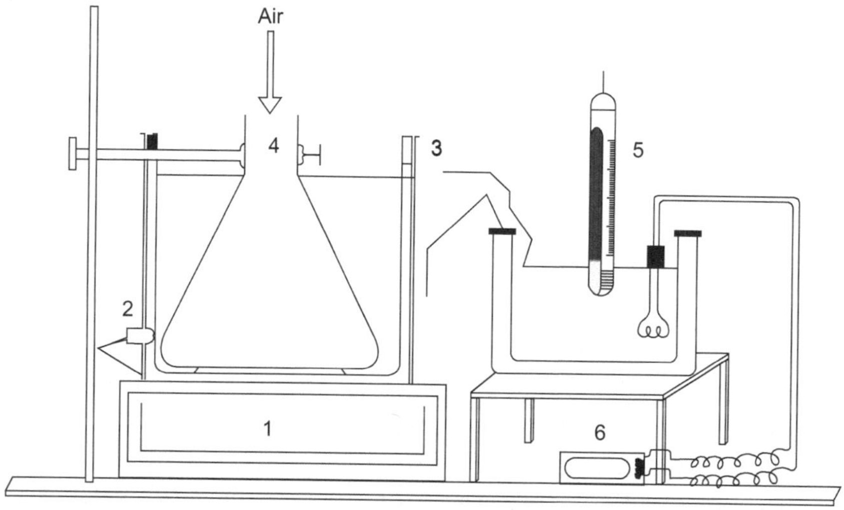

Fig. 3.1: Schematic diagram of the experimental set up for the kinetic study of S (IV) – O_2 oxidation reaction. 1. Magnetic Stirrer, 2. Water Inlet, 3. Water outlet, 4. Erlenmeyer Flask (Reaction mixture), 5. Thermometer, 6.Thermostat.

The kinetics was studied in buffered medium in which the pH remained fixed throughout the entire course of reaction. For this purpose 10 cm^3 buffer made from sodium acetate (0.07 mol L^{-1}) and acetic acid (0.03 mol L^{-1}) for acidic medium were used (total volume 100 cm^3) for obtaining the desired pH. The kinetics were followed by withdrawing the aliquot samples periodically and titrating the unreacted S(IV) iodometrically in slightly acidic medium (Brodzinsky *et al.*, (1980), Mudgal *et al.*, (2008), Prasad *et al.*, (1992) and Gupta *et al.*, (2008). For this purpose 5.0 ml aliquot samples were withdrawn periodically and added to a titration flask containing known quantity of iodine and sufficient acetic acid to make medium acidic. The unreacted iodine was titrated with standard sodium thio sulphate solution using starch as an indicator.

Treatment of Kenetic Data

In this study, the treatment of kinetics is based on first order rate constants (k_{obs}) In case of Ag(I) catalysed autoxidation studies, the first order rate constants were calculated from the linear plots of log [S(IV)] v/s time. All calculations were performed in MS Excel 7.0.

Reproducibility

The S(IV) autoxidation rates are known to have only satisfactory reproducibility. In our case, the duplicate rate determinations had a satisfactory reproducibility within 10%.

RESULTS AND DISCUSSION

Kinetics of organics inhibited uncatalysed and Ag (I) catalysed autoxidation of S (IV) in acidic medium.

The kinetics of atmospheric autoxidation of S (IV) by Ag (I) in the pH range 4.02-5.25 has been studied. The role of organics as inhibitor of Ag (I) catalysed autoxidation of S (IV) in acidic buffer medium has been identified. Based on the observed results a free radical mechanism has been proposed and following rate law has been given

$$-d\,[S(IV)]/dt = (k_1 + k_2[Ag])\,[S(IV)]/\,1 + B\,[Organics]$$

$$\Rightarrow \qquad R_{cat} = k_1\,[Ag(I)]\,[S(IV)]\,/\,\{k_9[x] + k_{10}[Organics]\}$$

Experiment were carried out at $30 \le t°C \le 45$, $4.02 \le pH \le 5.25$, 1×10^{-3} mol/dm$^3 \le [S(IV)] \le 10 \times 10^{-3}$ mol/dm^3, 5×10^{-6} mol/dm$^3 \le [Ag(I)] \le 2.5 \times 10^{-5}$ mol/dm^3, 5×10^{-6} mol/dm$^3 \le$ [organics] $\le 8 \times 10^{-4}$ mol/dm^3, Based on the experimental results, rate constants and order of the reactions were determined. Depending on the reaction conditions, the observed results for the Ag (I) catalysedS(IV) oxidation reaction in presence of organics has been tabulated and graphs have been plotted. The reaction order in S(IV) was first order for both reactions. The effect of Ag (I) ion and inhibitor concentrations as well as initial pH of the solution on S (IV) oxidation rate was discussed. It was found that the rate of the S(IV) oxidation depends on the initial pH of the solution but independent on pH change during reaction. The effect of temperature of solution on S (IV) oxidation catalysed by Ag(I) in presence of organics was discussed. The values of k_{obs} were determined at three different temperatures in the range of 30°C to 40°C By plotting a graph between log k v/s 1/T yield us an apparent empirical energy of activation for the reaction. In contrast our results conclusively showed that organicsstudied here(Formic *acid, Iso amyl alcohol, sodium benzoate, Benzamide, Iso propyl alcohol, aniline*) act as an inhibitor not catalyst for S (IV) autoxidation.The value of inhibition factor (B) of both uncatalysed and Ag(I) catalysed autoxidation of S(IV) in the present study are in the range of 10^3-10^4 as reported by Gupta *et al.*, (2008) and Prasad *et al.*, (2013). Isoamyl alcohol has highest inhibiting power may be due to formation of more stable radicals in reaction condition used and higher abundance in atmosphere as compare to other organics used.

Inhibiting effect of formic acid, sodium benzoate, benzamide, aniline, isopropyl alcohol, isoamyl alcohol on Ag (I) catalysed autoxidation of S (IV) in acidic medium are as follows:

Table 3.3: Calculated Value of B (Inhibition Parameter) in Absence and Presence of Ag (I)

Name of Organics	Inhibition parameter in the absence of Ag (I) (B) mol dm^{-3}	Inhibition parameter in the presence of Ag (I) (B) mol dm^{-3}
Formic acid	3.33×10^4	2.53×10^3
Sodium benzoate	3.68×10^4	1.48×10^3
Benzamide	4.78×10^4	1.91×10^3
Aniline	1.86×10^3	0.26×10^3
Isopropyl alcohol	4.92×10^3	2.03×10^3
Isoamyl alcohol	5.07×10^4	1.24×10^4

Table 3.4: Effect of Temperature k_{obs} Air Saturated Suspensions at [S(IV)] = 2×10^{-3} mol dm^{-3}, Ag (I) = 5×10^{-6} mol dm^{-3} [Organics] = 5.0×10^{-4} moldm^{-3},pH = 4.95

Name of Organics	Activation Energy kJ mol^{-1}
Formic acid	69.32
Sodium benzoate	24.11
Benzamide	17.05
Aniline	26.43
Isoamyl alcohol	71.83
Isopropyl alcohol	45.16

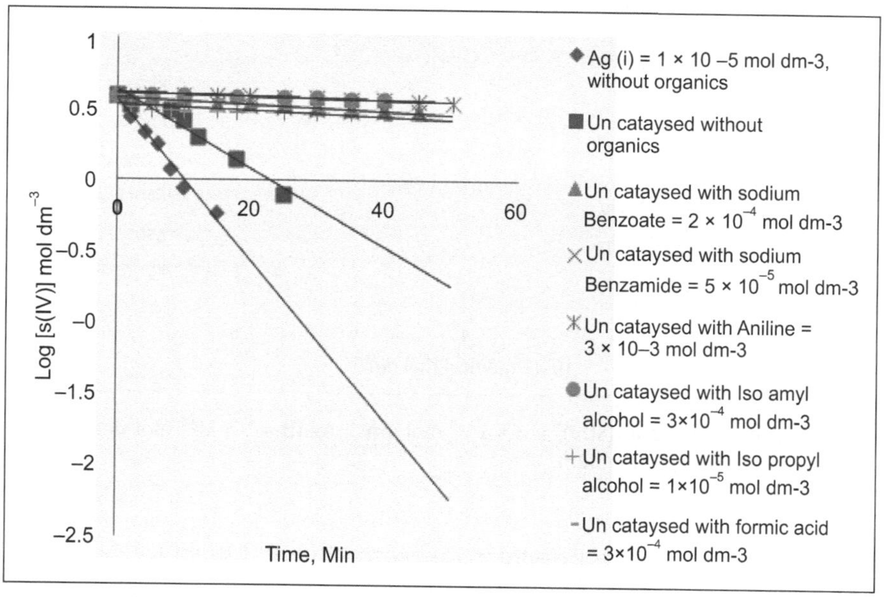

Fig. 3.2: The disappearance of [S(IV)] with time in air saturated suspensions at [S(IV)] = 2×10^{-3} mol dm^{-3} at pH = 4.95, t = 30° C

The inhibition power of these inhibitors are in the order of aniline < isopropyl alcohol < formic acid< sodium benzoate < benzamide < isoamyl alcohol. The inhibition parameter lies in the range of $10^3 – 10^4$ as reported by earlier workof Gupta *et al.*, Sameena *et al.*, Prasad *et al.*, these reactions follows free radical mechanism. These organic substances are potential inhibitors in the autoxidation of S (IV) in aqueous phase. Out of the six inhibitors undertaken for study in the present work, isoamyl alcohol shows higher inhibiting capacity as compared to other five inhibitors.

Table 3.5: Effect of pH at [S(IV)] = 2×10^{-3} mol dm^{-3}, Ag (I) = 5×10^{-6} mol dm^{-3}, [Organics] = 7.0×10^{-7} mol dm^{-3}, *t* = 30° C in acetate buffered medium

pH	$10^3 k_{benzamide}$ s^{-1}	10^3 k_{formic} s^{-1}	$10^3 k_{isopropylalco} s^{-1}$	10^3 $k_{isoamylalco.} s^{-1}$	$10^3 k_{sodiumbenzoate} s^{-1}$	$10^3 k_{aniline} s^{-1}$
4.02	0.489	0.315	0.401	0.172	0.354	0.470
4.35	0.559	0.365	0.523	0.214	0.392	0.514
4.56	0.627	0.426	0.611	0.272	0.484	0.564
4.75	0.714	0.469	0.726	0.328	0.659	0.607
4.95	0.842	0.491	0.859	0.373	0.853	0.686
5.25	0.901	0.553	0.925	0.422	0.926	0.717

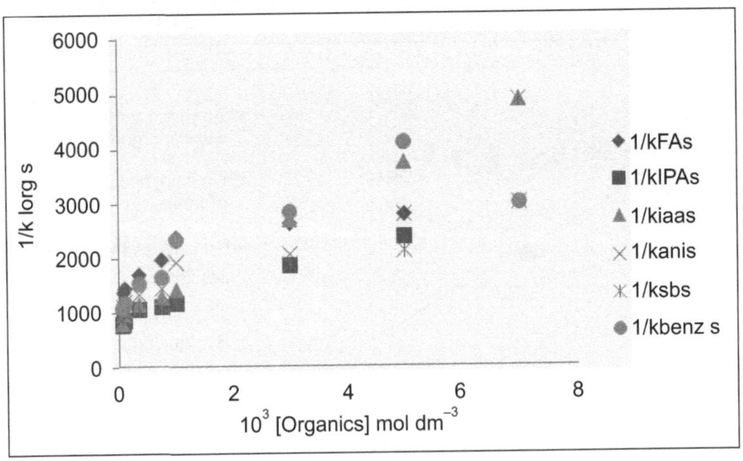

Fig. 3.3: Effect of Organics at [S(IV)] = 2×10^{-3} mol dm^{-3}, Ag (I) = 5×10^{-6} mol dm^{-3},pH = 4.95, *t* = 30°C in acetate buffered medium.

Mechanism

In aqueous solutions SO_2 is present in four forms $SO_2.H_2O$, HSO_3^{-1}, SO_3^{-2}, $S_2O_3^{-2}$ In the experimental range of pH the following equilibrium operates.

$$HSO_3^{-1}\ H^+ \rightleftharpoons SO_3^{-2} \quad ...(1)$$

$$HSO_3^{-1} \xrightleftharpoons{K_d} H^+ + SO_3^{-2}\ K_d = 5.01 \times 10^{-7,18} \quad ...(2)$$

$$Ag^+ + {}^-O_2CCH_3 \xrightleftharpoons{K_{oAc}} AgO_2CCH_3\ K_{oAc} = 2.29^{33} \quad ...(3)$$

$$Ag^+ + SO_3^{-2} \xrightleftharpoons{K_1} AgOSO_2^-K_1 = 2.51 \times 10^{5,29} \quad ...(4)$$

$$Ag^+ + HSO_3^{-1} \xrightleftharpoons{K_2} AgHSO_3 \quad ...(5)$$

$$AgOSO_2^- + O_2 \xrightleftharpoons{K_3} AgOSO_2^{-1}.O_2 \quad ...(6)$$

$$AgHSO_3 + O_2 \xrightleftharpoons{K_4} AgHSO_3.O_2 \quad ...(7)$$

$$AgHSO_3.O_2\,Ag^+ \longrightarrow HSO_5^- \quad ...(8)$$

$$HSO_5^- + HSO_3^{-1} \xrightarrow{K_2SO_4} SO_4 + SO_3 + H_2O \quad ...(9)$$

$$AgOSO_2^{-1}.O_2 \xrightarrow{k_3} Ag^+ + SO_{3+}O_2 \quad ...(10)$$

$$SO_3 + O_2 \xrightarrow{k_4} SO_5 \quad ...(11)$$

$$SO_5 + SO_3^{-2}\,SO_3 \xrightarrow{k_{5-2}} SO_5^{-2} \quad ...(12)$$

$$SO_5 + SO_3^{-2}SO_4 \xrightarrow{k_{6-2}} SO_4^{-2} \quad ...(13)$$

$$SO_5^{-2} + SO_3^{-2} \xrightarrow{k_7} 2SO_4^{-2} + SO_4^{-2} \quad ...(14)$$

$$SO_4 + SO_3^{-2} \xrightarrow{k_8} SO_3 + SO_4^{-2} \quad ...(15)$$

$$SO_4 + x \xrightarrow{k_9} \text{Non Chain product} \quad ...(16)$$

$$SO_4 + \xrightarrow{k_{10}} \text{OrganicsNon Chain product} \quad ...(17)$$

CONCLUSIONS

The following conclusions are deduced from the results of the benzamide inhibited Ag(I) catalysed autoxidation of S(IV) was that inhibit the oxidation with the fast influence. The value of Inhibition factor of both uncatalysed and Ag(I) catalysed autoxidation of S(IV) in the present study are in the range of 10^3 –10^4 which shows that free radical mechanism is operative.

Importance of Work

The results are useful for modeling rain water acidity and therefore a great use of meteorology and atmospheric chemistry.

This study is important in understanding the mechanism of the atmospheric oxidation of S(IV) by O_2.

REFERENCE

F. Dentener ,B. Ervens, C. George, J. E. Williams, G. V. Buxton, G. A. Salmon, M. Bydder, F. Wilkinson, P. Mirabel, R. Wolke, H. Herrmann, 2003, CAPRAM 2.4 (MODAC Mechanism) an Extended and Condensed Tropospheric Aqueous Phase Mechanism and its Application.*J. Geophys. Res.***108,** 4426.doi:10.1029/2002JD002202.

Acker K, Moller D,Wieprecht W,Auel R,Kalass D and Tscherwenka W, 2001, Nitrous and Nitric Acid Measurements Inside and Outside of Clouds at mt. Brocken *Water Air and Soil Pollution*, **130**, 331-336.

Acker K, Moller D,Wieprecht W, Auel R, Kalass D and Tscherwenka W, 2005, Concentrations of Nitrous Acid, Nitric Acid, Nitrite and Nitrate in the Gas and Aerosol Phase at a Site in the Emission Zone during ESCOMPTE 2001 Experiment, *Atmospheric Research*, **74**, 507-524.

Brimblecombe P., Spedding D.J., 1974, The Reaction Order of the Metal Ion Catalysed Oxidation of Sulphur Dioxide in Aqueous Solution. *Chemosphere*,**1**, 29-32.

Da-Jiongling,Qian Chun Huang Ying Ouyang, 2010, Impacts of Simulated Acid Rain on Soil Enzyme Activities in a Latosol, *Ecotoxicology and Environmental Safety*, 73,**8**,1914-1918.

Elissa Franzoni, Enrico Sassoni, 2011, Correlation Between Microstructural Characteristic and Weight Loss of Natural Stones Exposed to Simulated Acid Rain, *Science of the Total Environment*, **412**, 278-285.

Kulshrestha U.C., Sarkar A.K., Srivastava S.S., ParasharD.C., 1995, Wet-only and Bulk Deposition Studies at New Delhi (India), *Water Air and Soil Pollution*, **85**, 2137-2142.

Kulshrestha U.C., Sarkar A.K., Srivastava, S.S., Parashar,D.C., 1996, Investigation into Atmospheric Deposition through Precipitation Studies at New Delhi (India), *Atmospheric Environment*, **30**, 4149-4154.

Kulshrestha U.C, Kulshrestha M.J., Sekhar R, Sastry G.S. R., Vairamani M, 2003, Chemical Characterization of Rain Water at an Urban Site of South Central India, *Atmos. Environ.*, **37 (I)** 3019-3026.

Banerjee D., 2008, Study of Precipitation Chemistry Over an Industrial City, *Int J Environ Sci. Tech*, **5 (3)** , 331-338.

Saxena P, Turpin B.J., Andrews E., 2000, Measuring and Simulating Particulate Organics in the Atmosphere Problemsand Prospects. *Atmospheric Environment*, **34**, 2983–3013.

Khemani L.T., Momin G.A., Naik M.S., PrakasaRao P.S., Kumar R., Ramana Murty Bh.V., 1985a, Trace Elements and Sea Salt Aerosols Over the Sea Areas Around the Indian Sub Continent, *Atmospheric Environment*, **19**, 277.

Khemani L.T., Momin G.A., Naik M.S., Prakasa Rao P.S., Kumar R., Ramana Murty Bh.V., 1985b, Impact of Alkaline Particulates on pH of Rain-water in India, *Water Air and Soil Pollution*, **24**, 365.

Gupta K. S., Bhargava P., Manoj S. V. and Bhargava R., 2000, Kinetics and Mechanism of Silver(I) Catalyzed Oxidation of Aqueous Sulphur(IV) in Acetate Buffered Medium, *Transition Metal Chemistry*, **25**, 329-332.

A. J. Franck, F. Turecek, 1999, Study of Sulpfur Oxidation Product by Pyrolysis High Resolution Mass Spectrometer *Eur. Mass Spectrum*, **5**, 375-384.

Lee Y. J. and Rochelle G. T., 1987, Oxidative Degradation of Organic Acid Conjugated with Sulfite Oxidation in Flue Gas Desulphurization: Products, Kinetics and Mechanism, *Environment Science and Technology*, **21**, 266-271.

Brandt C. and van Eldik R., 1995, Transition Metal Catalyzed Oxidation of Aqueous Sulphur(IV) Oxides, Atmospheric Relevant Process and Mechanisms, *Chemical Reviews*, **95**, 119-190.

Calvert J. G. and Stockwell W. R., 1984, Mechanisms and Rates of Sulphur Dioxides in Atmosphere, In: *SO_2, NO and NO_2 Oxidation Mechanisms. Atmospheric Considerations*, J. G. Calvert (Ed.), Butterworths, Boston, pp. 1-62.

Hoffman M R and Edwards J O, 1975, Kinetics of the Oxidation of Sulphite by Hydrogen Peroxide in Acidic Medium, *Journal of Physical Chemistry*, **79**, 2096-2098.

Halperin J and Taube H, 1952, The Transfer of Oxygen Atoms in Oxidation Reductions IV The Reaction of Hydrogen Peroxide with Sulfite and Thiosulphate and of Oxygen, MnO_2 and of MnO_4^- with Sulfite, *J American Chemical Soc.*, **74**, 375-380.

Penkett S.A., Jones B.M.R., Eggleton A.E.J. 1979, A study of SO_2 Oxidation in Stored Rainwater Samplers, *Atmos. Environ.* **13**, 139–147.

Penkett S.A., Jones B.M.R., Brice K.A., Eggleton A.E.J., 1979, The Importance of Atmospheric Ozone and Hydrogen Peroxideinoxidising Sulphur Dioxide in Cloud and Rain-water, *Atmospheric Environment*, **13**, 123.

Larson T.V., 1976, The Kinetics of Sulphur Dioxide Oxidation by Oxygen and Ozone in Atmospheric Hydrometers, Ph.D. Thesis, University of Washington.

Martin L. R., 1984, In *SO_2, NO and NO_2 Oxidation Mechanisms, Atmospheric Considerations*, Calvert J. G. (Ed.), Butterworth, Boston. pp. 63-100.

Hoffman M. R. and Jacob D. J., 1984, In *SO_2, NO and NO_2 Oxidation Mechanisms, Atmospheric Considerations*, Calvert, J.G.(Ed.), Butterworth, Boston, pp. 101-172.

Hoffmann M. R. and Boyce S. D., 1983, In*Trace Atmospheric Constituents, Properties, Transformations and Fates*, S. E. Schwartz, (Ed.), John Wiley and Sons, New York, pp 147-189.

Kraft J. and Van Eldik R., 1989, Kinetics and Mechanism of the Iron(III)-Catalyzed Autoxidation of Sulphur(1V) Oxides in Aqueous Solution Formation of Transient Iron (III)-Sulphur (1V) Complexes, *Inorganic Chemistry*, **28**, 2297-2305.

28. Kuo D. T. F., Krik D. W. and Jia C. Q., 2006, The Chemistry of Aqueous S(IV)-Fe-O_2 System, State of the Art, *Journal of Sulphur Chemistry*, **27**, 461-530.

U. Schurath, J. Peeters, R. P. Wayne, G. K. Moortgat, I. Grgic,C. George, H. Herrmann, D. Poppe, 2003, *Towards Cleaner Air for Europe – Science, Tools and Applications Part 2, Overviews from the Final Reports of the EUROTRAC-2 Subprojects* (Eds P. M. Midgley, M. Reuther), pp. 73–98.

Manoj S. V., Mishra C. D., Sharma M., Rani A., Jain R.,Bansal S. P. and Gupta K. S., 2000, Iron, Manganese and Copper Concentrations in Wet Precipitations and Kinetics of the Oxidation of SO_2 in Rain Water at Two Urban Sites Jaipur and Kota in Western India, *Atmospheric Environment*, **34**, 4479-4486.

Fuzzi S., 1978, Study of Iron(III) Catalyzed Sulphur Dioxide Oxidation in Aqueous Solution Over a Wide Range of pH, *Atmospheric Environment*, **12**, 1439-1442.

Brimblecombe P., Spedding D.J., The Catalytic Oxidation of Micromolar Aqueous S(IV), *Atmospheric Environment*, **8**, 937-945.

Conklin M. H. and Hoffmann M. R., 1988, Metal ion-Sulphur(IV) Chemistry, 3, Thermodynamics and Kinetics of Transient Iron(III)-Sulphur (IV) Complexes, *Environ. Sci. Technol.* **22**, 899–907.

Huss Jr. A., Lim P. K. and Eckert C. A., 1982, Oxidation of Aqueous Sulphur Dioxide, Homogenous Manganese (II) and Iron (II) Catalysis at Low pH, *Journal of Physical Chemistry*, **86**, 4224-4228.

Wilkosz I., Konieczynski J., Zajusz-Zubek E.1999, Kinetic Studies of S(IV) Catalytic Oxidation in Aqueous Solutions at Concentrations Close to those Found in the Atmosphere, *Arch Environ Prot.*, **25**, 51–52.

I. Grgic R. Losno, W. Pasiuk-Bronikowska, in *EUROTRAC-2 CMD Final Report, 2003, Part III-1* (Eds U. Schurath, K.-H. Naumann).

Manoj S.V, Gupta K.S. and Bhargava P., 2000, Kinetics of Tetraamminecopper(II) Catalysed Oxidation of Sulphur(IV) by Peroxydisulphate in Ammonia Buffer, *Transition Metal Chemistry*, **25**, 274-278.

Connick R.E., Zhang Y.-X., 1996, Kinetics and Mechanism of the Oxidation of HSO_3^- by O_2, The Manganese(II)-Catalyzed Reaction. *Inorg. Chem.* **35**, 4613–4621.

Berglund J., Fronaeus S., Elding L.J., 1993, Kinetics and Mechanism for Manganese-catalyzed Oxidation of Sulphur(IV) by Oxygen in Aqueous Solution, *Inorg. Chem*,**32**, 4527–4538.

Podkrajsek B., Grgic I. and Tursic J., 2002, Determination of Sulphur Oxides Formed During the S(IV) Oxidation in the Presence of Iron, *Chemosphere*, **49**, 271–277.

S. Lunak, A.M. El-Wakil and J. Veprek-Siska, 1978, Autoxidation of Sulphite Catalysed by 3d Transition Metals and Inhibited by 2-propanol Mechanism of Inhibited and Induced Reactions Coll, *Czech. Chem. Commun.*, **43**, 3306.

Fuller E.C. and Crist R.H., 1941, The Rate of Oxidation of Sulfite Ions by Oxygen, *J American Chemical Soc.*,**63**,1644-1650.

Hobson D.B. Richardson P.J. and Robinson P.J., 1986, Kinetics and Mechanism of Co Catalysed Reaction of Oxygen and Sulfite at Very Low Concentrations, *J of Chem Soc.* Faraday Transactions 1, **82,** 869-881.

R.D. Srivastava, A.F. McMillan and I.J. Harris, Can. J. Chem., 1968, The Kinetics of Oxidation of Sodium Sulfite,*J of Chemical Engineering*, **46**, 181.

Gupta K.S., Bhargava P. and Manoj S.V., 1999, Kinetics of Silver(I) Catalysed Oxidation of Sulphur(IV) by Peroxodisulfate, *Indian Journal of Chemistry*, **38A**, 692-697.

Gupta K.S., Bhargava P. and Manoj S.V., 2001, Kinetics of Diamminesilver(I)-Catalysed Oxidation of Sulphur(IV) by Dioxygen in Ammonia Buffers, *Transition Metal Chemistry*, **26**, 71-75.

Gupta K. S., Jain U., Singh A., Mehta R. K., Manoj S. V., Prasad D. S. N., Sharma A., Parashar P., Bansal, S. P., 2004, Kinetics and Mechanism of the Osmium(VIII)-Catalysed Autoxidation of Aqueous Sulphur Dioxide in Acidic and Alkaline Media, *Journal of Indian Chemical Society*, **81**, 1083-1092.

D.E. Linn Jr., M.J. Dragan and D.E. Miller, 1990, Catalysis of Autoxidation of Aqueous Sulphur Dioxide Using $[Ni^{III}(cyclam)]$ Evidence for a Novel Radical Chain Mechanism,*Inorg. Chem.*, **29**, 4356.

Pasuik-Bronikowska W. Bronikowski, T. and Ulejczyk M., 1997, Solubilization of Organics un Water Coupled with Sulfite Autoxidation, *Water Research*, **31**, 1767-1775.

Rani A., Prasad D. S. N., Madnavat P. V. S., Gupta K. S., 1992, The Role of Free Fall Atmospheric Dust in Catalysing Autoxidation of Aqueous Sulphur Dioxide, *Atmospheric Environment*, **26A**, 667-673.

Prasad D. S. N., Rani A., Gupta K. S., 1992, Surface-Catalyzed Oxidation of Sulphur(IV) in Aqueous Silica and Copper(II) Oxide Suspensions, *Environmental Science and Technology*, **26,** 1361-1368.

Bhargava R., Rani A. and Gupta K. S., 1993, Oxidation of Aqueous Sulphur Dioxide in Suspensions of Magnesium Dioxide, Removal of SO_2 from Flue Gases, *Indian Journal of Chemistry*, **32A,** 713-716.

Rani A., Prasad D. S. N., Jain U. and Gupta K. S., 1991, Dynamics of Multiphase Glass Powder Catalysed Autoxidation Sulphur Dioxide in Bulk in Aqueous Phase, *Indian Journal of Chemistry*, **30A**, 756-764.

Gupta K.S., Mehta R.K., Sharma A.K., Mudgal P.K., Bansal S.P., 2008, Kinetics of the Uninhibited and Ethanol-inhibited CoO, Co_2O_3 and Ni_2O_3 Catalyzed Autoxidation of Sulphur(IV) in Alkaline Medium, *Transition Metal Chemistry*, **33**,809-817.

Prasad D. S. N., Rani A., Madnavat P. V. S., Bhargava R. and Gupta K. S., 1991, Kinetics of Surface Catalyzed Oxidation of Sulphur(IV) by Dioxygen in Aqueous Suspensions of Cobalt (II) oxide, *Journal of Molecular Catalysis*, **69**, 395-405.

Gupta K. S., Singh R., Saxena D., Manoj S. V. and M. Sharma, 1999, Role of Manganese Dioxide in the Autoxidation of Sulphur(IV) in Toxic and Anoxic Suspensions, *Indian Journal of Chemistry*, **38A**, 1129-1138.

Bhargava R., Prasad D. S. N., Rani A., Bhargava P. Jain U. and Gupta K. S., 1992, Kinetics of Autoxidation of Aqueous Sulphur Dioxide in Suspensions of Nickel(III) Oxide, *Transition Metal Chemistry*, **17**, 238-241.

Manoj S.V., Sharma M. and Gupta K.S. 1999, Role of Cuprous Oxide in Autoxidation of Aqueous Sulphur Dioxide and Its Atmospheric Implications, *Atmospheric Environment*, **33**, 1503-1512.

Prasad D. S. N., Mehta R. K., Parashar P., Madnawat P. V. S., Rani A., Singh U., Manoj, S. V., Bansal S. P. , Gupta K. S., 2003, Kinetics of Surface-catalysed Autoxidation of Aqueous Sulphur Dioxide in Cobalt(III) Oxide Suspensions, *Journal of Indian Chemical Society*, **80**, 391-394.

Cohen S, Chang S.G. Markovitz S S and Novakov T., 1981 Role of Fly Ash in Catalytic Oxidation of S (IV) Slurries, *Environmental Sc. and Tech.* **15**, 1498-1502.

Madnavat P.V.S., Rani A., Sharma M. Prasad D.S.N., and Gupta K.S., 1993, Role of Surface and Leached Metal Ion Catalysis in Autoxidation of S(IV) in Power Plant Flyash Suspensions, *Atmospheric Environment*, **27A**, 1985-1991.

Saxena D., Sharma M., Rani A. and Gupta K.S. 1995, Studies on Rates of Autoxidation of Aqueous Sulphur Dioxide in Several Fly Ash Suspensions. Implications for Acid Rain, *J Environment Sc. And Health*, **A-30**, 1191-1210.

Brodzinsky R, Chang SG, Mankovitz SS, Novakov T, 1980, Kinetics and Mechanism of Catalytic Oxidation of Sulphur di oxide on Carbon in Aqueous Suspension, *J of Physical Chemistry*, **84**, 3353-3358.

Gupta K.S., Madnawat P.V.S.,Bhargava R., Prasad D.S.N., Sharma M. rani A, 1992, Autoxidation of Aqueous Sulphur di oxide in Suspensions of Minerals and Rocks, Precip, Scavenging *Atmos-surf-exch*, 153-160.

Saxena D., Sharma M., Rani A., Singh R, Gupta K.S., 1993, Kinetics of Oxidation of Aqueous Sulphurdioxide by lead Dioxide in Aqueous Suspensions, *Indian Journal of Environmental Protection*, **15**, 575-579.

Prasad D. S. N., Rani A., Sharma M. and Gupta K. S., 1994, Rates of Autoxidation of Sulphur(IV) in Aqueous Suspensions of Limestone Powder, Implications for Scrubber Chemistry, *Indian Journal of Chemistry*, **1**, 87-92.

R.E. Connick, Y.X. Zhang, S. Lee, R. Adamic and P. Cheing, 1995, Kinetics and Mechanism of Oxidation of HSO_3^- by O_2 the Uncatalysed Reactions, *Inorg. Chem.*, 34, 4543.

Berresheim H, Talbot R.W., Andreae M.O., Jacob D.J., Beecher, K.M., 1990, Source and Sink of Formic and Acetic and Pyruvic Acids Over Central Amazon, *Journal of Geophysical Research*, **95**, 16799–16811.

Huss A., Jr. Lim P. K. and Eckert C. A., 1978, on the 'Uncatalyzed' Oxidation of Sulphur(IV) in Aqueous Solutions, *Journal of American Chemistry Society*, **108**, 6253.

Huss Jr. A. Lim, P. K. and Eckert, C. A., 1982, Oxidation of Sulphur Dioxide, High Pressure Studies and Proposed Reaction Mechanisms, *Journal of Physical Chemistry*, **86**, 4229-4233.

Huss Jr. A, Lim P. K. and Eckert C. A., 1982, Oxidation of Sulphur Dioxide, The Effects of Chelating Agents and Phenolic Anti-oxidants, *Journal of Physical Chemistry*, **86**, 4233-4237.

Huie R. E. and Peterson, N. C., 1983, In *Trace Atmospheric Constituents, Properties, Transformations & Fates*, S. E. Schwartz, (Ed.), John Wiley and Sons, New York, pp. 118-143.

Huie R. E. and Neta P., 1984, Chemical Behaviour of SO_3^- and SO_5^- Radicals in Aqueous Solutions, *Journal of Physical Chemistry*, **23**, 5665-5669.

Backstrom H. L. J., 1934, The Chain Mechanism of the Autoxidation of Sodium Sulfite Solutions, *J. Phys. Chem.*(B), **25**, 122-138.

Hayon E.,Treinin A. and Wilf J., 1972, Electronic Spectra, Photochemistry and Autoxidation Mechanism of the Sulfite-bisulfite Pyrosulfite Systems. The SO_2^-, SO_3^-, SO_4^- and SO_5^- Radicals, *Journal of American Chemical Society*, **94**, 47-57.

Manoj S.V., Mudgal P.K. and Gupta K.S., 2008, Kinetics of Iron (III) Catalysed Autoxidation of S(IV) in Acetate Buffered Medium, *Transition Meat Chemistry*, **33**,311-316.

Altwicker E. R., 1980, In *Advances in Environmental Sciences and Engineering*, Vol. **3.** J. R. Pfaffin and E. N. Zieglar (Eds.), Gordon and Breach Science Publishers, New York, pp. 80-91.

LeeRaja, S. Raghunathan, R. Yu, X.-Y. T., Chen J., Kommalapati, R.R., Murugesan, K., Shen X., Qingzhong Y., Valsaraj K.T., Collett Jr. J.L., 2008, Fog Chemistry in the Texas–Louisiana Gulf Coastcorridor, *Atmos. Environ.* **42**, 2048–2061.

Grgic I., Dovzan A., Bercic G., and Hudnik V., 1998, The Effect of Atmospheric Organic Compounds on the Fe-catalyzed S(IV) Autoxidation in Aqueous Solution, *J. Atmos. Chem.* **29**, 315–337.

Podkrajsek B., Grgic I., and Tursic J., 2002, Determination of Sulphur Oxides Formed During the S(IV) Oxidation in the Presence of Iron, *Chemosphere* **49**, 271–277.

Ziajka J., Beer F. and Warneck P., 1994, Iron-catalyzed Oxidation of Bisulfite Aqueous Solution: Evidence for a Free Radical Chain Mechanism, *Atmospheric Environment,* **28(15)**, 2549-2552.

W. Pasiuk-Bronikowska, J. Ziajka, T. Bronikowski, 1992, *Autoxidation of Sulphur Compounds,* (Ellis Horwood, New York).

J. Ziajka, W. Pasiuk-Bronikowska, 1998, Effect of α-pinene and Cis-verbenol on the Rate of S (IV) Oxidation Catalysed by Fe, Proceedings of EUROTRAC Symposium 98 Transport and Chemical Transformation in the Troposphere, Gramisch Partenkirchen Germany, 756-764.

Pasuik-Bronikowska, W. Bronikowski, T. Ulejczyk, M., 1998, Chemical Interactions of Aqueous Phase Pollutants, Sulphur Dioxide and Sobrerol in U. Schurath and R. Roselieb (Eds.), Proc. 2nd Workshop of the EUROTRAC-2 Subproject Chemical Mechanism Development, Forschungszentrum Aachen, Aachen, pp. A12, 1-4.

Pasuik-Bronikowska W.,Bronikowski, T., Ulejczyk, M., 2000, Transformation of Atmospheric Constituents and Pollutants Induced by S(IV) Autoxidation. Chemistry and Kinetics. In:

EUROTRAC-2 Annual Report, CMD Chemical Mechanism Development, ISS, Munich, pp. 123-126.

Rudzinski K. A. and Pasuik-Bronokowska, Isoprene Inhibition of S(IV) Autoxidation Initiated by Peroxydisulfate, In, *Transport and chemical Transformation in the Troposphere, Proc. EUROTRAC-2 Symp. 2000*, P. M. Midgley; M. J. Reuther and M. Williams (Eds.), Springer, Berlin, pp. 1-4.

Herrmann H., Ervens B., Jacobi H.W., Wolke R., Nowacki P., Zellner R., 2000, A Chemical Aqueous Phase Radical Mechanism for Tropospheric Chemistry, *Journal of Atmospheric Chemistry*, **36**, 231–3284.

Bravo H, 2002, Concentration of Benzene and Toluene in the Atmosphere of Southwestern Area at Mexico City Metropolitan Zone, Atmospheric Environment, **36**, 3843-3849.

Bigelow S. L., 1988, Catalytic Effects in the Oxidation of Sodium Sulfite by Air Oxygen, *Zeitschriftfuer Physikalische Chemie*, **26**, 493-532.

Alyea H. N. and Backstrom H. L. J., 1929, The Inhibitive Action of Alcohols on the Autoxidation of Sodium Sulfite. *Journal of American Chemical Society*, **51**, 90-107.

Ziajka J and Pasiuk-Bronikowska W, 2003, Fe Catalysed Autoxidation of S (IV) Inhibited by Aliphatic Alcohols, Nonterlinic and Substituted with α-pinene Skeleton, In Proceedings of the Joint Workshop EC Cluster 3 Chemical Process and Mechanism. EC Shaping of the Future of Atmospheric Chemistry Research in Europe, University of Paris, Paris.

Wolf A., Deutsch F., Hoffmann P. and Ortner H. M., 2000, The Influence of Oxalate on Fe-catalyzed S(IV) Oxidation by Oxygen in Aqueous Solution, *Journal of Atmospheric Chemistry*, **37**, 125-135.

Pasuik-Bronikowska W.,Bronikowski T.,Ulejczyk M., 1999, Oscillations in the Rate of S(IV) Autoxidation Inhibited by Sobrerol, in R. Vogt and G. Axelsdottir (Eds.), Proc. Joint Workshop, Ford Forschungszentrum Aachen, Aachen, pp. 195-198.

W. Pasiuk-Bronikowska, T. Bronikowski, M. Ulejczyk, 2003, Inhibition of the S(IV) Autoxidation in the Atmosphere by Secondary Terpenic Compounds, *J. Atmos. Chem.*,**44**, 97. doi:10.1023/A:1022164702310.

Manoj S.V., Bhargava R., Rani A. and Gupta, K. S., 1992, Surface-mediated Oxidation of Aqueous Sulphur Dioxide in Ceramic Powder Suspensions, *Indian Journal of Chemistry*, **31A,** 683-687.

Mudgal P.K., Bansal S.P. and Gupta K.S., 2007, Kinetics of Atmospheric Oxidation of Nitrous Oxide by Oxygen in Aqueous Medium, *Atmospheric Environment*, **41**, 4097-4105.

Ashmore P. G., 1963, *Catalysis and Inhibition of Chemical Reactions*. Butterworths, London.

Gilvert B. C., Stell J. K., Peet W. J. and Radford, K. J., 1988, Generation and Reaction of the Chlorine Atom in Aqueous Solution, *Journal of Chemical Society, Faradey Transactions*, **1**, 84, 3319-3330.

Dogliotti L. and Hayon E., 1967, Flash Photolysis of Persulfate Ions in Aqueous Solution, Study of Sulfate and Ozonide Radical Anions, *Journal of Physical Chemistry*, **71**, 2511-2516.

Clifton C. L. and Huie, R. E. 1989, Rate Constants for Hydrogen Abstraction Reactions of the Sulfate Radical, SO^-_4, Alcohols, *International Journal of Chemical Kinetics*, **21**, 677-687.

Wine L Zhu, J. M. Nicovich, P. H., 2003, Temperature-Dependent Kinetics Studies of Aqueous Phase Reactions of $SO_4^{''}$ Radicals with Dimethyl Sulfoxide, Dimethylsulfone and Methane Sulfonate, *J. Photochem. Photobiol.Chem.*, **157**, 311. doi:10.1016/S1010-6030(03)00064-9.

J. Ziajka, P.Warneck, 1995, Reaction Mechanism of the Iron(III)-Catalyzed Autoxidation of Bisulfite in Aqueous Solution, Steady State Description for Benzene as Radical Scavenger. *Ber. Bunsenges. Phys. Chem., 99*, 59.

J. Ziajka W. Pasiuk-Bronikowska, 2003, Autoxidation of Sulphur Dioxide in the Presence of alcohols Under Conditions Related to the Tropospheric Aqueous Phase, *Atmos. Environ*, **37**, 3913. 104.–l

J. Ziajka W. Pasiuk-Bronikowska, 2005, Rate Constants for Atmospheric Trace Organics Scavenging SO_4-in the Fe-catalysed Autoxidation of S(IV). *Atmos. Environ.*, **39**, 1431.

Sameena Begam, Faiyaz Huusain, D.S.N. Prasad, 2013, Kinetics of Formic Acid Inhibited Uncatalysed and CO_2O_3 Catalysed Autoxidation of S(IV) in Alkaline Medium, *Pelagia Research Library*, **4**(1), 122-131.

Yogpal Dayal, K.S. Gupta, 2014, Role of Some Organic Inhibitors on Oxidation of SO_2 in Rain Water Medium, *Env. Sc. Pollu Res*, Vol. **21**, 3474-3483.

Yogpal Dayal, K.S. Gupta, 2014. The Influence of Hydroxyl Organic Compounds on the Oxidation of SO_2 by Oxygen, *Env. Sc. Pollu Res*, Vol. **21**, 7808-7817.

Anast J. M. and Margerum D. W., 1981, Trivalent Copper Catalysis of the Autoxidation of Sulfite, Kinetics and Mechanism of the Copper (III/II) Tetraglycine Reactions with Sulfite, *Inorganic Chemistry*, **20**, 2319.

Clemitshaw, K. C. 2006, Coupling Between the Trophospheric Photochemistry of Nitrous Acid (HONO) and Nitric Acid (HNO_3), *Environmental Chemistry*, **3**, 31-34.

Brandt C., Van Eldik R., 1995, Transition Metal-catalyzed Oxidation of Sulphur(IV) Oxides. Atmospheric Relevant Processes and Mechanisms *Chemical Review*, **95**, 119–190.

Gupta K. S., 2002, Acid Rain Precursors, Sources Control and Damaging Effects, In: *Proceedings Second SERC School on Mathematical Modelling of Atmospheric Pollution*, Sapna Book House, Bangalore, pp. 7-12.

A.I. Vogel, 1982, *A Textbook of Quantitative Inorganic Analysis* Longman Green, London, pp. 357-370.

Jeffery G H, Basset J, Mendham J and Denney R.C., 1989, Vogles Textbook of Quantitative Chemical analysis, Addison Wesley Long man Limited Essex pp. 383-385.

Brodzinsky R, Chang S.G., Mankovitz S.S., Novakov T., 1980, Kinetics and Mechanisms of the Catalytical Oxidation of Sulphur Dioxide on Carbon in Aqueous Suspensions, *Journal of Physical Chemistry* **84,** 3353-3358.

Mudgal P.K., Sharma A.K., Mishra C.D., Bansal S.P. and Gupta K.S., 2008, Kinetics of Ammonia and Ammonium Ion Inhibition of the Atmospheric Oxidation of Aqueous Sulphur Dioxide by Oxygen, *Journal of Atmospheric Chemistry*, **61,** 31-55.

Gupta K.S., Mehta R.K., Sharma A.K., Mudgal P.K., Bansal S.P., 2008, Kinetics of Uninhibited and Ethanol Inhibited CoO, Co_2O_3 Catalysed Autoxidation of S(IV) in Alkaline Medium, *Trans Metal Chem.*, **33**, 809-817 doi 10.1007/s 11243-008-9115-6.

D.S.N. Prasad, A. Rani and K.S. Gupta, 1992, *Environ. Sci. Technol.*, **26**, 1361, doi10.1021/es 00031a013.

A.K. Sharma, P. Parashar, A.K. Gupta, R. Sharma and D.S.N. Prasad, Formic Acid Inhibited Ag (I) Catalysed Autoxidation of S (IV) in Acidic Medium, J. Chem. & Chemi Sci. 5 (2015) 760-771.

A.K. Sharma, P. Parashar, A.K. Gupta, R. Sharma and D.S.N. Prasad, Ag (I) Catalysed Autoxidation of S (IV) and Its Inhibition by Iso Propyl Alcohol in Acidic Medium, Chem. Sci. Rev Lett. 17(5) (2016) 14-23.

A.K. Sharma, R. Sharma and D.S.N. Prasad, Kinetics and Mechanism of Uncatalysed and Ag (I) Catalysed Autoxidation of S (IV) and Its Inhibition by Iso Amyl Alcohol in Acidic Aqueous Solutions, Int. J. Mod. Sci. Eng. Technol. 2 (12) (2015) 31-40.

Sharma, A.K., Sharma, R., Prasad, D.S.N. and Parashar, P. The Inhibitive Action of Aniline on the Autoxidation of Sodium Sulfite in Acidic Medium. *J. Anal. Phar. Res.*, 2016, 17(5), 14-23.

Sharma, A.K.; Sharma, R.; Prasad, D.S.N. The Effect of Atmospheric Aromatic Amides on the Ag (I) Catalyzed S(IV) Autoxidation in Aqueous Solution. *The Experiment*, 2017, 40(1), 2354-2363.

Sharma, A.K.; Parasher P., Sharma, R.; Prasad, D.S.N.Ag (I) Catalyzed Oxidation of SO_2 in Aqueous Solution Differing Effect of Benzoate Ions in Acidic Medium. *Current Phy chem.* 2017, 7, 1-10 (in Press)

Sharma, A.K.; Sharma, R.;Prasad, D.S.N. Kinetics of Isoamyl Alcohol and Aniline Inhibited Uncatalysed and Ag (I) Catalysed Autoxidation of S (IV) in Acidic Medium. *Asian J. Research Chem.* 2017,10 (3),251-258. **DOI: 10.5958/0974-4150.2017.00040.2**

Sharma, A.K.; Sharma, R.; Prasad, D.S.N.Role of Organics in Atmospheric Catalytic Autoxidation of Aqueous Sulphur Dioxide in Acidic Medium. *Malaysian Journal of Chemistry*, 2017, 19(1), 1–12

Analytical Techniques in Chemical and Biological Sciences **Page: 42-49**
Edited by: Dr. Deep Mala and Dr. Pawan Kumar 'Bharti'
ISBN: 978-93-86841-59-9
Edition: 2018
Published by: Discovery Publishing House Pvt. Ltd., New Delhi (India)

4

Drinking Water quality Analysis of two Natural Springs at Nganglam, Bhutan

Pawan K. Bharti[1]

ABSTRACT

The study area is surrounded by hills and mountains at high elevation near Nganglam in Eastern Himalayas. The DCCL project site is located at about 4.5 km north of Nganglam and 10 km from indo-Bhutan border. The assessment of drinking water quality has been carried out to estimate the suitability of spring water with special reference to Heavy Metals and microbiological aspects. Heavy Metals like Cadmium, copper, iron, manganese, lead and zinc were found nil or in very low concentration at both sites during every season. Cadmium, manganese and copper was absolutely absent in all seasons, while lead concentrations were also found below detection limit in maximum samples. The concentration of iron was maximum observed 0.13 mg/l during the entire study. Zinc concentration was also found below the standards limit.

The present study deals with the preliminary physico-chemical characteristics of the spring water and exhibits the natural quality of water with minimum anthropogenic activities, which contribute in microbial contamination and pollution load of natural water. In the bacteriological test, both the samples water does not confirm to the prescribed standards. Analysis shows that the water is unfit for drinking purpose due to the microbial contamination.

Key words: Microbial contamination, MPN, Water quality, Heavy Metals, Pollution status.

INTRODUCTION

The major rivers of the country flow north to south, with their source in the alpine zone and flowing right down to the tropical zone on the border with India. The rivers of Bhutan generally have steep gradients and narrow steep-sided valleys, which occasionally open up to give small areas of flat land for cultivation. The topography is rugged and characterized by swift flowing of rivers. Bhutan has abundant water resources, but these resources will face new, complex and

[1] Shriram Institute for Industrial Research, Delhi-7

pervasive challenges caused by population growth, climate change and socio-economic development. Bhutan has enormous water resources as a result of the many glaciers and glacial lakes, vast forest cover and high precipitation. Royal government of Bhutan appointed the National Environment Commission (NEC) as the apex body for coordinating the water resources management of the country.

As the water, the most abundant and vital natural resource is extremely essential for survival of all living organisms, but today clean water has become a precious commodity and its quality is threatened by numerous sources of pollution. Water pollution creates physical, chemical and biological changes in the water, and further affects the water quality for a long time of period (Malik and Bharti, 2005a). Water resources in the study area may be classified in to stream/ spring water, and surface water. The villagers use mostly spring water as their principal source for domestic consumption and other daily activities. In some villages the spring water is collected in a tank and supplied by pipelines to different houses as protected water supply for both drinking and cooking purpose. Assessment of microbial quality of water in the area was carried out once in every season. Water quality study of water resources with reference to bacteriological contamination proved the suitability of spring water as drinking water.

To assess the water quality of study area two number of spring water samples from different stations were drawn and analyzed for various physico-chemical parameters, Heavy Metals and microbiological parameters. The assessment has been carried out to estimate the effect of any anthropogenic activities on the water quality of the study area and to formulate mitigation measures to prevent the surface water bodies and stream water from further pollution. There are no lake and ponds and even no well and borewell were found in the study area. In most part of the study area, the water streams are moving from north to south direction. There are many natural springs near Nganglam which join the tributary of Kirung Ri, Kurung Ri river, Bidungri and Bodari stream and ultimately join the Manas river.

The Himalayas are the cradle of a large number of streams and mighty rivers (Bharti, 2004). Near Indo-Bhutan border, 150 Km. far away from Guwahati city, Nganglam (Bhutan) is the study site for the accounting of physico-chemical parameters, Heavy Metals and microbiological parameters in natural water and fluctuations at the different season. The DCCL project site is located at Lower Chenkari village of Nganglam, Pemagatsel district in Eastern Himalayas in Bhutan. The project site is surrounded by hills and mountains at high elevation. The project site is located at about 4.5 Km north of Nganglam and 10 km from indo-Bhutan border. The geo-co-ordinates of the study area is 26°52′ to 26°55′ N Latitude and 91°12′ to 91°14′ E Longitude. The maximum temperature in summer is 32°C and minimum 5°C in winters.

There are no industrial activities existing in the area and ecosystems are quite natural.

The present study deals with the microbial characteristics of the spring water of Nganglam area influenced by anthropogenic activity and to determine the nature and degree of anthropogenic impacts on quantitative variations in microbes in relation to physico-chemical parameters and Heavy Metals of spring water.

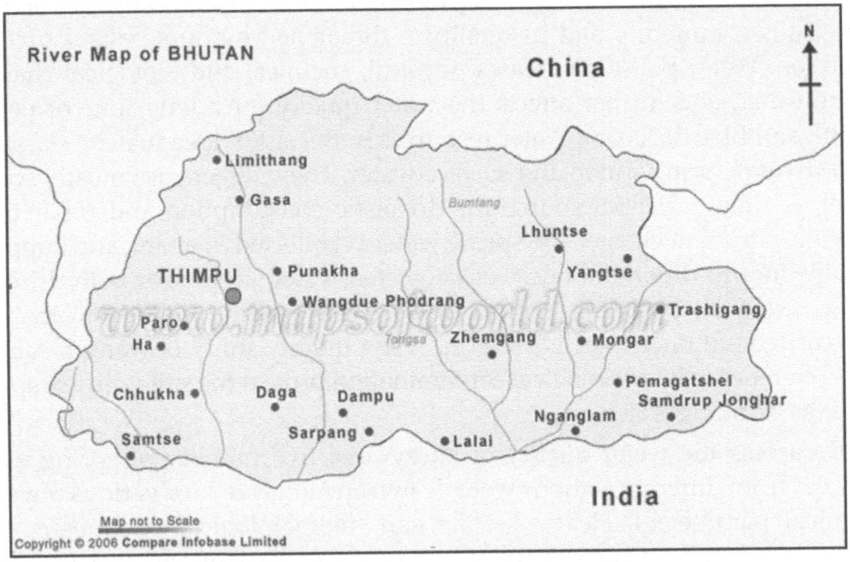

Map-1: Showing the water resources near Nganglam

MATERIALS AND METHODS

The water samples were collected from spring source Nganglam (sampling site A) and Chenkari spring (sampling site B) near DCCL project site according to the analytical requirement in morning period 9:00 Hrs. to 10:00 Hrs. The samples for physico-chemical parameters and Heavy Metals were collected by using rinsed Borosil glassware, and analyzed with the help of the procedure described by APHA (1998) and Trivedi and Goel (1984). Grab water samples were collected in 5 litre plastic jerry canes and 250 ml sterilized clean glass/ pet bottles for physico-chemical parameters and bacteriological test respectively from selected sampling locations. Water quality parameters were analyzed as per standard procedures/ method given in IS:3025 (revised part) and APHA (1998).

Colour, odour, turbidity, velocity, temperature and Dissolved oxygen were analysed on sampling sites. Samples were collected from selected sites and immediately preserved in ice boxes, and transfer to the lab for further analysis. Water samples were digested and Heavy Metals were detected using Atomic absorption spectrophotometer.

RESULTS AND DISCUSSION

Nutrients concentrations, Heavy Metals, bacteriological parameters and related physico-chemical parameters from selected sites are depicted in tables. Both the spring water has the spatio-temporal variations of water parameters, which play a vital role in all physico-biochemical reactions and self-purification power of aquatic system (Malik and Bharti, 2005b). Turbidity is the basic characteristic of the physical status of the water bodies. Although both of the spring water is clear because there is no more pollution, siltation was the main source of turbidity (Malik and Bharti, 2005c).

Table 4.1: Physical Characteristics of Spring Waters

S.No.	Para-meters	Unit	Nganglam Spring				Chenkari Spring				Desirable Limit
			Winter	Summer	Mon-soon	Post-mon-soon	Winter	Summer	Mon-soon	Post-mon-soon	
1.	Colour	-	Clear	Clear	Clear	Clear	Clear	Clear	Clear	Clear	-
2.	Odour	-	Nil	Nil	Nil	Nil	Nil	Nil	Nil	Nil	-
3.	Turbi-dity	NTU	<1	<1	<1	<1	<1	2	<1	<1	5
4.	TDS	Mg/l	217	167	618	167	101	105	86	102	500

Table 4.2: Chemical Characteristics of Spring Waters

Sl. No.	Parameters	Unit	Nganglam Spring				Chenkari Spring				Desirable Limit
			Winter	Summer	Mon-soon	Post-mon-soon	Winter	Summer	Mon-soon	Post-mon-soon	
1.	pH	-	7.7	8.2	7.8	7.8	7.9	8.3	8.2	7.6	6.5-8.5
2.	Alkalinity	Mg/l	174	143	112	125	76	77	65	65	200
3.	Total Hardness	Mg/l	161	148	109	157	77	80	64	89	300
4.	Calcium	Mg/l	44	44	33	50	26	28	22	27	75
5.	Magnesium	Mg/l	12	9	6	7	3	3	3	5	30
6.	Chlorides	Mg/l	5	4	3	2	5	5	5	8	250

Maximum turbidity was recorded <1 NTU during all season at Nganglam spring and 2 NTU in summer season at Chenkari spring. Total dissolved solids were found in the range of 167 mg/l in to 618 mg/l at Nganglam spring and 86-105 mg/l at Chenkari spring. The pH of natural water was controlled in a great extent by the interaction of hydroxyl ions arising from the hydrolysis of bicarbonate (Sharma, 1986). The pH of river water was recorded slightly alkaline (7.7 – 8.2) at Nganglam spring and (7.6-8.3) at Chenkari spring. Total hardness is mainly due to percentage of calcium and magnesium salts of bicarbonates, carbonates, sulphates and chlorides, while the value of alkalinity occured due to presence of bicarbonates. The total hardness was analyzed 109-161 mg/l at Nganglam spring and 64-89 mg/l at Chenkari spring during the study period. Alkalinity was found 65-174 mg/l with a small fluctuation. A positive relationship between hardness and alkalinity was recorded in river Ganga at Rishikesh (Chopra and Patric, 1994). Chloride concentration was recorded (2-5 mg/l) at Nganglam spring and (5-8 mg/l) at Chenkari spring. Chloride and hardness showed a positive relationship (Chopra and Patric, 1994). Chloride was found in the form of chloride ion, and one of the major inorganic anion present in natural water (Malik and Bharti, 2009).

Table 4.3: Heavy Metals in Spring Waters

Sl. No.	Para-meters	Unit	Nganglam Spring				Chenkari Spring				Desirable Limit
			Winter	Summer	Mon-soon	Post-mon-soon	Winter	Summer	Mon-soon	Post-mon-soon	
1.	Cadmium	Mg/l	BDL	BDL	BDL	BDL	BDL	BDL	BDL	BDL	0.01
2.	Copper	Mg/l	BDL	BDL	BDL	BDL	BDL	BDL	BDL	BDL	0.05
3.	Iron	Mg/l	BDL	0.08	0.08	BDL	0.06	0.1	BDL	0.13	0.3
4.	Lead	Mg/l	BDL	0.02	BDL	BDL	BDL	0.02	BDL	BDL	0.05
5.	Manga-nese	Mg/l	0.01	BDL	BDL	BDL	BDL	BDL	BDL	BDL	0.1
6.	Zinc	Mg/l	0.01	0.2	0.4	BDL	0.02	0.02	BDL	0.05	5.0

Table 4.4: Bacteriological Characteristics of Spring Waters

Sl. No.	Para-meters	Nganglam Spring				Chenkari Spring				Desirable Limit
		Winter	Summer	Mon-soon	Post-monsoon	Winter	Summer	Mon-soon	Post-monsoon	
1.	MPN Coli. / 100 ml	40	25	142	210	23	92	46	140	10 orga-nisms
2.	Tests for E. Coli detec-tion	Nega-tive	Positive	Posi-tive	Nega-tive	Nega-tive	Posi-tive	Posi-tive	Nega-tive	Negative

Calcium and magnesium the dominant cations, and these represent the main weathering products, but significant hydro-chemical differences between the two sampling sites associated with the bedrock geology exist (Jenkins *et al.*, 1995) Calcium is one of the essential nutrients, which plays an important role in biological system. Calcium concentration was recorded (33-50 mg/l) at Nganglam spring and (22-28 mg/l) at Chenkari spring. Magnesium is also an essential element but it is toxic at higher concentration. The concentration of magnesium in river was found maximum (12 mg/l) and minimum (3 mg/l). During the summer season nutrients concentration in hill-streams and natural spring water became more. Miller *et al.*, (1997) described the nutrients availability in selected environmental settings of the Potomac River and Cameron (1996) showed the similar type of fluctuation in Fraser river of British Columbia. Bond (1979) described similar nutrients concentration pattern in a stream draining a mountain ecosystem in Utah. Bharti *et al.*, (2010) described the similar environmental conditions in Kempty fall in Uttarakhand.

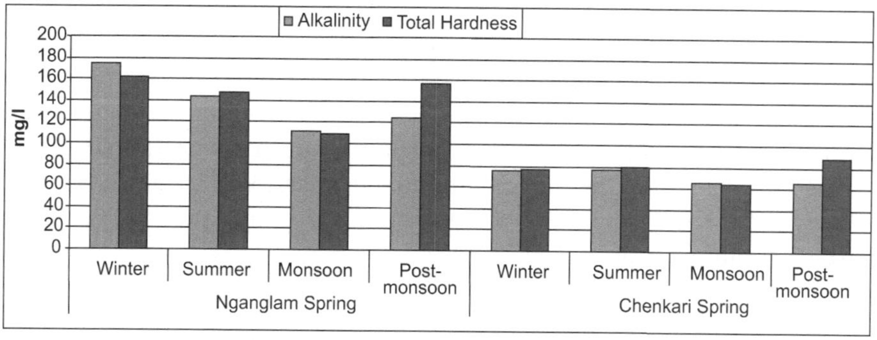

Fig. 4.1: Total hardness and Alkalinity trend of spring waters.

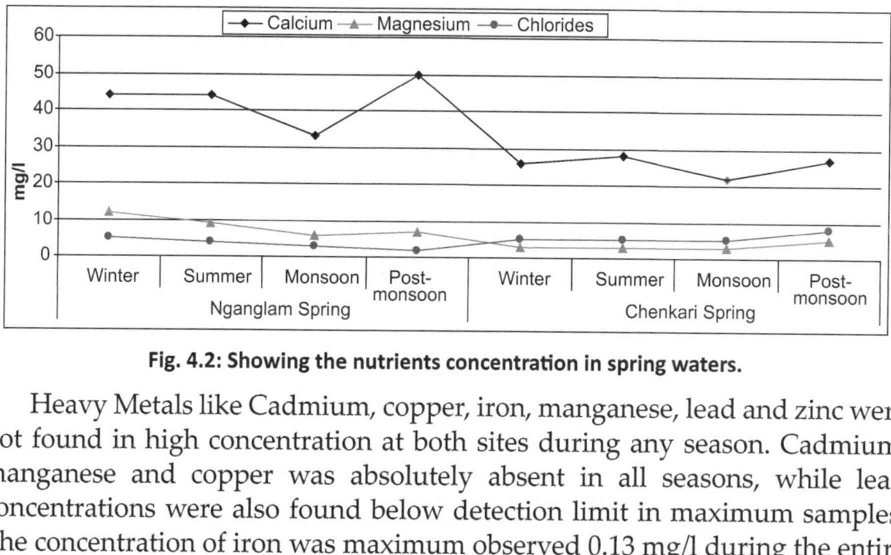

Fig. 4.2: Showing the nutrients concentration in spring waters.

Heavy Metals like Cadmium, copper, iron, manganese, lead and zinc were not found in high concentration at both sites during any season. Cadmium, manganese and copper was absolutely absent in all seasons, while lead concentrations were also found below detection limit in maximum samples. The concentration of iron was maximum observed 0.13 mg/l during the entire study. Zinc concentration was also found below the standards limit and it was found 0.4 mg/l. Malik *et al.*, (2009) described the role of Heavy Metals in the surface water of north India. The results of Bharti *et al.*, (2010) were also indicated the relation of Heavy Metals and phytoplankton in a north Indian water body.

The present results conclude that significant differences in spring water nutrient concentrations exist among different environmental settings within the two subunits. The environmental setting with the highest potential by more soluble nutrients, fluctuations in nutrient concentrations were the land use and carbonate bedrock that was predominated in the Bhutanese valley. Absence or low concentration of Heavy Metals shows that the water is still industrial pollution free. Heavy Metals were found almost nil or in very low concentrations at both selected site. The present study deals with the preliminary physico-chemical characteristics of the spring water and exhibits the natural quality of water with minimum anthropogenic activities, which contribute in pollution load of an ecosystem. However, the Indian standards are not so strict (Bharti, 2007), but Heavy Metals never cross the limits during the study period. On the basis of nutrients and Heavy Metals, the water may be considered for drinking and other purposes, but in the bacteriological test, both the samples water does not confirm to the prescribed standards (IS: 10500-1991). Analysis shows that the water is unfit for drinking purposes due to the microbial contamination.

REFERENCE

APHA (1995): Standard methods for examination of water and waste water. *American Public Health Association, 19th edition. Inc, New York.* pp:1970.

Baron, J. & Bricker, O.P. (1990) Hydrological and chemical flux in Loch Vale watershed, Rocky Mountain National Park. In: Biogeochemistry of major rivers. SCOPE 42. Wiley and sons, New York, USA.

Bharti, P.K. (2004): Limnobiological study of Sahastradhara hill-stream at Dehradun, *M.Sc. Dissertation*, submitted to Gurukula Kangri University, Hardwar, pp: 102.

Bharti, P.K. (2007): Why Indian standards are not so strict?, *Current Science,* 93(9): 1202.

Bharti, P.K., Malik, D.S. and Rashmi Yadav (2010): Influence of Heavy Metals on Abundance of Cyanophyceae Members in Three Spring-fed Lake in Kempty, Dehradun, In: 'Advances in Aquatic Ecology, Vol-III' ed. by V.B. Sakhare, *Daya Publishing House, New Delhi,* pp: 107-111.

Bond, H. B. (1979): Nutrient concentrations patterns in a stream draining a montane ecosystem in Utah. *Ecology.* 60(6): 1184-1196.

Cameron, E. M. (1996): Hydrogeo-chemistry of the Fraser River British Columbia: Seasonal variation in major and minor components. *J. Hydrol.* 182(1-4): 209-255.

Chopra, A. K. and Patrick, N. J. (1994): Effect of domestic sewage on self-purification of Ganga water at Rishikesh. *A. Bio. Science.* 13(11): 75-82.

Jenkins, A., Sloan W.T. & Cosby, B.J. (1995) Stream chemistry is the middle hills and high mountain of the Himalaya, Nepal. *Journal of Hydrology.* Vol-166, No-1-4: 61-79.

Khanna, D.R and Singh. R.K. (2000). Seasonal fluctuations in the plankton of Suswa River at Raiwala Dehradun. *Env. Conservations J.* 1(2 & 3): 89-92.

Malik, D. S. and Bharti, P. K. (2005b): Fluctuation in planktonic population of Sahastradhara hill-stream at Dehradun (Uttaranchal), *Aquacult.* 6 (2): 191-198.

Malik, D. S. and Bharti, P. K. (2005c): Primary production efficiency of Sahstradhara hill-stream, Dehradun, *Env. Cons. J.* 6 (3): 117-121.

Malik, D. S. and Bharti, P. K. (2009): Ecology of Sahastradhara Hill-stream at Dehradun (Uttaranchal), In: 'Advances in Aquatic Ecology, Vol-I' ed. by V.B. Sakhare, *Daya Publishing House, New Delhi,* pp: 1-11.

Malik, D. S. and Bharti, P. K., Negi, K.S. and Rashmi Yadav (2009): Distribution of Metals in Water of an Artificial Lake at Mussoorie, Uttarakhand, In: 'Aquatic biology and aquaculture' edited by V.B. Sakhare, Ambajoagi, MS, *Manglam Publication, New Delhi*, pp: 77-95.

Malik, D. S. and Bharti, Pawan K. (2005a): Nutrient dynamics in Rhithron zone of Shivalik Himalayan stream Sahastradhara, Dehradun (Uttaranchal), *Env. Cons. J.* 6 (2): 63-68.

Miller, C. V.; Denis, J. M.; Ator, S. W. and Brakebill, J. W. (1997): Nutrients in stream during baseflow in selected environmental settings of the Potomac river basin. *J. American Wat. Resources Association.* 33(6): 1155-1171.

Odum, E. P. (1971): Fundamentals of Ecology. New York. W. B. *Saunders and Co.* pp:1-344.

Psenner, R. (1989). Chemistry of high mountain lakes in siliceous catchments of central Alps. *Aquatic Sci.* 51: 108-128.

Shrama, R.C. (1986). Effect of physico-chemical factors on benthic fauna of Bhagirathi River Garhwal Himalaya. *Indian. J.Ecol.* 13(1): 133-137.

Subramanian, V. (1979) Chemical and suspended sediment characteristics of river of India. *J. Hydrol*, 44: 37-55.

Trivedi, R. K. and Goel, P. K. (1984): Chemical and biological methods for water pollution studies. Karad. Environmental publication. pp: 1-25.

Xue, H.B. and Schooner, J.L. (1994) Acid deposition and lake chemistry in southwest China. *Wat. Air, Soil Pollut.* 75: 61-78.

Analytical Techniques in Chemical and Biological Sciences **Page: 50-68**
Edited by: Dr. Deep Mala and Dr. Pawan Kumar 'Bharti'
ISBN: 978-93-86841-59-9
Edition: 2018
Published by: Discovery Publishing House Pvt. Ltd., New Delhi (India)

5

Inductively Coupled Plasma Mass Spectrometry (ICP-MS)

Prasann Kumar and Sunil Kumar[1]

ABSTRACT

Inductively coupled plasma mass spectroscopy is routinely used in many diverse research fields, such as earth, environmental, life and forensic sciences and in food, material, chemical, semiconductor and nuclear industries. The high ion density and the high temperature in a plasma provide an ideal atomizer and element ionizer for all types of samples and materials introduced by a specialized deviceoutstanding properties such as high sensitivity, relative salt tolerance, compound-independent element response and highest quantitation accuracy lead to the unchallenged performance of ICPMS in efficiently detecting, identifying and reliably quantifying trace element. The increasing availability of relevant reference compounds and high separation selectively extend the molecular identification capability of ICPMS hyphenated to species – specific separation techniques.

Keywords: Coupled, Diverse, Environment, Forensic, Material, Semiconductor.

INTRODUCTION

Inductively coupled plasma mass spectrometry (ICPMS) is an analytical technique that performs elemental analysis with excellent sensitivity. The ICP-MS instrument employs argon plasma (ICP) as the ionization source and a mass spectrometer (MS), usually with a quadrupole mass filter, to separate the ions produced.It can simultaneously measure most elements in the periodic table and determine analyte concentrations down to the sub nanogram per litre or parts per trillion (PPT), level. It can perform qualitative, semi quantitative, and quantitative analysis, and compute isotopic ratios on water samples, and in waste extracts and digest in an ICP-MS instrument, liquid samples are introduced by a peristaltic pump to the nebulizer where a sample aerosol is formed. Argon gas is introduced through a series of concentric quartz tubes, known as the ICP torch. The torch is located in the center of an RF coil. A Tesla coil ionizes the argon gas and free electrons are accelerated by a 27 MHz radio frequency field.

[1] Department of Agronomy, School of Agriculture, Lovely Professional University, Jalandhar, Punjab, 144411, India

Collisions between the accelerated electrons and the argon gas to generate high temperature plasma. The sample aerosol is instantaneously decomposed in the plasma to form analyte atoms, some of which are ionized. The ions produced are extracted from the plasma into the mass spectrometer region, which is

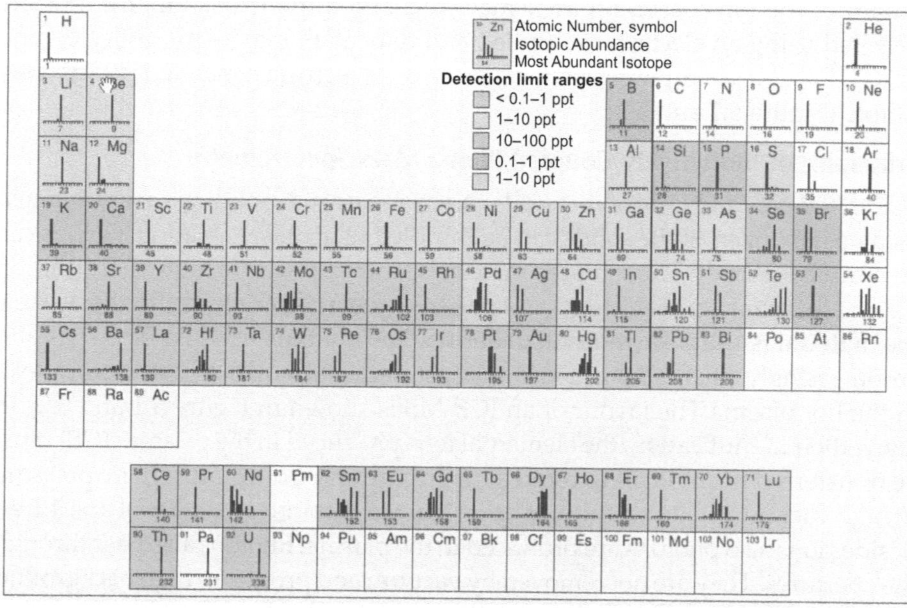

Fig. 5.1: Approximate detection capabilities of the ELAN 6000/6100 quadrupole ICP-MS (Source: Perkin Elmer, Inc)

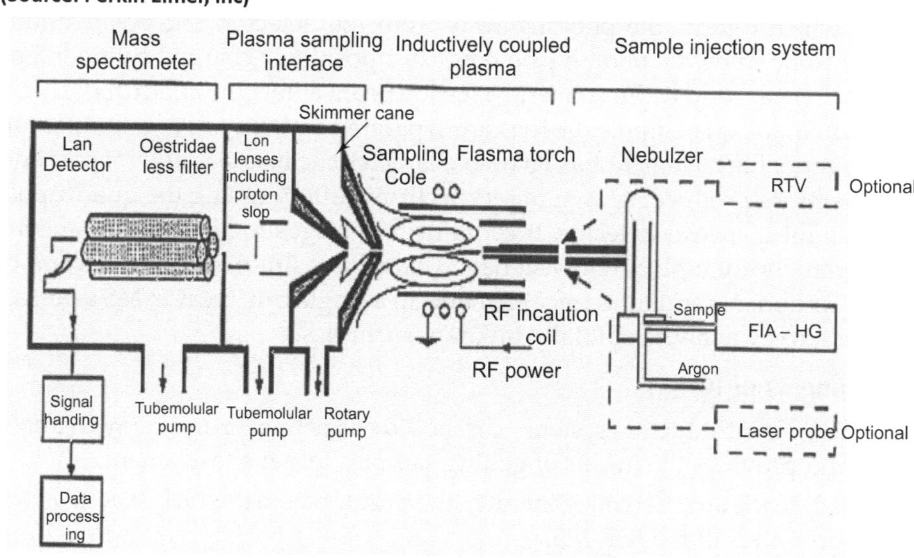

Fig. 5.2: Schematic diagram of ICP-MS

(Source: Review Literature)

maintained at a high vacuum (typically 10-6torr) using differential pumping. The analyte ions are extracted through a pair of orifices, approximately 1 mm in diameter, known as the sampling cone and the skimmer cone. The analyte ions are then focused by a series of lenses into a quadrupole mass analyzer which separates the ions based on their mass-tocharge ratio (m/z). Finally, ions are detected using an electron multiplier, and data at all masses are collected and stored through a computer interface. The mass spectrum generated is extremely simple (Figure 5.1 and 5.2).

Principles of Induvtively Coupled Plama Mass Spectrometry

Using ICP-MS, all kinds of materials can be measured. Solutions are vaporized using a nebulizer, while solids can be sampled using laser ablation. Gasses can be sampled directly. The sampled material is introduced into high-energy argon plasma that consists of electrons and positively charged argon ion. In the plasma, the material is split into individual atoms. These atoms will lose electrons and become (singly) charged positive ions. Most elements ionize very efficiently (>90) in the hot plasma.The layout of an ICP-MS is shown in Figure 5.1 and 5.2. To allow their identification, the elemental ions produced in the plasma (ICP) must be transferred from 7000K to room temperature and from atmospheric pressure to high vacuum. To do so, the ions are extracted through a number of apertures. Besides ions also photons are produced in the plasma. Photons also pass through the apertures. They are not removed by vacuum and produce a high background signal when they reach the detector. To minimize this background, also called photon stop is present this is a small metal plate placed in the centre of the ion beam, which reflects the photons away from the detector. The positive ions are not stopped by the photon stop because a positively charged cylinder lens guides them around it. Subsequently, the ion beam enters the quadrupole mass analyser. In the quadrupole the ions are separated on the basis of their mass-to charge ratio. Each element has its own characteristic isotopes and masses and will therefore produce its own mass spectrum. After passing the quadrupole the ions hit a special detector. It contains two stages to allow simultaneous measurements of high and low signals. This allows simultaneous detection of main components and ultra trace elements in a single run, the ICP-MS a perfect tool for survey analysis of totally unknown samples.

Components pf ICP-MS

- Sample introduction system – composed of a nebulizer and spray chamber and provides the means of getting samples into the instrument.
- ICP torch and RF coil–generates the argon plasma, which serves as the ion source of the ICP-MS.
- Interface – links the atmospheric pressure ICP ion source to the high vacuum mass spectrometer.

- Vacuum system – provides high vacuum for ion optics, quadrupole, and detector.
- Collision/reaction cell – precedes the mass spectrometer and is used to remove interferences that can degrade the detection limits achieved. It is possible to have a cell that can be caused both in the collision cell and reaction cell modes, which is referred to as a universal cell.
- Ion optics – guides the desired ions into the quadrupole while assuring that neutral species and photons are discarded from the ion beam.
- Mass spectrometer – acts as a mass filter to sort ions by their mass-to-charge ratio (m/z).
- Detector – counts individual ions exiting the quadrupole.
- Data handling and system controller- controls all aspects of instrument control and data handling to obtain final concentration results.

Application of Inductive Coupled Plasma Mass Spectroscopy

One of the largest volume uses for ICP-MS is in the medical and forensic field, specifically, toxicology. A physician may order a metal assay for a number of reasons, such as suspicion of heavy metal poisoning, metabolic concerns, and even hepatological issues. Depending on the specific parameters unique to each patient's diagnostic plan, samples collected for analysis can range from whole blood, urine, plasma, serum, to even packed red blood cells. Another primary use for this instrument lies in the environmental field. Such applications include water testing for municipalities or private individuals all the way to soil, water and other material analysis for industrial purposes. In the forensic field, glass ICP-MS is popular for glass analysis] Trace elements on glass can be detected using the LA-ICP-MS. The trace elements from the glass can be used to match a sample found at the crime scene to a suspect.In recent years, industrial and biological monitoring has presented another major need for metal analysis via ICP-MS. Individuals working in plants where exposure to metals is likely and unavoidable, such as a battery factory, are required by their employer to have their blood or urine analyzed for metal toxicity on a regular basis. This monitoring has become a mandatory practice implemented by osha, in an effort to protect workers from their work environment and ensure proper rotation of work duties (i.e. rotating employees from a high exposure position to a low exposure position). Regardless of the sample type, blood, water, etc., it is important that it be free of clots or other particulate matter, as even the smallest clot can disrupt sample flow and block or clog the sample tips within the spray chamber. Very high concentrations of salts, e.g. sodium chloride in sea water, can eventually lead to blockages as some of the ions reunite after leaving the torch and build up around the orifice of the skimmer cone. This can be avoided by diluting samples whenever high salt concentrations are suspected, though at a cost to detection limits. ICP-MS is also used widely in the geochemistry field for radiometric dating, in which it is used to analyze the relative abundance of different isotopes, in particular uranium and lead. ICP-MS is more suitable for this application than the previously used thermal ionization mass spectrometry, as species with high ionization energy such as osmium and tungsten can be easily ionized. For high precision ratio work, multiple collector instruments are normally used to reduce the effect noise on the calculated ratios.In the field of flow cytometry, a new technique uses ICP-MS to replace the traditional fluorochromes. Briefly, instead of labelling antibodies (or other biological probes) with fluorochromes, each antibody is labelled with a distinct combinations of lanthanides. When the sample of interest is analysed by ICP-MS in a specialised flow cytometer, each antibody can be identified and quantitated by virtue of a distinct ICP "footprint". In theory, hundreds of different biological probes can thus be analysed in an individual cell, at a rate of ca. 1,000 cells per second. Because elements are easily distinguished in ICP-MS, the problem of compensation in multiplex flow cytometry is effectively eliminated.In the pharmaceutical industry, ICP-MS is used for detecting inorganic impurities in pharmaceuticals and their ingredients. New and reduced maximum permitted exposure levels of heavy metals form dietary supplements, introduced in USP (United States Pharmacopeia) <232>Elemental Impurities—Limits and USP <233> Elemental Impurities—Procedures, will increase the need for ICP-MS technology, where, previously, other analytic methods have been sufficient. Laser ablation inductively coupled plasma mass spectrometry (LA-ICP-MS) is a powerful technique for the elemental analysis of a wide variety of materials encountered in forensic casework. (LA-ICP-MS) has already successfully been applied to applications in forensics, metals, glasses, soils, car paints, bones and teeth, printing inks, trace elemental, fingerprint, and Paper. Among these, forensic glass analysis stands out as an application for which this technique has great utility to provide highly. Car hit and runs, burglaries, assaults, drive-by shootings and bombings such as these situations may cause glass fragments that could be used as evidence of association in glass transfer conditions. LA-ICP-MS is considered one of the best techniques for analysis of glass due to the short time for sample preparation and sample, small sample size of less than 250 nanograms. In addition, there is no need for complex procedures and handling of dangerous materials that is used for digestion of the samples. This allows detecting major, minor and tracing elements with a high level of precision and accuracy. There are set of properties that are used to measure glass sample such as physical and optical properties including color, thickness, density, refractive index (RI) and also, if necessary, elemental analysis can be conducted in order to enhance the value of an association. Cosmetics, such as lipstick, recovered from a crime scene may provide valuable forensic information. Lipstick smears left on cigarette butts, glassware, clothing, bedding; napkins, paper, etc. may be valuable evidence. Lipstick recovered from clothing or skin may also indicate physical contact between individuals. Forensic analysis of recovered lipstick smear evidence can provide valuable information on the recent activities of a victim or suspect. Trace elemental analysis of lipstick smears could be used to complement existing visual comparative procedures to determine the lipstick brand and color.Previous forensic techniques employed for the organic analysis of lipsticks by compositional comparison include thin layer chromatography (TLC), gas chromatography (GC), and high-performance liquid chromatography (HPLC). These methods provide useful information regarding the identification of lipsticks. However, they all require long sample preparation times and destroy the sample. Nondestructive techniques for the forensic analysis of lipstick smears include UV fluorescence observation combined with purge-and-trap gas chromatography, microspectrophotometry and scanning electron microscopy-energy dispersive spectroscopy (SEM-EDS), and Raman spectroscopy (Figure 5.3).

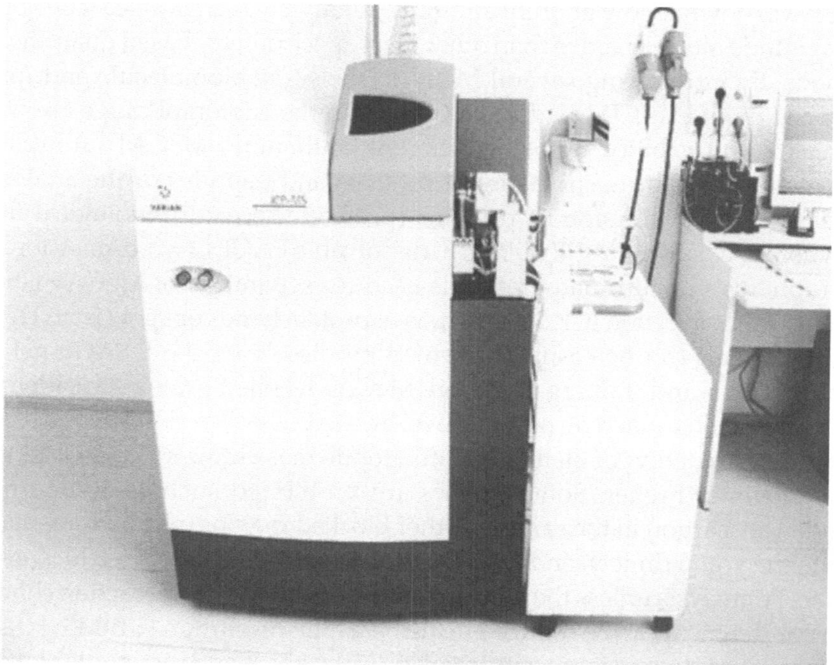

Fig. 5.3: Instruemnt Inductive Coupled Plasma Mass Spectroscopy

(Source: Review of Literature)

Quantification of Protein and Biomolecules

A growing trend in the world of elemental analysis has revolved around the speciation, or determination of oxidation state of certain metals such as chromium and arsenic. One of the primary techniques to achieve this is to separate the chemical species with high-performance liquid chromatography

(HPLC) or field flow fractionation (FFF) and then measure the concentrations with ICP-MS.There is an increasing trend of using ICP-MS as a tool in speciation analysis, which normally involves a front end chromatograph separation and an elemental selective detector, such as AAS and ICP-MS. For example, ICP-MS may be combined with size exclusion chromatography and quantitative preparative native continuous polyacrylamide gel electrophoresis (QPNC-PAGE) for identifying and quantifying native metal cofactor containing proteins in biofluids. Also the phosphorylation status of proteins can be analyzed. In 2007, a new type of protein tagging reagents called metal-coded affinity tags (MeCAT) were introduced to label proteins quantitatively with metals, especially lanthanides. The MeCAT labelling allows relative and absolute quantification of all kind of proteins or other biomolecules like peptides. MeCAT comprises a site-specific biomolecule tagging group with at least a strong chelate group which binds metals. The MeCAT labelled proteins can be accurately quantified by ICP-MS down to low attomol amount of analyte which is at least 2–3 orders of magnitude more sensitive than other mass spectrometry based quantification methods. By introducing several MeCAT labels to a biomolecule and further optimization of LC-ICP-MS detection limits in the zeptomol range are within the realm of possibility. By using different lanthanides MeCAT multiplexing can be used for pharmacokinetics of proteins and peptides or the analysis of the differential expression of proteins (proteomics) e.g. in biological fluids. Breakable PAGE SDS-PAGE (DPAGE, dissolvable PAGE), two-dimensional gel electrophoresis or chromatography is used for separation of MeCAT labelled proteins. Flow-injection ICP-MS analysis of protein bands or spots from DPAGE SDS-PAGE gels can be easily performed by dissolving the DPAGE gel after electrophoresis and staining of the gel. MeCAT labelled proteins are identified and relatively quantified on peptide level by MALDI-MS or ESI-MS.The ICP-MS allows determination of elements with atomic mass ranges 7 to 250 (Li to U), and sometimes higher. Some masses are prohibited such as 40 due to the abundance of argon in the sample. Other blocked regions may include mass 80 (due to the argon dimer), and mass 56 (due to ArO), the latter of which greatly hinders Fe analysis unless the instrumentation is fitted with a reaction chamber. Such interferences can be reduced by using a high resolution ICP-MS (HR-ICP-MS) which uses two or more slits to constrict the beam and distinguish between nearby peaks. This comes at the cost of sensitivity. For example, distinguishing iron from argon requires a resolving power of about 10,000, which may reduce the iron sensitivity by around 99%. A single collector ICP-MS may use a multiplier in pulse counting mode to amplify very low signals, an attenuation grid or a multiplier in analogue mode to detect medium signals, and a Faraday cup/bucket to detect larger signals. A multi-collector ICP-MS may have more than one of any of these, normally Faraday buckets which are much less expensive. With this combination, a dynamic range of 12 orders of magnitude, from 1 ppq to 100 ppm is possible. ICP-MS is a method of choice for the determination of cadmium in biological samples.Unlike atomic absorption spectroscopy, which can only measure a single element at a time, ICP-MS has the capability to scan for all elements simultaneously. This allows rapid sample processing. A simultaneous ICP-MS that can record the entire analytical spectrum from lithium to uranium in every analysis won the Silver Award at the 2010 Pittcon Editors' Awards. An ICP-MS may use multiple scan modes, each one striking a different balance between speed and precision. Using the magnet alone to scan is slow, due to hysteresis, but is precise. Electrostatic plates can be used in addition to the magnet to increase the speed, and this, combined with multiple collectors, can allow a scan of every element from Lithium 6 to Uranium Oxide 256 in less than a quarter of a second. For low detection limits, interfering species and high precision, the counting time can increase substantially. The rapid scanning, large dynamic range and large mass range is ideally suited to measuring multiple unknown concentrations and isotope ratios in samples that have had minimal preparation (an advantage over TIMS), for example seawater, urine, and digested whole rock samples. It also lends well to laser ablated rock samples, where the scanning rate is so quick that a real time plot of any number of isotopes is possible.This also allows easy spatial mapping of mineral grains. In terms of input and output, ICP-MS instrument consumes prepared sample material and translates it into mass-spectral data. The actual analytical procedure takes some time; after that time the instrument can be switched to work on the next sample. A series of such sample measurements requires the instrument to have plasma ignited, meanwhile a number of technical parameters have to be stable in order for the results obtained to have feasibly accurate and precise interpretation. Maintaining the plasma requires a constant supply of carrier gas (usually, pure argon) and increased power consumption of the instrument. When these additional running costs are not considered justified, plasma and most of auxiliary systems can be turned off. In such standby mode only pumps are working to keep proper vacuum in mass-spectrometer.The constituents of ICP-MS instrument is designed to allow for reproducible and/or stable operation.The first step in analysis is the introduction of the sample. This has been achieved in ICP-MS through a variety of means.The most common method is the use of analytical nebulizer. Nebulizer converts liquids into an aerosol, and that aerosol can then be swept into the plasma to create the ions. Nebulizers work best with simple liquid samples (i.e. solutions). However, there have been instances of their use with more complex materials like a slurry. Many varieties of nebulizers have been coupled to ICP-MS, including pneumatic, cross-flow, Babington, ultrasonic, and desolvating types. The aerosol generated is often treated to limit it to only smallest droplets, commonly by means of a Peltier cooled double pass or cyclonic spray chamber. Use of autosamplers makes this easier and faster, especially for routine work and large numbers of samples. A Desolvating Nebuliser (DSN) may also be used; this uses a long heated capillary, coated with a fluoropolymer membrane, to remove most of the solvent and reduce the load on the plasma. Matrix removal introduction systems are sometimes used for samples, such as seawater, where the species of interest are at trace levels, and are surrounded by much more abundant contaminants.Laser ablation is another method. While being less common in the past, is rapidly becoming popular has been used as a means of sample introduction, thanks to increased ICP-MS scanning speeds. In this method, a pulsed UV laser is focused on the sample and creates a plume of ablated material which can be swept into the plasma. This allows geochemists to spacially map the isotope composition in cross-sections of rock samples, a tool which is lost if the rock is digested and introduced as a liquid sample. Lasers for this task are built to have highly controllable power outputs and uniform radial power distributions, to produce craters which are flat bottomed and of a chosen diameter and depth. For both Laser Ablation and Desolvating Nebulisers, a small flow of Nitrogen may also be introduced into the Argon flow. Nitrogen exists as a dimer, so has more vibrational modes and is more efficient at receiving energy from the RF coil around the torch.Other methods of sample introduction are also utilized. Electrothermal vaporization (ETV) and in torch vaporization (ITV) use hot surfaces (graphite or metal, generally) to vaporize samples for introduction. These can use very small amounts of liquids, solids, or slurries. Other methods like vapor generation are also known.

The ICP Torch Making Ions

The plasma used in an ICP-MS is made by partially ionizing argon gas (Ar Ar^{+} $^{+}$e). The energy required for this reaction is obtained by passing an electrical current in wires that surround the argon. After the sample is injected, the plasma's extreme temperature causes the sample to separate into individual atoms (atomization). Next, the plasma ionizes these atoms (M $M^{+} + e^{-}$) so that they can be detected by the mass spectrometer. Inductively coupled plasma (ICP) for spectrometry is sustained in a torch that consists of three concentric tubes, usually made of quartz. The end of this torch is placed inside an induction coil supplied with a radiofrequency electric current. A flow of argon gas (usually 14 to 18 litres per minute) is introduced between the two outermost tubes of the torch and an electrical spark is applied for a short time to introduce a free electronsintothe gas stream. These electrons interact with the radio-frequency magnetic field of the induction coil and are accelerated first in one direction, then the other, as the field changes at high frequency (usually 27.12 MHz). The accelerated electrons collide with argon atoms, and sometimes a collision causes an argon atom to part with one of its electrons. The released electron is in turn accelerated by the rapidly changing magnetic field. The process continues until the rate of release of new electrons in collisions is balanced by the rate of recombination of electrons with argon ions (atoms that have lost an electron). This produces a 'fireball' that consists mostly of argon atoms with a rather small fraction of free electrons and argon ions.

Advantage of Argon

Making the plasma of argon, instead of other gases, has several advantages. First, argon is abundant (in the atmosphere, as a result of the radioactive decay of potassium) and therefore cheaper than other noble gases. Argon also has a higher first ionization potential than all other elements except He, F, and Ne. Because of this high ionization energy, the reaction ($Ar^+ + e^- \rightarrow Ar$) is more energetically favorable than the reaction ($M^+ + e^- \rightarrow M$). This ensures that the sample remains ionized (as M^+) so that the mass spectrometer can detect it.Argon can be purchased for use with the ICP-MS in either a refrigerated liquid or a gas form. However, it is important to note that whichever form of argon purchased, it should have a guaranteed purity of 99.9% Argon at a minimum. It is important to determine which type of argon will be best suited for the specific situation. Liquid argon is typically cheaper and can be stored in a greater quantity as opposed to the gas form, which is more expensive and takes up more tank space. If the instrument is in an environment where it gets infrequent use, then buying argon in the gas state will be more appropriate as it will be more than enough to suit smaller run times and gas in the cylinder will remain stable for longer periods of time, whereas liquid argon will suffer loss to the environment due to the venting of the tank when stored over extended time frames. However, if the ICP-MS is to be used routinely and is on and running for eight or more hours each day for several days a week, then going with liquid argon will be the most suitable. If there are to be multiple ICP-MS instruments running for long periods of time, then it will most likely be beneficial for the laboratory to install a bulk or a micro bulk argon tank which will be maintained by a gas supply company, thus eliminating the need to change out tanks frequently as well as minimizing loss of argon that is left over in each used tank as well as down time for tank changeover.There are rare ICP-MS solutions that utilize helium for plasma generation.

Transfer of Ions into Vaccum

The carrier gas is sent through the central channel and into the very hot plasma. The sample is then exposed to radio frequency which converts the gas into a plasma. The high temperature of the plasma is sufficient to cause a very large portion of the sample to form ions. This fraction of ionization can approach 100% for some elements (e.g. sodium), but this is dependent on the ionization potential. A fraction of the formed ions passes through a ~1 mm hole (sampler cone) and then a ~0.4 mm hole (skimmer cone). The purpose of which is to allow a vacuum that is required by the mass spectrometer. The vacuum is created and maintained by a series of pumps. The first stage is usually based on a roughing pump, most commonly a standard rotary vane pump. This removes most of the gas and typically reaches a pressure of around 133 Pa. Later stages have their vacuum generated by more powerful vacuum systems, most often turbomolecular pumps. Older instruments may have used oil diffusion pumps for high vacuum regions.

Ion Optics

Before mass separation, a beam of positive ions has to be extracted from the plasma and focused into the mass-analyzer. It is important to separate the ions from UV photons, energetic neutrals and from any solid particles that may have been carried into the instrument from the ICP. Traditionally, ICP-MS instruments have used transmitting ion lens arrangements for this purpose. Examples include the Einzel lens, the Barrel lens, Agilent's Omega Lens and Perkin-Elmer's Shadow Stop. Another approach is to use ion guides (quadrupoles, hexapoles, or octopoles) to guide the ions into mass analyzer along a path away from the trajectory of photons or neutral particles. Yet another approach is Varian patented used by Analytik Jena ICP-MS 90 degrees reflecting parabolic "Ion Mirror" optics, which are claimed to provide more efficient ion transport into the mass-analyzer, resulting in better sensitivity and reduced background. Analytik Jena ICP-MS PQMS is the most sensitive instrument on the market.A sector ICP-MS will commonly have four sections: an extraction acceleration region, steering lenses, an electrostatic sector and a magnetic sector. The first region takes ions from the plasma and accelerates them using a high voltage. The second uses may use a combination of parallel plates, rings, quadropoles, hexapoles and octopoles to steer, shape and focus the beam so that the resulting peaks are symmetrical, flat topped and have high transmission. The electrostatic sector may be before or after the magnetic sector depending on the particular instrument, and reduces the spread in kinetic energy caused by the plasma. This spread is particularly large for ICP-MS, being larger than Glow Discharge and much larger than TIMS. The geometry of the instrument is chosen so that the instrument the combined focal point of the electrostatic and magnetic sectors is at the collector, known as Double Focussing (or Double Foccussing).If the mass of interest has a low sensitivity and is just below a much larger peak, the low mass tail from this larger peak can intrude onto the mass of interest. A Retardation Filter might be used to reduce this tail. This sits near the collector, and applies a voltage equal but opposite to the accelerating voltage; any ions that have lost energy while flying around the instrument will be decelerated to rest by the filter.

Interface Sampling Ions

Placing a plasma, operating at 6000 °C, near an ion focusing device operating near room temperature is a bit like placing the earth about a half-mile away from the sun. In addition to a large temperature difference, the plasma operates at a pressure that is much higher than the vacuum required by the ion lens and allows mass spectrometer portions of the instrument. The interface the plasma and the ion lens system to coexist and the ions generated by the plasma to pass into the ion lens region. The interface consists of two or three inverted funnel-like devices called cones.Until recently, all commercially available ICP-MS systems used the two-cone design. Such a design requires down-stream focusing of the beam that exits the interface region. This focusing has been achieved through the use of a single or a series of charged devices called ion lenses. With a two-cone design, there can only be a two-step reduction in the pressure between the plasma and filtering quadrupole. A recent innovation has introduced a third cone into the interface which greatly reduces the divergence of the ion beam as it exits the interface region. The third cone, called the hyper-skimmer, provides a threestep reduction in pressure between the plasma and the filtering quadrupole, resulting in a substantial reduction in the divergence of the emerging ion beam. With the three-cone design, conventional ion lenses can be completely eliminated from the instrument, resulting in greater ion transmission, improved long-term stability, and reduced instrument maintenance. In the three-cone design, none of the cones have a voltage applied such as may exist on an extraction lens. Since the cones are electrically neutral, any build up of material on their surfaces will not significantly impact their function. In addition, experience has shown that the threecone design requires no more maintenance than a conventional two-cone design. Cones are most often produced from nickel or platinum. While nickel cones have a lower purchase price, platinum cones provide longer life, are more resistant to some acids, and provide a small improvement in instrument performance. The orifice openings of the cones should be large enough to allow for the passage of the ion beam, while, at the same time, not allow so much gas to enter the instrument that the instrument's vacuum system is taxed. Experience has shown that orifice openings of approximately 1 mm are ideal.

Transfer of Ions into Vaccum

The carrier gas is sent through the central channel and into the very hot plasma. The sample is then exposed to radio frequency which converts the gas into a plasma. The high temperature of the plasma is sufficient to cause a very large portion of the sample to form ions. This fraction of ionization can approach 100% for some elements (e.g. sodium), but this is dependent on the ionization potential. A fraction of the formed ions passes through a ~1 mm hole (sampler cone) and then a ~0.4 mm hole (skimmer cone). The purpose of which is to allow a vacuum that is required by themass spectrometer.The vacuum is created and maintained by a series of pumps. The first stage is usually based on a roughing pump, most commonly a standard rotary vane pump. This removes most of the gas and typically reaches a pressure of around 133 Pa. Later stages have their vacuum generated by more powerful vacuum systems, most often turbo molecular pumps. Older instruments may have used oil diffusion pumps for high vacuum regions.

Collision Reaction Cell

The collision reaction cell is used to remove interfering ions through ion/neutral reactionsCollision/reaction cells are known under several trade names. The dynamic reaction cell was introduced by Perkin-Elmer on their Elan DRC (followed by Elan DRC II and Elan DRC-e) instrument and is located before the quadrupolein the ICP-MS device. The chamber has a quadrupole and can be filled-up with reaction (or collision) gases (ammonia, methane, oxygen or hydrogen), with one gas type at a time or a mixture of two of them, which reacts with the introduced sample, eliminating some of the interference. The collisional reaction interface (CRI) technology used in the Bruker(former Varian) ICP-MS is another effective approach to removing ions.Axial field technology (AFT) is a DRC modification by Perkin-Elmer, which consists in two supplementary rods placed in the DRC cell that move the ions faster through the cell and improving analysis speed. Thermo Scientific's XSeries2 instrument utilizes a collision/reaction cell for interference removal, consisting of a non-consumable hexapole and chicane ion deflector, which takes the ion beam offaxis. The Agilent octopole reaction system (ORS)) uses only helium or hydrogen and the volume of the cell is smaller than that of a DRC, but is based only on collision reactions and not on chemical reactions.

Collisional Reaction Interface (CRI)

The proprietary collisional reaction interface (CRI) used in the Bruker ICP-MS destroying interfering ions. These ions are removed by injecting a collisional gas (He), or a reactive gas (H_2), or a mixture of the two, directly into the plasma as it flows through the skimmer cone and/or the samplercone.Supplying the reactive/collisional gas into the tip of the skimmer cone and/or into the tip of the sampler cone induces extra collisions and reactions that destroy polyatomic ions in the passing plasma. Fundamentally, CRI is a micro Collision/Reaction Cell (mCRC) destroying ICP-MS interferences using a collisional Kinetic Energy Discrimination (KED) phenomenon and chemical reactions with interfering ions similarly to traditionally used larger Collision.

Ion Optics

Before mass separation, a beam of positive ions has to be extracted from the plasma and focused into the mass-analyzer. It is important to separate the ions from UV photons, energetic neutrals and from any solid particles that may have been carried into the instrument from the ICP. Traditionally,ICP-MS instruments have used, transmitting ion lens arrangements for this purpose. Examples include the Einzel lens,the Barrel lens, Agilent's Omega Lens and Perkin-Elmer's Shadow stop.Another approach is to use ion guides (quadrupoles, hexapoles, or octopoles) to guide the ions into the mass analyzer along a path away from the trajectory of photons or neutral particles. Yet another approach is Varian patented used by Bruker 90 degrees reflecting "Ion Mirror" optics, which are claimed to provide more efficient ion transport into the massanalyzer, resulting in better sensitivity and reduced background.

The Mass Spectrometer-Seperating Ion

The mass spectrometer separates the singly charged ions from each other by mass, serving as a mass filter. Three main types of mass spectrometers are used in commercial ICP-MS systems: quadrupole, time-of-flight, and magnetic sector. For overall performance and economic value, most laboratories choose an ICP-MS with a quadrupole mass spectrometer. A quadrupole works by setting voltages and radio frequencies to allow ions of a given mass-to-charge ratio to remain stable within the rods and pass through to the detector. Ions with different mass to charge ratios are unstable in the cell and are ejected.To cover the full mass range, the electronics rapidly change the conditions of the quadrupole to allow different mass-to-charge ratio ions to pass through. Under the control of the instrument software, the mass spectrometer can move to any m/z needed to measure the elements of interest in the sample analyse.

Data Handling and System Controller

All ICP-MS instruments require computers and sophisticated software to control the mass spectrometer as well as perform calculations on the data collected. Additionally, the operating parameters of the spectrometer, including the proper ignition of the plasma, pressure within the high vacuum region, and the voltage applied to the detector, are to be constantly monitored by the controller, and the operator is to be alerted if any parameter falls outside of the proper working range and mass response of the instrument. All in all, the controller should monitor more than 100 separate parameters of the spectrometer.

Data Handling and Calculation

The software translates he ion counts measured by the detector into information that may be more useful to the operator. The ICP-MS instrument can provide data in one of four ways – semi-quantitative analysis, quantitative analysis, isotope dilution analysis, and isotope ratio. Results can be generated using customized report formats or easily transferred to a laboratory information management system (LIMS) or other data handling system.

ICPMS Spectrum

Is a plot of ion intensity (y-axis) versus mass to charge ratio.In an argon plasma, predominantly singly charged ions are produced.This means in practice that the mass-to-charge ratio can be replaced by mass in the spectrum.Most elements have more than one isotope and each isotope has a specific mass. Copper(Cu),or example, has two isotopes: 63 Cu with 34 neutrons and 65 Cu with 36 neutrons in the nucleus thus, the mass spectrum of copper consists of two peaks, mass 63 and mass 65. The natural ratio of the different isotopes of an element is constant in nature. Therefore, it is not difficult to correct for overlap of isotopes of different elements. In addition, a noninterfered isotope is present for almost all elements. Remaining interfering signals are removed by "inhouse" software. This approach makes fast overview analysis of the total elemental composition.

Interferences

Although interferences do occur in ICP-MS, they are relatively few in number (when compared to some other analytical techniques such as for example inductively coupled plasma atomic emission spectrometry, ICP-AES), generally predictable and can often be corrected for, may be minimized by optimizing instrument operating conditions, or are relatively insignificant. The three types of interferences that occur are isobaric, molecular (or polyatomic) and doubled-charged ion interferences.

Isobaric Interferences

Occur for equal mass isotopes of different elements. Examples include the following: 58Fe on 58Ni,64Ni on 64Zn,48Ca on 48Ti. They are best avoided by choosing alternatives, noninterfered analyte isotopes, if available. Given acknowledge of the natural abundances of the isotopes of all elements, isobaric interferences are easily corrected by measuring the intensity of another isotope of the interfering element and subtracting the appropriate correction factor from the intensity of the interfered isotope.

Molecular Interferences

Are due to the recombination of sample and matrix ions with air or other matrix components (e.g. O, N, Cl, etc.) in the cooler regions of the plasma. Examples include the following: 40Ar16O on 56Fe, 47Ti16O on 63Cu, 40Ar35Cl on 75As, 40Ar2 on 80Se. Most molecular ions formed by matrix components are predictable and may be corrected for by applying correction factors determined by analysing interference solutions. Molecular interferences may also be avoided by using alternative, non-interfered analyte isotopes. In some cases, they can be reduced in severity or even eliminated completely by using more appropriate sample introduction systems or optimizing instrument operating conditions.

Doubly-Charged Ion Interferences

Are due to relatively rare doubly-charged matrix or sample ions with twice the mass of the analyte and hence the same mass/charge ratio. The following is an example: $90Zr^{++}$ on 45Sc. The formation of doubly-charged species can generally be minimized by optimizing instrument operating conditions. Luckily, the first ionisation potential of Ar, although high enough to efficiently ionise most elements once, is not high enough to produce doubly-charged ions of most elements, thus limiting their numbers in Ar plasmas.

Matrix Effects

Clogging of the orifices in either or both of the interface cones may be a problem when samples with high total dissolved solid (TDS) contents are analysed. The high salt content of seawater samples represents a common example of this type of matrixdependent effect. The problem may be overcome by sample dilution or by avoiding solutions with TDS concentrations above 0.1 wt.%. Alternatively, a sample introduction system capable of removing dissolved salts may be used (e.g. an ultrasonic nebuliser with a desolvation unit).The presence of abundant, easily ionised matrix components such as Na in seawater may lead to a suppression in the ionisation efficiency of analytes. Once again, this effect may be reduced by sample dilution or by removal of the easily ionised matrix component.Mass-charge effectsbetween abundant heavy matrix ions (e.g. Pb, U) with high kinetic energies and lighter analyte ions may also result in decreased analyte signal intensities.

Lab Cautions for ICP - MS

- Make sure that all samples are well mixed prior to analysis.
- Label all sample tubes and caps.
- Calculate the exact added standard concentration in each sample.
- After completion of the experiment, remove all sample tubes and caps from the ICP-MS instrument area.

Current ICP-MS Offers

There are several ICP-MS systems that are presently promoted for various application markets. Although quadrupole ICP-MS is the vast majority of ICP-MS instruments produced and sold,the other two types of ICP-MS instruments available include sector field and time-of-flight (TOF). "In terms of the numbers produced, you can think of quadrupole ICP-MS as being like gasoline engine cars, sector field ICP-MS as diesel cars, and TOF-ICP-MS as being like hybrid cars," according to Steven Beres, Perkin Elmer ICPMS Specialist/Expert. Asseen, PerkinElmer's ICP-MS system is continually evolving. The current ICP-MS instruments offered include the ELAN 9000, ELAN DRC-e, and ELAN DRC II.Agilent Technologies currently markets the 7500 series2, including the 7500cx, which is a wide-range sampler, whereas the 7500csis specifically for the semiconductor industry. ICP-MS systems from Thermo Fisher Scientific include the XSERIES 2, ELEMENT GD, ELEMENT XR, and ELEMENT2 HRICP- MS. The ELEMENT models are sector field ICPMS units. In July 2008, Thermo Fisher published a poster demonstrating the capability of collision cellbased ICP-MS to analyze multi elemental environmental and geological samples with the use of the XSERIES 2 collision cell-based ICP-MS analyzer. Varian, currently offers the 810-MS, for trace and elemental analysis, and the 820-MS, which uses a collision reaction interface system to overcome spectroscopic interferences. GBC Scientific (Dandenong, Victoria, Australia) offers the GBC OptiMass 9500 ICP-TOF-MS, a second-generation time-of-flight mass spectrometer. Its main areas of application include both environmental and forensic analysis.

Expanding Markets

The market size for the number of ICP-MS units sold, including both quadrupole and high-resolution systems, is currently 900–1000 per year. ICP-MS has been widely used for testing drinking water, wastewater, soil and other parts of the environment, body fluids, tissues, and the materials that make electronic chips. ICP-MS technology has revolutionized many industries, including the semiconductor and environmental industries, by enabling laboratories to run more precise, sensitive analyses, more economically and more quickly. In fact, today's three major applications served by ICPMS technology include environmental monitoring, biomonitoring, and elemental analysis in the semiconductor industry.Environmental monitoring and biomonitoring go somewhat hand-in-hand, since both involve testing for chemicals in the environment. Environmental monitoring is of fundamental importance because it provides the basis on which we make our assessments of the quality of our environment. Biomonitoring is an important application on a personal level since it involves testing human blood, urine, and other body fluids and tissue samples to assess the degree of exposure and absorption of natural, synthetic, and toxic chemicals in the environment.The semiconductor industry is another important application market for ICP-MS. Over the past several decades, computer chips have been introduced into the majority of electronic devices manufactured in the world today— mobile phones, TVs, DVD players, and more. Throughout the years, the application of ICP-MS to test the materials that make electronic chips has allowed semiconductor chips to become more powerful, smaller, and affordable. "ICP-MS has allowed them to achieve greater densities with fewer defects per wafer so that the cost per chip could decrease," noted Steven Beres. ICP-MS is influencing new ways of thinking in other markets. One market involves the observation of life science and biological applications. Cells and other intracellular components interact with elements and metals for signaling, function, and maintenance. As a result, ICP-MS would be a potential tool to analyze molecular interactions occurring within the cells, which includes binding interactions between proteins and other metals.

Applications Quantitative Analysis

The ICP-MS accurately determines how much of a specific element is in the material analyzed. In a typical quantitative analysis, the concentration of each element is determined by comparing the counts measured for a selected isotope to an external calibration curve that was generated for that element. Liquid calibration standards are prepared in the same manner as used in AA and ICP-OES analysis. These standards are analyzed to establish the calibration curve. The unknown samples are then run, and the signal intensities are compared to the calibration curve to determine the concentration of the unknown.

Isotope Ratio

Since ICP-MS instruments measure specific isotopes of an element, the ratio of two or more isotopes can readily be determined. Isotope-ratio determinations are used in a variety of applications, including geological dating of rocks, nuclear applications, determining the source of a contaminant, and biological tracer studies.

Isotope Dilution

Isotope dilution experiments can also be performed by ICP-MS. In isotope dilution, the sample is spiked with an enriched isotope of the element of interest. The enriched isotope acts as both a calibration standard and an internal standard. Because the enriched isotope has the same chemical and physical properties as the analyte element, it is the best possible internal standard. For this reason, isotope dilution is recognized as being the most accurate type of all analyses and is often used to certify standard reference materials.

Semi-quantitative Analysis

For some analyses, it is not necessary to calibrate the ICP-MS for each element. After the instrument has been calibrated using a single solution containing as few as three elements, a high-quality semiquantitative analysis for 82 elements can be performed in just a few minutes. Semi-quantitative analysis provides a fingerprint of the elements present in a sample and the approximate concentrations of each element. This information can help determine what standards are necessary for quantitative analysis. Additionally, semi- quantitative analysis can provide valuable information on what other elements are present in a sample that could cause interferences and potentially affect the results. The software does this by comparing the measured spectrum of the unknown sample to the known isotopic fingerprints for each element and mass response of the instrument. When a match is obtained, the element is identified and the concentration estimated by comparing the measured signal to a stored response file for that element.

CONCLUSION

Inductively coupled plasma mass spectrometry (ICPMS) is an analytical technique that performs elemental analysis with excellent sensitivity. The ICP-MS instrument employs argon plasma (ICP) as the ionization source and a mass spectrometer (MS), usually with a quadrupole mass filter, to separate the ions produced. It can simultaneously measure most elements in the periodic table and determine analyte concentrations down to the sub nanogram per litre or parts per trillion (PPT), level. It can perform qualitative, semi quantitative, and quantitative analysis, and compute isotopic ratios on water samples, and in waste extracts and digest in an ICP-MS instrument, liquid samples are introduced by a peristaltic pump to the nebulizer where a sample aerosol is formed. Argon gas is introduced through a series of concentric quartz tubes, known as the ICP torch. The torch is located in the center of an RF coil.

REFERENCES

Valdimir, N.Epov, R. Douglas Evans, Jian Zheng, Masatoshiyamada, Chemistry of 322 Lma nual, http://www.csun.edu/~hcchm003/322l/ 322lmicp.pdf,41

Inductively Coupled Plasma Mass Spectrometry (ICP-MS), Philips Research, Materialanalysis, http://www.research.philips.com/technologie s/matanalysis/downloads/icp-ms.pdf

The 30 Minute Guide to ICPMS, ICP Mass Spectroscopy, http://www.perkinelmer.co m/PDFs/ Downloads/tch_icpmsthirtyminuteg uide.pdf,2001,2

V. Baranov, S. Tanner , "A Dynamic Reaction Cell for ICP-MS. Part 1: The Rf-field Energy Contribution in Thermodynamics of Ionmolecule Reactions". J. Anal. At. Spectrom. http://en.wikipedia.org/wiki/Inductively_cou pled_plasma_mass_spectrometry, 1993 1133– 1142,

A Beginner's Guide to ICP-MS R. Thomas,http://en.wikipedia.org/wiki/Inductively_ coupled_ plasma_mass_spectrometry.

Wang, XueDong; IouriKalinitchenko, "Principles and Performance of the Collision Reaction Interface for the" (PDF),Varian.Jan,http://en.wikipedia.org/ wiki/Inductively_coupled_ plasma_mass_spectrometry, 2010.

Kenichi Sakata *et al.*, Inductively Coupled Plasma Mass Spectrometer and Method, US Patent 6265717 B1,http://en.wikipedia.org/wiki/Inductively_coupled_plasma_mass_ spectrometry.

Iouri Kalinitchenko Ion Optical System for a Mass Spectrometer, United States PatentNumber 6,614,021B1, http://en.wikipedia.org/wiki/Inductively_cou pled_plasma_mass_ spectrometry, 2003.

Shane Elliott, Michael Knowles, and Iouri Kalinitchenko, A Change in Direction in ICPMS, published on Mar, http://en.wikipedia.org/wiki/Inductively_cou pled_plasma_mass_ spectrometry, 2004.

Inductively Coupled Plasma Mass Spectrometry (ICP-MS), Philips Research, Material Analysis, http://www.research.philips.com/technologie s/matanalysis/downloads/icp-ms.pdf

Potts, In: Handbook of Silicate Rock Analysis. Blackie, Glasgow Inductively coupled Plasmamass Spectrometry - Methodology 2, http://web.uct.ac.za/depts/geolsci/facilities/ ic pms/lectures/lec2.html, 1987, 575-586

Valdimir N. Epov, R. Douglas Evans, Jian Zheng, Masatoshi Yamada, Chemistry of 322L Manual, http://www.csun.edu/~hcchm003/322l/322l micp.pdf,45

Maugh, T. H. http://shop.perkinelmer.com/content/related materials/articles/atl_icpms 25 years-american laboratory september 2008.pdf, 1983, 178-9.

https://en.wikipedia.org/wiki/Inductively_coupled_plasma_mass_spectrometry

Analytical Techniques in Chemical and Biological Sciences **Page: 69-76**
Edited by: Dr. Deep Mala and Dr. Pawan Kumar 'Bharti'
ISBN: 978-93-86841-59-9
Edition: 2018
Published by: Discovery Publishing House Pvt. Ltd., New Delhi (India)

6

Analysis of Water Quality of Kirung Ri River at Nganglam, Pemagatshel Bhutan

Pawan K. Bharti and P. Kumar[1]

ABSTRACT

The project site is surrounded by hills and mountains at high elevation near Nganglam in Eastern Himalayas. The project site is located at about 4.5 Km north of Nganglam and 10 km from indo-Bhutan border. The assessment of water quality has been carried out to estimate the effect of any anthropogenic activities on the environment of the study area and to formulate mitigation measures to prevent the surface water bodies and stream water from further pollution.

Heavy Metals like Cadmium, copper, iron, manganese, lead and zinc were not found in high concentration at both sites during any season. Cadmium, manganese and copper was absolutely absent in all seasons, while lead concentrations were also found below detection limit in maximum samples. The concentration of iron was maximum observed 0.1 mg/l during the entire study. Zinc concentration was also found below the standards limit.

The present study deals with the preliminary physico-chemical characteristics of the river water and exhibits the natural quality of water with minimum anthropogenic activities, which contribute in pollution load of an ecosystem.

Key words: Physico-chemical characteristics, Water quality, Heavy Metals, Pollution status.

INTRODUCTION

Bhutan is blessed with enormous water resources as a result of the many glaciers and glacial lakes, vast forest cover and high precipitation. Royal government of Bhutan (RGoB) appointed the National Environment Commission (NEC) as the apex body for coordinating the water resources management in the country. The topography is rugged and characterized by swift flowing of rivers. The climate of Bhutan is dominated by monsoon, which sweeps in from the way of Bengal during June, is intense during July and August and finally peters out during September. The period from November to January is normally dry. During April

[1] Shriram Institute for Industrial research, Delhi-7

and May pre-monsoon showers occur often with substantial rainfall along the southern border with India. The major rivers of the country flow north to south, with their source in the alpine zone and flowing right down to the tropical zone on the border with India. The rivers of Bhutan generally have steep gradients and narrow steep-sided valleys, which occasionally open up to give small areas of flat land for cultivation. Bhutan has abundant water resources, but these resources will face new, complex and pervasive challenges caused by population growth, climate change and socio-economic development.

Water resources in the study area may be classified in to two major categories, (1) stream/spring water, and (2) surface water. The villagers use mostly spring water as their principal source for domestic consumption. In some villages the spring water is collected in a tank and supplied by pipelines to different houses as protected water supply for both drinking and cooking purpose. Assessment of background quality of water in the area was carried out once in every season. Water quality study of water resources with reference to quantity and quality depicts impacts of anthropogenic activities.

To assess the water quality of study area two number of river water samples from different stations were drawn and analyzed for various physico-chemical parameters, Heavy Metals and biological parameters. The assessment has been carried out to estimate the effect of any anthropogenic activities on the environment of the study area and to formulate mitigation measures to prevent the surface water bodies and stream water from further pollution. There are no lake and ponds and even no well and borewell were found in the study area. In most part of the study area, the water streams are moving from north to south direction. Kirung Ri river flows from Nganglam towards Chenkari entrance bridge and Dungsam Cement Corporation Limited (DCCL) project site. Kirung Ri river passes adjacent to DCCL project site at a distance of 0.1 Km. Kirung Ri river meets the Manas river which is a major tributary of Brahmaputra after traveling around 36 Km after confluence point of Kirung and Kurung rivers.

The present study reveals to characteristics the water nutrient chemistry, influenced by anthropogenic activity & quarrying of the geologically sediment environments and to determine the nature and degree of anthropogenic impacts on quantitative variations in nutrients in relation to physico-chemical parameters and Heavy Metals of river water.

Study Area

Bhutan is situated in the Eastern Himalayas. The DCCL project site is located at Lower Chenkari village of Nganglam, Pemagatsel Dzonkhag (district) in Eastern Bhutan. The project site is surrounded by hills and mountains at high elevation. The project site is located at about 4.5 Km north of Nganglam and 10 km from indo-Bhutan border. The topography of surrounding area of DCCL project site has an undulating terrain with hills, covered by thick vegetation. Towards west there are some agriculture fields along with some rocks and hilly terrain. The geo-co-ordinates of the study area is 26°52′ to 26°55′ N Latitude and 91°12′ to 91°14′ E Longitude. The average sea level is 1588 meter. The maximum temperature in summer is 32°C and minimum 5°C in winters. There are no industrial activities exist in the area. Nganglam's economy is mainly based on agriculture and animal husbandry. The study area has no transport linkage at present. The villages spread over different hillocks.

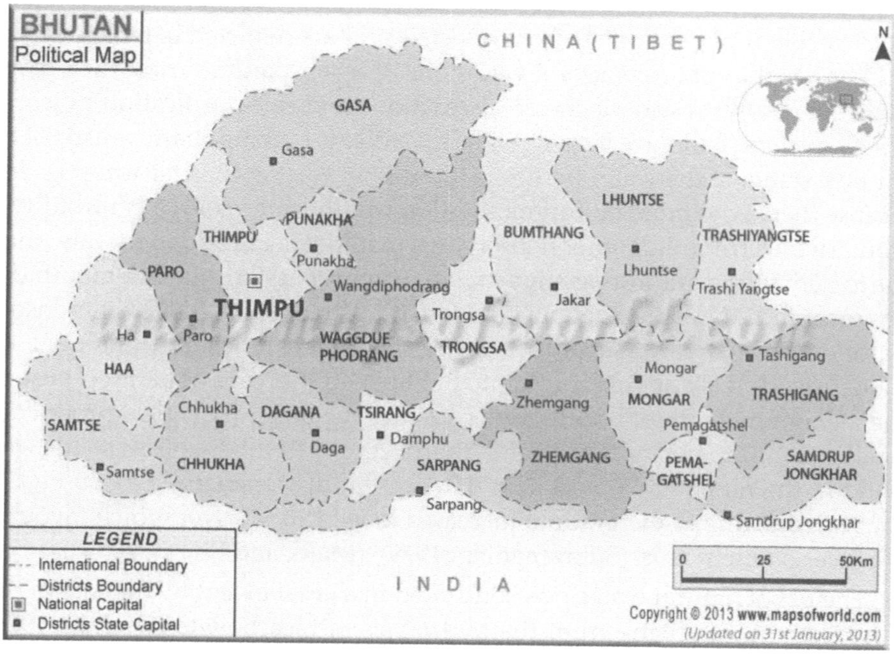

Map-1: showing the districts of Bhutan including Pemagatshel

MATERIALS AND METHODS

Grab water samples were collected in 5 litre plastic jerry canes and 250 ml sterilized clean glass/ pet bottles for physico-chemical parameters and bacteriological test respectively from selected sampling locations. Water quality parameters were analyzed as per standard procedures/ method given in IS:3025 (revised part) and APHA (1998).

The water samples were collected from Kirung Ri River upstream (U/S sampling site A) Near Military camp and downstream (D/S sampling site B) near DCCL project site according to the analytical requirement in morning period 9:00 Hrs. to 10:00 Hrs. The samples for physico-chemical parameters and Heavy Metals were collected by using rinsed Borosil glassware, and analyzed with the help of the procedure described by APHA (1995) and Trivedi and Goel (1984). Colour, odour, turbidity, velocity, temperature and

Dissolved oxygen were analysed on sampling sites. Samples were collected from selected sites and immediately preserved in ice boxes, and transfer to the lab for further analysis. Water samples were digested and Heavy Metals were detected using Atomic absorption spectrophotometer.

RESULTS AND DISCUSSION

Kirung Ri river is flowing throughout a valley of hills chain near the Indo-Bhutan Border, enriched with limestone and lignite rocks, which affect the water quality of stream according to the locations. Nutrients concentration and related physico-chemical parameters from selected sites are depicted in tables. Kirung Ri river has the spatio-temporal variations of water parameters, which play a vital role in all physico-biochemical reactions and self-purification power of aquatic system (Badola & Singh, 1981). Turbidity is striking characteristic of the physical status of the water bodies. Although in Kirung Ri river water is clear because there is no more pollution, siltation was the main source of turbidity in tributaries. Detritus and other non-organic material being added to water mass due to rainfall and anthropogenic activities (Camron, 1996). Maximum turbidity was recorded 2 NTU during rainy season at upstream and 4 NTU in monsoon season at downstream. Turbidity reduce the transparency and minimize the photic zone and always obstructs into light penetration in a aquatic ecosystem. The maximum depth of photic zone provides the better biological production for all aquatic organisms (Malik and Bharti, 2005b). Total dissolved solids were found in the range of 65 mg/l in to 110 mg/l at upstream and 97-135 mg/l at downstream, due to the gradual increases in velocity of river which favoured effective sedimentation (Subramanian, 1979), (Malik and Bharti, 2005c).

The pH of natural water was controlled in a great extent by the interaction of hydroxyl ions arising from the hydrolysis of bicarbonate (Sharma, 1986). The pH of river water was recorded slightly alkaline (7.8 – 8.2) at upstream and (7.9-8.4) at downstream. Total hardness is mainly due to percentage of calcium and magnesium salts of bicarbonates, carbonates, sulphates and chlorides, while the value of alkalinity occured due to presence of bicarbonates. The concentration of hardness was analyzed 48-92 mg/l at upstream and 75-110 mg/l at downstream during the study. Alkalinity was also found 40-99 mg/l with a small fluctuation. A positive relationship between hardness and alkalinity was recorded in river Ganga at Rishikesh (Chopra and Patric, 1994). Chloride concentration was recorded (3-7 mg/l) at upstream and (4-6 mg/l) at downstream. Chloride and hardness showed a positive relationship (Chopra and Patric, 1994). Chloride was found in the form of chloride ion, and one of the major inorganic anion present in natural water (Malik and Bharti, 2009).

Calcium and magnesium the dominant cations, and these represent the main weathering products, but significant hydro-chemical differences between the two sampling sites associated with the bedrock geology exist (Jenkins *et al.*,

1995) Calcium is one of the essential nutrients, which plays an important role in biological system. Calcium concentration was recorded (11-26 mg/l) at upstream and (20-28 mg/l) at downstream. Magnesium is also an essential element but it is toxic at higher concentration. The concentration of magnesium in river was found maximum (11 mg/l) and minimum (5 mg/l). During the summer season nutrients concentration in rivers and hill-streams became more. Miller *et al.,* (1997) described the nutrients availability in selected environmental settings of the Potomac River and Cameron (1996) showed the similar type of fluctuation in Fraser river of British Columbia. Bond (1979) described similar nutrients concentration pattern in a stream draining a mountain ecosystem in Utah.

Heavy Metals like Cadmium, copper, iron, manganese, lead and zinc were not found in high concentration at both sites during any season. Cadmium, manganese and copper was absolutely absent in all seasons, while lead concentrations were also found below detection limit in maximum samples. The concentration of iron was maximum observed 0.1 mg/l during the entire study. Zinc concentration was also found below the standards limit. Malik *et al.,* (2009) described the role of Heavy Metals in the surface water of north India. The results of Bharti *et al.,* (2010) were also indicated the relation of Heavy Metals and phytoplankton in a north Indian water body.

Table 6.1: Physical Characteristics of Kirung Ri River Water

S.No.	Para-meters	Unit	Kirung Ri Upstream				Kirung Ri Downstream				Desi-rable Limit
			Winter	Summer	Mon-soon	Post-mon-soon	Winter	Summer	Mon-soon	Post-mon-soon	
1.	Colour	-	Clear	Clear	Clear	Clear	Clear	Clear	Clear	Clear	-
2.	Odour	-	Nil	Nil	Nil	Nil	Nil	Nil	Nil	Nil	-
3.	Turbidity	NTU	2	1	1	1	4	2	3	1	5
4.	Velocity	m/s	0.9	0.8	1.0	0.8	0.7	0.6	0.8	0.8	-
5.	TDS	Mg/l	90	65	110	85	120	97	135	115	500

Table 6.2: Chemical Characteristics of Kirung Ri River Water

S.No.	Para-meters	Unit	Kirung Ri Upstream				Kirung Ri Downstream				Desirable Limit
			Winter	Summer	Mon-soon	Post-mon-soon	Winter	Summer	Mon-soon	Post-mon-soon	
1.	pH	-	8.2	8.1	8.1	7.8	8.3	8.4	7.9	7.9	6.5-8.5
2.	Alkalinity	Mg/l	65	84	40	55	85	99	78	75	200
3.	Total Hardness	Mg/l	70	92	48	64	96	110	75	105	300
4.	Calcium	Mg/l	15	26	11	14	25	28	20	24	75
5.	Mag-nesium	Mg/l	7	8	5	7	8	10	6	11	30
6.	Chlorides	Mg/l	3	4	7	6	4	4	5	6	250

Table 6.3: Heavy Metals in Kirung Ri River Water

S.No.	Parameters	Unit	Kirung Ri Upstream				Kirung Ri Downstream				Desirable Limit
			Winter	Summer	Monsoon	Post-monsoon	Winter	Summer	Monsoon	Post-monsoon	
1.	Cadmium	Mg/l	BDL	BDL	BDL	BDL	BDL	BDL	BDL	BDL	0.01
2.	Copper	Mg/l	BDL	BDL	BDL	BDL	BDL	BDL	BDL	BDL	0.05
3.	Iron	Mg/l	BDL	0.1	BDL	0.05	0.1	0.1	0.08	BDL	0.3
4.	Lead	Mg/l	BDL	0.02	BDL	BDL	BDL	0.02	BDL	BDL	0.05
5.	Manganese	Mg/l	BDL	BDL	BDL	BDL	BDL	BDL	BDL	BDL	0.1
6.	Zinc	Mg/l	BDL	0.03	BDL	0.04	0.02	0.02	0.02	BDL	5.0

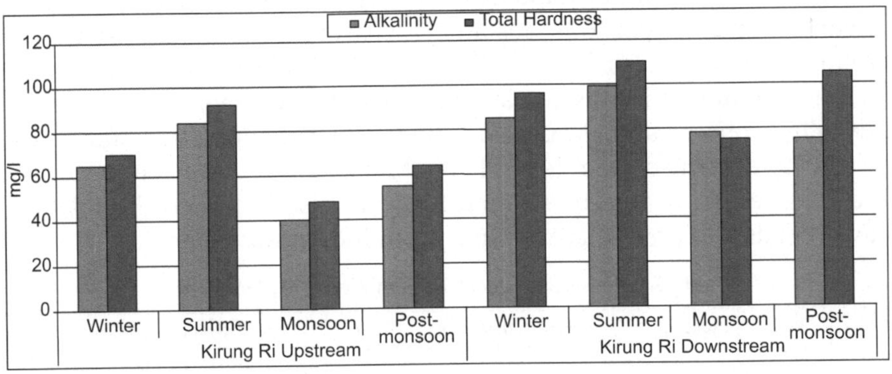

Fig. 6.1: Total hardness and Alkalinity trend of Kirung Ri river water.

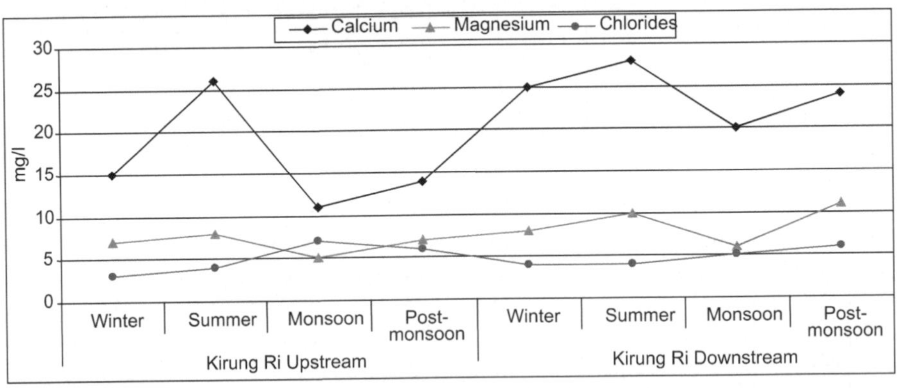

Fig. 6.2 : Showing the nutrients concentration in Kirung Ri river during the study period.

The present results conclude that significant differences in river water nutrient concentrations exist among different environmental settings within the two subunits. The environmental setting with the highest potential by more soluble nutrients, fluctuations in nutrient concentrations were the land use and carbonate bedrock that was predominated in the Bhutanese valley.

The spatial variations in TDS are attributed to climatic and lithological control over the ionic concentrations. Absence or low concentration of Heavy Metals shows that the water is still industrial pollution free. Heavy Metals were found almost nil or in very low concentrations at both selected site. The present study deals with the preliminary physico-chemical characteristics of the river water and exhibits the natural quality of water with minimum anthropogenic activities, which contribute in pollution load of an ecosystem. However, the Indian standards are not so strict (Bharti, 2007), but Heavy Metals never cross the limits during the study period. On the basis of nutrients and Heavy Metals, the water may be considered for drinking and other purposes.

Analysis of the water has been conducted at both sampling locations on the river basins. The natural water quality of Kirung Ri River can be characterized as highly oxygenated, slightly alkaline with low conductivity and no salinity was recorded. The mountain streams and rivers are free of salinity and suitable for irrigation.

REFERENCE

APHA (1995): Standard Methods for Examination of Water and Waste Water. *American Public Health Association, 19th edition. Inc, New York.* pp. 1970.

Badola, S.P. and Singh, H.R. (1981) Hydrobiology of the River Alaknanda of Garhwal Himalaya. *Indian J. Ecol.*, 8(2): 269-276.

Baron, J. & Bricker, O.P. (1990) Hydrological and Chemical Flux in Loch Vale Watershed, Rocky Mountain National Park. In: Biogeochemistry of Major Rivers. SCOPE 42. Wiley and Sons, New York, USA.

Bharti, P.K. (2007): Why Indian Standards are not so Strict?, *Current Science,* 93(9): 1202.

Bharti, P.K., Malik, D.S. and Rashmi Yadav (2010): Influence of Heavy Metals on Abundance of Cyanophyceae Members in Three Spring-fed Lake in Kempty, Dehradun, In: 'Advances in Aquatic Ecology, Vol-III' ed. by V.B. Sakhare, *Daya Publishing House, New Delhi,* pp. 107-111.

Bond, H. B. (1979): Nutrient Concentrations Patterns in a Stream Draining a Montane Ecosystem in Utah. *Ecology.* 60(6): 1184-1196.

Cameron, E. M. (1996): Hydrogeo-chemistry of the Fraser River British Columbia: Seasonal Variation in Major and Minor Components. *J. Hydrol.* 182(1-4): 209-255.

Chopra, A. K. and Patrick, N. J. (1994): Effect of Domestic Sewage on Self-purification of Ganga Water at Rishikesh. *A. Bio. Science.* 13(11): 75-82.

Jenkins, A., Sloan W.T. & Cosby, B.J. (1995) Stream Chemistry is the Middle Hills and High Mountain of the Himalaya, Nepal. *Journal of Hydrology.* Vol-166, No-1-4: 61-79.

Khanna, D.R and Singh. R.K. (2000). Seasonal Fluctuations in the Plankton of Suswa River at Raiwala Dehradun. *Env. Conservations J.* 1(2 & 3): 89-92.

Malik, D. S. and Bharti, P. K. (2005b): Fluctuation in Planktonic Population of Sahastradhara Hill-Stream at Dehradun (Uttaranchal), *Aquacult.* 6 (2): 191-198.

Malik, D. S. and Bharti, P. K. (2005c): Primary Production Efficiency of Sahstradhara Hill-Stream, Dehradun, *Env. Cons. J.* 6 (3): 117-121.

Malik, D. S. and Bharti, P. K. (2009): Ecology of Sahastradhara Hill-Stream at Dehradun (Uttaranchal), In: 'Advances in Aquatic Ecology, Vol-I' ed. by V.B. Sakhare, *Daya Publishing House, New Delhi*, pp. 1-11.

Malik, D. S. and Bharti, P. K., Negi, K.S. and Rashmi Yadav (2009): Distribution of Metals in Water of an Artificial Lake at Mussoorie, Uttarakhand, In: 'Aquatic Biology and Aquaculture' Edited by V.B. Sakhare, Ambajoagi, MS, *Manglam Publication, New Delhi*, pp. 77-95.

Malik, D. S. and Bharti, Pawan K. (2005a): Nutrient Dynamics in Rhithron Zone of Shivalik Himalayan Stream Sahastradhara, Dehradun (Uttaranchal), *Env. Cons. J.* 6 (2): 63-68.

Miller, C. V.; Denis, J. M.; Ator, S. W. and Brakebill, J. W. (1997): Nutrients in Stream During Baseflow in Selected Environmental Settings of the Potomac River Basin. *J. American Wat. Resour. Association.* 33(6): 1155-1171.

Odum, E. P. (1971): Fundamentals of Ecology. New York. W. B. *Saunders and Co.* pp:1-344.

Psenner, R. (1989). Chemistry of High Mountain Lakes in Siliceous Catchments of Central Alps. *Aquatic Sci.* 51: 108-128.

Shrama, R.C. (1986). Effect of Physico-chemical Factors on Benthic Fauna of Bhagirathi River Garhwal Himalaya. *Indian. J.Ecol.* 13(1): 133-137.

Subramanian, V. (1979) Chemical and Suspended Sediment Characteristics of River of India. *J. Hydrol*, 44: 37-55.

Trivedi, R. K. and Goel, P. K. (1984): Chemical and Biological Methods for Water Pollution Studies. Karad. Environmental Publication. pp. 1-25.

Xue, H.B. and Schooner, J.L. (1994) Acid Deposition and Lake Chemistry in Southwest China. *Wat. Air, Soil Pollut.* 75: 61-78.

Analytical Techniques in Chemical and Biological Sciences **Page: 77-82**
Edited by: Dr. Deep Mala and Dr. Pawan Kumar 'Bharti'
ISBN: 978-93-86841-59-9
Edition: 2018
Published by: Discovery Publishing House Pvt. Ltd., New Delhi (India)

7

Impact of Textile Industrial Effluent on Agricultural Soil Quality at Panipat, India

Pawan K. Bharti[1, 2*], Vijender Singh[3] and Pawan Kumar Tyagi[4]

ABSTRACT

Textile industries of Panipat city are famous for handloom business in abroad as well as in India. The monitoring of agricultural soil quality was carried out for the assessment of effects of textile effluents on some environmental components. Samples of soils and crop plants have been analyzed for seven heavy metals, viz. Cadmium, Copper, Iron, Lead, Manganese, Nickel and Zinc using AAS. The results show the presence of some of the heavy metals in agricultural soil comparatively higher than the soil from 10 km far from industrial area. Metal transfer factor from soil to vegetation was calculated for all heavy metals. Transfer factor was found maximum 3.27 for Zn, while for manganese transfer factor was evaluated 0.78. The present paper deals with the distribution of heavy metals in irrigated agricultural soil and crop plant tissues in the territory of Panipat textile industrial area.

Key words: Heavy metals, agriculture soil, accumulation, transfer factor, crop plants.

INTRODUCTION

In the last two decades, the rapid growth of industrialization, urbanization and development have created negative impacts on lithosphere, atmosphere and hydrosphere of the environment. In most parts of India, textile handloom business including cotton, woolen, dying, printing, weaving, etc. are the main source of economy and employments for a major low income group. Textile industries consume a large quantity of water and generate a huge amount of wastewater, which generally discharged into a common effluent drain of industrial area. The composite effluents from textile industries in Panipat city

[1] Department of Zoology and Environmental Science, Gurukula Kangri, University, Hardwar- 249404
[2] Shriram Institute for Industrial Research, Delhi-7, India
[3] Green Environmental Consultancy and Services, 3263, Urban Estate, Safido Bypass, Jind (Haryana), India
[4] Econ Laboratory, Dehradun, India

consisting high concentrations of heavy metals, organic pollutants and toxic colours, which may affect the quality of surface water, soil, ground water and plant tissues of the region.

Textile effluent when discharged into the pond and through pond they percolated to the ground water (Malik *et al.*, 2006). When this water is used for irrigation purpose affects our crop health. The textile effluent had consisting high concentration of trace heavy metals and through its accumulation in different trophic levels in food chains of ecosystem ultimately cause the health hazards among livestock and human beings (Malik *et al.*, 2004). Ground water contaminated by textile effluents, has deteriorated immensely the post agriculture irrigation, drinking utilities and impacts on agricultural soil systems and crop plant vegetation.

The sediments existing as the bottom of the water column play a major role in the pollution scheme of an aquatic system by heavy metals (Forstner, 1985). They reflect the current quality of the water system and can be used in detecting the presence of contaminants that do not remain soluble after discharge into surface water. As a result of complex physical, chemical and biological processes a major fraction of heavy metals (contributed naturally as well as through various anthropogenic activities) is found to be associated with bottom sediments (Baruah *et al.*, 1996). Bed sediments in surface water systems thus act both as a sink and source of metals. Metal accumulation in sediments provides a record of the spatial and temporal history of pollution (Martin and Whitfield, 1983). Hence, sediment monitoring can provide important information on various pollution events.

Discharges of textile waste on land and used for agricultural purpose have also affected the crop and soil productivity due to high dissolved salts. The suspended solids, which are present in the waste, may carry out clogging of soil pores. The sodium, which is present in the waste, may lead to hardening of texture of soil, thereby preventing penetration of roots in soil (Malik and Bharti, 2010).

Textile effluent pollution may also alter the characteristics of sediment and soil of industrial area directly or indirectly. Composite effluents from textile industries and dye houses of Panipat industrial area normally discharged openly into a common effluent drain without any adequate treatment and commences in a large pond near Binjhole village near to industrial area, which may change the quality of bottom sediments of drain , pond sediment quality and also the physico-chemical characteristics of surrounding agricultural soil (Bharti, 2007).

MATERIAL AND METHODS

Panipat is situated on the bank of river Yamuna, it lies between 29′ 09′ 50″ and 29′ 50′ North latitude and 76° 31′ 15″ and 77° 12′ 45″ East longitude with a height of 255 masl. Panipat town is located on the national highway no. 1 about 90 km toward north of Delhi has a population of about 0.27 million. Average population density of the urban area of Panipat city is 25,278 per Sq. Km., while the area of town is 10.8 Sq. Km. Study points in Panipat city is situated on Jatal road in industrial area near GT Road. Soil samples were collected in polythene bags from the agricultural fields of the area, and 10 km far from industrial area on Jatal road. Root and shoot samples of Radish (*Raphanus sativus)* were also picked up for heavy metals analysis. Ground water samples were also collected for heavy metals analysis. All samples were analyzed by the standard methods (APHA, 1995) and Trivedi and Goel (1984). Transfer factor between plants and soil was calculated for each metal according to the following formula: TF = *Ps* (mg g–1 dry wt)/*St* (mg g–1 dry wt), Where, *Ps* is the plant metal content originating from the soil and *St* is the total metal content in the soil.

Fig. 7.1: Satellite imagery showing industrial area and affected pond

RESULTS AND DISCUSSION

As the major source of heavy metals pollution are dye houses of textile industries in Panipat region. Metal reach in pond water and percolate down to ground water (Malik *et al.*, 2006). Because the ground water is mostly used for irrigation of agricultural fields in most part of Haryana state, so, due to the repeated irrigation practices, agricultural soil quality may be altered. Some heavy metals may accumulate in the tissues of agricultural crop vegetations from these contaminate soils. Agricultural soil is indirectly in touch of point source of metal pollution, because no one is irrigating the agricultural fields directly with textile effluents. Soil samples of irrigated land used for growing crops and vegetables showed the presence of all seven metals considered in the study. Concentration of Mn, Fe, Zn, Cu, Ni, Cr, Pb and Cd (mg g^{-1}) is depicted in Table 7.1. These values are higher in soil samples compared to vegetable samples, except for Zn. The reason might be due to its weak adsorptive nature in the soil (Lokeshwari and Chandrappa, 2006). Plants can absorb the higher quantity of zinc. The average total concentration of all metals in soil samples was lower than the concentrations in ground water. However, in some agricultural soils heavy metals present in trace amount naturally (Nongkynrih *et al.*, 1996).

Table 7.1: Heavy Metals in Agricultural Soil in Industrial Area.

Metals (in µg/g)	Agricultural soil					Control soil	Ground water
	Soil 1	Soil 2	Soil 3	Mean	SD	(in µg/g)	(in mg/l)
Cd	0.001	0.007	0.04	0.016	0.0210	BDL	0.006
Cu	0.05	0.28	0.42	0.25	0.1868	0.155	0.303
Fe	0.14	0.39	0.92	0.483	0.3983	0.357	2.767
Mn	0.02	0.08	0.15	0.083	0.0650	0.065	0.26
Ni	0.04	0.05	0.11	0.067	0.0378	0.045	0.072
Pb	0.16	0.21	0.73	0.367	0.3156	0.258	0.74
Zn	0.04	0.09	0.23	0.12	0.0985	0.089	0.101

It was found that the average concentrations of heavy metals in surface soils, i.e. Mn, Ni, Fe, Cu, Cd, Pb and Zn were 0.08, 0.06, 0.48, 0.25, 0.016, 0.36 and 0.12 mg g^{-1} respectively, in which Fe, Pb, Cu were found in excess level due to their cumulative and adsorptive nature in soil after repeated irrigation by contaminated ground water. Cd and Zn were found minimum due to their weak adsorptive nature in soil (Mido and Satake, 2003). Soils near textile industries having comparatively high concentrations of Mn and Zn, while cadmium minimum (Kasem and Singh, 1999). Due to the soil and plant interactions some toxic metals may accumulate in the tissues of crop plants (Henning *et al.*, 2001). Most of the laboratory research on biosorption of heavy metals indicates that no single mechanism is responsible for metal uptake. In general, two mechanisms are known to occur, viz. 'adsorption', which refers to binding of materials onto the surface and 'absorption', which implies penetration of metals into the inner matrix (Ramraj *et al.*, 2000). Either one of these or both the mechanisms might take place in the transportation of metals into the body tissues of crop plant vegetations. Roots and shoots of radish were analysed for total metal content. The order of toxic heavy metal contamination in crop plants is as follows: Zn > Fe, > Mn > Ni > Pb> Cu > Cd. Cadmium was not found in the samples of plant parts. Accumulation of these heavy metals in vegetable plant might be due to the use of contaminated ground water for their cultivation. Zn was present in appreciable amounts in the shoots part of the vegetable.

Table 7.2: Mean Values of Heavy Metals in Vegetation Tissues (in μg/g).

Plants parts	Cd	Cu	Fe	Mn	Ni	Pb	Zn
Radish root	BDL	0.012	0.148	0.043	BDL	0.019	0.143
Radish shoot	BDL	0.0005	0.128	0.022	0.019	BDL	0.249
Transfer factor	0	0.05	0.57	0.78	0.28	0.05	3.27

BDL = Below Detection Limit

Heavy metals in plant tissues were found to be lower in comparison to irrigated soil. Fe, Zn, Pb and Mn were found 0.148, 0.143, 0.019 and 0.043 μg g^{-1} respectively maximum in plant roots, while in plants shoots only Zn and Fe were found 0.25 and 0.128 μg g^{-1}. Cd was almost absent in plant tissues, however shoots may contain comparatively high concentrations of Cd in few plant species (Olaniya *et al.*, 1998). The concentrations of Zn and Cd in crops increased with the degree of contamination of the soil. Different vegetable species accumulate different metals depending on environmental conditions, metal species and plant available forms of heavy metals. Studies have shown that uptake and accumulation of metals by plant species depend on several factors, and various researchers have identified several reasons (Bingham *et al.*, 1975; Dowdy *et al.*, 1978). Transfer factor was found to be more for Zn, Mn, Fe and Ni 3.27, 0.78, 0.57 and 0.28 respectively from agricultural soils to vegetation. It is found that the average total concentration of metals in plant shoots is higher than the plant roots. Overall results on comparison reveal that metals in water had impact on soil quality and crop plant vegetations also.

Soil quality and composition may also alter in irrigated agricultural crop fields and thus metals accumulated in plants body, which may seriously caused health hazards to livestock and ultimately to human beings by direct consumption or by uptake the food products originated by cattle (De, 2002). Irrigation with contaminated ground water containing variable amounts of heavy metals leads to increase in concentration of metals in the soil and vegetation. Concentration of metals in vegetation will provide baseline data and there is a need for intensive sampling of the same for quantification of the results.

REFERENCES

APHA (1995). Standard Methods for Examination of Water and Waste Water. *American Public Health Association,* 19th edition. Inc, New York, pp. 1170.

Bingham, F. T., Page, A. I., Hahler, R. J. and Ganje, T. J. (1975). Growth and Cadmium Accumulation of Plants Grown on Soil Treated with Cadmium Enriched Sewage Sludge. *J. Environ. Qual.*, 4, 207–210.

Bharti, P.K. (2007): Effect of Textile Industrial Effluents on Ground Water and Soil Quality in Panipat Region (Haryana), *Ph.D. Thesis*, Submitted to Gurukula Kangri University, Hardwar, pp. 191.

De, A. K. (2002). Environmental Chemistry, *New Age International (Ltd) Publishers, New Delhi*, pp: 392.

Dowdy, R. H., Larson, W. E., Titrud, J. M. and Latterel, J. J. (1978). Growth and Metal Uptake of Snap Beans Grown on Sewage Sludge Amended Soil – A Four Year Field Study. *J. Environ. Qual.*, 7, 252–257.

Henning, B.J.; Snyman, H.G and Aveling, T.A.S. (2001). Plant-Soil Interactions of Sludge Borne Heavy Metals and the Effect on Maize (*Zea mays* L.) Seedlings Growth, *Wat. SA*, 27(1): 71-78.

Kashem, M.A. and Singh, B.R. (1999). Heavy Metal Contamination of Soil and Vegetation in the Vicinity of Industries in Bangladesh, *Water, Air and Soil Pollution*, 115: 347-361.

Lokeshwari, H. and Chandrappa, G.T. (2006). Impact of Heavy Metal Contamination of Bellandur Lake on Soil and Cultivated Vegetation, *Current Science*, 91(9): 622-627.

Malik, D.S.; Bharti, P.K. and Grover, S. (2006). Alteration in Surface Water Quality Near Textile Industries at Panipat (Haryana), *Environment Conservation J.*, 7(2): 65-68.

Malik, D.S.; Yadav, R. and Bharti, P.K. (2004). Accumulation of Heavy Metals in Crop Plants Through Irrigation of Contaminated Ground Water in Panipat Region, *Environmental Conservation Journal*, 5 (3): 101-104.

Malik, D.S. and Bharti, P.K. (2010). Textile Pollution, Daya Publishing House, Delhi, pp. 383.

Mido, Y. and Satake, M. (2003) Chemicals in the Environment, In: *Toxic Metals* (eds Sethi, M. S. and Iqbal, S. A.), Discovery Publishing House, New Delhi, pp. 45–68.

Nongkynrih, P. D.; Khar, P.S. And Khating, D.T. (1996). Micronutrients Elements in Acid Aflisols of Meghalaya Under Rice Cultivation, *J. Soil Sci.*, 44(3): 455-457.

Olaniya, M. S., Sur, M. S., Bhide, A. D. and Swarnakar, S. N. (1998). Heavy Metal Pollution of Agricultural Soil and Vegetation Due to Application of Municipal Solid Waste – A Case Study. *Indian J. Environ. Health*, 40, 160–168.

Ramraj, Athiya Afshan, Halappa Gowda, T. P. and Karanth, N. G. K. (2000). Sorption of Copper(II) and Lead(II) by Microbial Cultures During Growth. *Indian J. Environ. Health*, 42, 95–99.

Trivedi, R.K. and Goel, P.K. (1984). Chemical and Biological Methods for Water Pollution Studies, *Environmental Publication*, Karad, pp. 251.

Analytical Techniques in Chemical and Biological Sciences
Edited by: Dr. Deep Mala and Dr. Pawan Kumar 'Bharti'
ISBN: 978-93-86841-59-9
Edition: 2018
Published by: Discovery Publishing House Pvt. Ltd., New Delhi (India)

Page: 83-88

8

Biochemical Studies in Cat fish (Clarious lazera) Infected with *Flavobacterium columnare* and Treated with Probiotic

Mona S. Zaki[1], Nabila EL Battrawy[2] and Samy IShalaby

ABSTRACT

The present study was planned to investigate the effect of Flavobacterium columnare infection on some hematological, serum biochemical and pathological alterations of Clarious lazera. Forty five fish were divided into three equal groups. Fish of first group served as a control. Fish of group (2&3) were naturally infected by Flavobacterium columnare. Fish of group (3) were treated after 7 days of post-infection using the probiotic bacterium, Lactobacillus rhamonsus for 10 days. Sampling was done after 1 and 7 days of post-infection (gps 1 & 2) and 10 days of post-treatment (gps 1 & 3). The results revealed a non significant changes in the hematological and the biochemical parameters after 1 day of infection, but after 7 days of post-infection and 10 days of post-treatment, a significant decrease in RBCs, Hb, PCV and significant increase in AST, ALT, urea, creatinine, sodium, potassium, cortisol, insulin and glucose were seen. Iron showed a significant decrease at the same period of sampling. The infected skin loses its natural sheen and a gray, white or yellowish margin surrounds the foal lesion. The mouth and inner walls of the oral cavity may be covered with a yellowish mucoid material. In scaly-less fishes, the lesions start with simple ulcers which predominately end with extensive saddleback-like ulcers exposing the underlying musculatures. Fin and gill rot is another lesion of the progressive infection in both scaly and scaly-less fishes. These reactions were evident, after 7 days of post-infection and the severity of the lesions were markedly decreased after 10 days of post-treatment. It could be concluded that, Flavobacterium columnare infections induced marked tissue alterations as well as some hematological and serum biochemical changes. Although probiotic treated the infected cases and allowed the regenerative processes but it does not progress the hematological and serum biochemicalparameters.

Key words: Cat fish; *Flavobacterium columnare*; Biochemical changes.

---

[1] Department of Aquaculture, National Research Centre, Dokki Giza Egypt
[2] Department of Microbiology, Animal Reproduction Institute, Giza Egypt 1Department of Reproduction, National Research Centre, Dokki Giza Egypt

INTRODUCTION

Columnaris disease is a predominant bacterial disease of both cultured and wild freshwater fish. Many commercially important fish species are susceptible to columnaris disease, such as (but not limited to) salmonids, eels, carp, goldfish, tilapia and channel catfish. This disease also poses a problem for many freshwater fish. F. columnare is mentioned in most books of tropical aquarium fish diseases as the cause of cotton-wool disease. Post reported fish exhibiting greyish-white discoloration especially on the head and around the mouth. These may evolve into whitish filaments emerging from the lesions, hence the name mouth fungus. Although F. columnare is described as being an important pathogen, as far as we know, it has never been actually isolated from tropical aquarium fish, nor has its significance and pathogenicity been studied in any way.

F. columnare infections may result in skin lesions, fin erosion and gili necrosis, with a high degree of mortality, leading to severe economic losses.

The term probiotic was firstly used to denominate microorganisms that have effects on other microorganisms.

Probiotics can provide some solutions to this problem through different mechanisms or properties such as the production of inhibitory compounds such as bacteriocins, competition for adhesion sites with opportunistic or pathogen microorganisms, competition for nutrients with other bacteria or an improvement of the immune status (e.g. increase of production of immunoglobulins, acid phosphatase, antimicrobial peptides, improvement of cellular activities, etc.).

Use of microbial probiotics to promote health maintenance and disease prevention and control is now widely accepted as the new ecofriendly alternative measures for sustainable aquaculture.

The present work aimed to study the effect of *F. columnare* on biochemical and skin disease clinicopathological findings of infected *cat fish* before and after treatment with probiotic.

MATERIALS AND METHODS

Fish: Forty five fish *naturally infected* with *F. columnare* average body weight of 100-150 gm/fish were obtained from River Nile and transported to the laboratory and reared in 3 equal glass aquaria (115 liter capacity), fed a balanced ration and provided with continuous aireated and renued tap water.

Fish were kept one week for acclimatization and mean time subjected to mycological, bacteriological and pathological examinations.

The probiotic bacterium, Lactobacillus rhamonsus (ATCC 53103) was cultured in MRS broth at 26.8C for 48 h, centrifuged and washed with sterile PBS 2 times.

Bacterial pellets were measured in PBS and their densities were determined. Under sterile conditions, the bacteria were manually incorporated into commercial dry pellets at rates of 108 and 1010 CFU/g in feed for low and high LAB diets, respectively. Fish fed only commercial dry pellets served as a control. Fish were fed approximately 0.8% of body weight once a day. The probiotic groups ingested an average of 3.8 × 106 and 3.8 × 108 cells day-1.

Table 8.1: Effect of Naturally Infected Fish with *F. columnare* on Some Hematological Parameters of Catfish Before and After Treatment in Comparison with Control (Mean ± SE)

Parameters	Control gp.	Infect 1 dayP.I.	ed gp.7 days P.I.	Treated gp. (10 days P.T)
RBCs (106/mm^3)	2.42	2.43	1.94	1.73
Hb (gm/dl)	8.03	8.21	8.29	7.63
PCV	19.03	18.01	16.01	15.01
MCV (FL)	37.03	34.28	29.10	28.01
Reticulocytes (%)	1.60	1.40	1.22	1.54

**Significant at P < 0.01, P.I. = Post-infection, P.T. = Post-treatment, gp. = group

Experimental infection: Fish were divided into 3 equal groups. Fish of group (1) were kept without treatment to serve as a control. Fish of groups (2 and 3) were naturally infected by *F. columnare*. Fish of group (3) were treated after 7 days of infection using probiotic (2.9 × 106) for 10 days.

Table 8.2: Effect of Naturally Infected fish with *F. column are* on Some Serum Biochemical Parameters of Catfish Before and after Treatment Incomparison with Control (Mean ± SE)

Parameters	Control gp.	Infec 1 day P.I.	ted gp.7 days P.I.	Treated gp. (10 days P.T)
AST (U/L)	80.00±0.64	80.00±0.15	125.00±0.38	127.00±0.57*
ALT (U/L)	20.00±0.15	22.00±0.17	32.00±0.17*	37.00±0.13*
Urea (mg%)	3.03±0.30	3.07±0.34	4.05±0.52*	4.03±0.81*
Creatinine (mg%)	0.61±0.20	0.63±0.32	0.83±0.21*	0.89±0.12*
Sodium (mfg/dl)	125.00±0.32	135.00±0.71	148.00±1.10*	155.90±1.72*
Potassium (mfg/dl)	3.00±0.21	3.20±0.39	5.62±0.72*	6.30±0.70*
Cortisol (μg/dl)	0.70±0.18	0.75±0.17	1.02±0.64*	1.01±0.70*
Insulin (μg/dl)	9.20±0.14	10.60±0.70	12.20±0.40*	11.90±0.60*
Glucose (mfg/dl)	60.30±0.34	63.80±0.70	80.00±0.73*	82.80±0.70*
Iron (mg/dl)	221.00±0.10	223.00±1.10	212.00±1.10*	194.00±1.14*

*Significant of p<0.01

Sampling: Blood samples and tissue specimens were taken at first and seventh days of infection (gp2) and also after ten days of treatment (gp3).

Sampling was also done at the same tome from control group (gp1). Blood samples were taken in heparinised microhematocrit tube and other tubes to be centrifuged at 3000 r. p. m. for 10 min. for serum separation. The serum stored at 20°C until analysis.

Hematological examinations: The erythrocytic indices (RBCs, Hb, PCV and MCV) and reticulocytes were determined according to Schalm (19).

Serum biochemical analysis: Serum aspirateaminotransferase (AST) and alanin aminotransferase (ALT) also serum urea, creatinine and glucose were estimated using kits supplied from Biomerieux (France). Sodium and potassium were determined by flame photometer according the method described by silversmith (20). Serum cortisol level was determined using radio immunoassay technique (21). Insulin was estimated by radioimmunoassay using kits obtained from diagnostic products corporation (Los Angeles, USA). Iron was determined using atomic absorption according to Joseph and Roger (22).

RESULTS

F. columnare, after 1 of day post-infection, induced non significant changes in the hematological and serum biochemical parameters. A significant decrease in RBCs, Hb and PCV was observed in cat fish, after 7 days of post- infection and 10 days of post-treatment, while MCV and a period of reticulocytes showed a high significant decrease at the same period of sampling in comparison with control. A significant increase in AST, ALT, urea, creatinine, sodium, potassium, cortisol, insulin and glucose was noticed in cat fish after 7 days of post-infection by *F. columnare* and 10 days of post-treatment while iron showed a significant decrease at the same period of sampling in comparison withcontrol.

Clinically, cat fish infected by *F. columnare showed* he infected skin loses its natural skin and a gray, white or yellowish margin surrounds the foal lesion. The mouth and inner walls of the oral cavity may be covered with a yellowish mucoid material. In scaly fish, the lesions start with simple ulcers which predominately end with extensive saddleback-like ulcers exposing the underlying musculatures. Fin and gill rot is another lesion of the progressive infection in both scaly and scaly fish.

DISCUSSION

It is apparent that, Nile cat fish infected with *F. columnare* caused a significant increase in glucose and insulin levels only during 7 days of infection and 10 days of treatment probiotic. It is well known that, any stress factor such as handling, incubation, or anathesia have been shown to cause hyperglycemia followed by hyperinsulinemia [19].

The present work revealed that, serum glucose was elevated during 7 days of infection and 10 days of treatment. One consistent effect of cortisol was the reduction in the haemoglobin, PCV, RBCs and iron level as a result of dease in appetite in the cat fish or more likely to be the direct of catabolic effect of cortisolon the fish (24).

The experiment showed that sodium (Na) and potassium (K) concentrations were significantly increased, this retention may be attributable to kidney impairment where the kidney is the normal passway for Na and K, this may explain the main cause for elevation of serum creatinine and urea in the treated groups which also microscopically exhibited vacuolar degeneration of renal tubules. This confirms the previous results recorded by Osfor *et al.* (25), Zaki *et al.* (26) and Abdel Aziz *et al.,* (27). This led to temporal changes in plasma insulin concentration which did not mirror those for glucose. One of the reasons may be the high sensitivity to glucose of pancreatic cells producing somatostatin which in turn inhibits insulin secretion during the initial period after *F. columnare* (28). *F. columnare* infection causes a significant increase of cortisol level which may be due to the activation of hypothalamus pituitary internal axis. These results coincide with those observed by Jauncey and Ross (29) and Zaki et al. (30), who stated that, hyphae of *F. columnare* may invade deep tissues of the fish and penetrate the vital organs as kidney, liver and even the central nervous system and eye.

Marked elevations were noticed in the activity of (AST) and (ALT). The liver is the primary organ of detoxification as well as a major site for detoxification reaction, therefore, a significant increase in liver *F. columnare* explanations for the presence of the *F. columnare* or its toxins in liver. This picture was confirmed histopathologically by the marked vacuolar degeneration of hepatocytes.

As primary pathogen for stressed fish, this is in agree with Zaki *et al.* (26) and Badran *et al.,* (31). Who stated that hyphae of *F. columnare* may invade deep tissues of fish and penetrate the vital organs even the central nervous system.

The clinical signs and postmortem lesions that reported among infected cat fish were similar to those reported by Aly and Ashram (33) and Attia [34] and Ferguson [35].

REFERENCES

Rehulka J. & M inarik B. (**2007**). *Aquaculture Research* 38, 1182-1197.

Soto E., M auel M .J., Karsi A. & Lawrence M.L. **2008**. *Journal of Applied Microbiology* 104, 1302-1310.

Suomalainen L.R., Bandilla M. & Valtonen E.T. **2009**. *Journal of Fish Diseases* 32, 723—726.

Post G. **1987**. Bacterial Diseases of Fish. In: Textbook of Fish Health. T. F. H. Publications, Ascot, Berkshire, UK, pp. 51-56.

Decostere A., Haesebrouck F. and Devriese L.A. **1998**. *Veterinary Microbiology* 62, 35-45.

Bassleer, G., **1983**. Wegwijs In Visziekten. B.V.W.J. Thieme and Cie, Zutphen, pp. 42-43.

Tomey, W.A., **1985**. Ziekten bij aquariumvissen. Zuid Boekprodukties B.V., Best, Nederland, pp. 53-54.

Butcher, R.L., **1992**. Manual of Ornamental Fish. British Small Animal Veterinary Association, Gloucestershire, pp. 92-93.

Lilly DM, Stilwell H. **1965**. *Science*; 147(3659) 747-748.

Gram L. Prospects of Fish Probiotics. In: *Microbial Ecology in Growing Animal*. **2005**. p. 379-417.

Panigrahi A, Kiron V, Puangkaew J, Kobayashi T, Satoh S, Sugita H. **2005**. *Aquaculture*; 243 241-254.

Balcázar JL, De Blas I, Ruíz-Zarzuela I, Cunningham D, Vendrell D, Múzquiz JL. **2006**. *Veterinary Immunology*; 114173-186.

Vine NG, Leukes WD, Kaiser H. **2006**. *FEMS Microbiology Reviews*; 30 404-427.

Balcázar JL, Decamp O, Vendrell D, De Blas I, Ruíz-Zarzuela I. **2006**. *Microbial Ecology in Health and Disease*;18 65-70.

Nayak SK. **2010**. *Fish and Shellfish Immunology*; 29 02-14.

Mohapatra S, Crakraborty T, Kumar V, Deboeck G, Mohanta KN. **2013**. *Journal of Animal Physiology and Animal Nutrition*; 97405-430.

Pandiyan P, Balaraman D, Thirunavukkarasu R, George EGJ, Subaramaniyan K, Manikkam S, Sadayappan B. **2013**. *Drug Invention Today*; 5 55-59.

Ram C. Sihag and Parvati Sharma, **2012**.. *Journal of Fisheries and Aquatic Science, 7: 72-103.*

Willoughby, L. and A. Pickering, **1977**. Transactions of the British Mycology Society, 68:91.

Schalm, O., **1986**. Schalm's Veterinary Hematology, 4th Edition 524.

Silversmit, *A.B. Med*. **1965**. 45:175.

Pickering A.D. and P. Pottinger, **1983**. *Gen. com. Endocrinol.*, 49:232.

Joseph, A. and W.G. Roger, **1976**. Clinical Chemistry Principal and Procedures, pp. 168-197.

Musa, S.O. and F. Omeregie, **1995**. *J. of Aquatic Sciences*, 14:3742.

Osfor, M.H., M.S. Zaki and A.Z. Saleh, **1998**. *Bull. NRC. Egypt*, 23 (2):128-192.

Zaki, M.S., M.H. Osfor, F.S. Bayumi and F.N. Aboul Gheit **2003**. *Bull. NRC, Egypt*, 28 (2):245-257.

Abdel Aziz, E.S., A Ayanis and M.M. Ali, **2002**. *Egypt J. Comp. Clinic. Pathology*, 15 (2):108-125.

Sheridan, M.A., C.D. Eilerston and E.M. Plisetskaya, **1991**. *Endocrinol.*, 81:36.

Juncey, K. and B. Ross, **1982**. A Guide to Tilapia Feed and Feeding Institute of Aquaculture Univ. of Striling, Scotland.

Zaki, M.S., Fawzi, O. M and El-Jacky,J, **2008**. *Am-Euras. J. Agric.& Environ. Sci.*, 3(5): 677-680.

Badran, A.F., M. Ezzat and M. El-Tarabili, **1991**. *Zagazig. Vet. J.*, 19 (1):26-40.

Aly, S. and A. El Ashram, **2000**. *Alex. J. Vet. Science*, 16 (1):165-174. [33] Aly, S. and A. El Ashram, **2000**.. *Alex. J. Vet. Science*, 16 (1):165-174.

Attia, Y., **2000**. Studies on Scales of Healthy and Diseased Fish. MVSc, Zagazig Univ., Egypt.

Ferguson, H., **1989**. Textbook of Systemic Pathology of Fish. 1st Ed. Lowa State Univ. Press., Ames, Lowa, Canada.

Analytical Techniques in Chemical and Biological Sciences
Edited by: Dr. Deep Mala and Dr. Pawan Kumar 'Bharti'
ISBN: 978-93-86841-59-9
Edition: 2018
Published by: Discovery Publishing House Pvt. Ltd., New Delhi (India)

Page: 89-106

9

Optimal Protein Intake Exerts Trade-offs for Improved Lifespan in Different Species of Drosophila

*[1]B.P. Harini, [2]Yarajarla R Babu and [3]S. Rajashekar

ABSTRACT

The present investigation claims that protein plays a central role followed by carbohydrates and amino acid. Carbohydrate and amino acid are also indirectly essential in determining the lifespan of *Drosophila melanogaster, Drosophila nasuta nasuta* and *Drosophila nasuta albomicans*. As there is a decrease in longevity of control flies, one can assume that the additional dietary nutrients have an impact on extending lifespan. In addition to this irrespective of diet and concentrations the females have shown increased lifespan than males.

Key words: *Drosophila* species, Dietary restriction, carbohydrate, amino acid, protein Longevity.

INTRODUCTION

Dietary restriction (DR), a reduction in the amount of food or particular nutrients eaten, is the most consistent environmental manipulation to extend lifespan and protect against age related diseases. Current evolutionary theory explains this effect as a shift in the resolution of the trade-off between lifespan and reproduction. However, recent studies have questioned the role of reproduction in mediating the effect of DR on longevity and no study has quantitatively investigated the effect of DR on reproduction across species (Joshua *et al.*, 2016).

Dietary restriction (DR) refers to a moderate reduction of food intake that leads to extension of life span beyond that of normal, healthy individuals. This intervention has principally been studied in rodents, but it also extends the life span of a wide range of organisms including the fruit fly, *Drosophila melanogaster* (Magwere *et al.*, 2004). Food availability, the nutritional status

[1] Department of Zoology, Bangalore University, Jnanabharathi Campus, Bengaluru-560 056, Karnataka, India.
[2] Department of Applied Genetics, Karnatak University, Dharwad.
[3] Centre for Applied Genetics, Bangalore University, Jnanabharathi Campus, Bengaluru-560 056.
* Corresponding Author.

of the organism and their effects upon reproductive rate plays a key role in lifespan-determination and are central to evolutionary life history theory.

Animals and plants grow and reproduce surrounded by nutritional variation, where food is often scarce or key nutrients are lacking. Because the juvenile nutritional environment has major effects on the adult phenotype, linking nutrition and fitness is an increasingly important aspect of ecology, evolution and life-history theories (Raubenheimer *et al.*, 2009; Morehouse *et al.*, 2010).

The fruit fly *Drosophila* is a useful organism for the investigation of the mechanisms by which dietary restriction (DR) extends lifespan. Its relatively short generation time, well-characterized molecular biology, genetics and physiology and ease of handling for demographic analysis are all major strengths. Lifespan has been extended by DR applied to adult *Drosophila*, by restriction of the availability of live yeast or by co-ordinate dilution of the whole food medium. Lifespan increases to a maximum through DR with a progressive dilution of the food and then decreases through starvation as the food is diluted further. Daily and lifetime fecundities of females are reduced by food dilution throughout the DR and starvation range. Standard *Drosophila* food ingredients differ greatly between laboratories and fly stocks can differ in their responses to food dilution, and a full range of food concentrations should therefore be investigated when examining the response to DR. Flies do not alter the time that they spend feeding in response to DR (Partridge *et al.*, 2005).

The fruit fly has long served as a model for human health, with over 2000 publications in the field of aging. The fly's short lifespan and well-documented genetics have made it an attractive model for studying human health, aging, and disease. The *Drosophila* genome has many homolog's with humans, e.g., 60% of human disease genes are shared with the fruit fly (Schneider, 2000). This genetic relationship between human and fly genetics facilitates the use of *Drosophila* to uncover mechanisms that improve human health and lifespan. Using *Drosophila* to study aging mechanisms will inform future interventions of human health, including the reduction of food intake.

When nutritional scarcity is encountered in an environment, reduced rates of senescence are often observed in animals, resulting in an extension in lifespan whilst reproductive effort is reduced or arrested (Weithoff, 2007; Carey *et al.*, 2005). By avoiding the cost of reproduction and allocating available nutrients to somatic upkeep during unfavorable dietary conditions, organisms may improve their fitness by surviving until successful reproduction can begin or resume (Barrett *et al.*, 2009).

Caloric restriction (CR), or dietary restriction, is a dietary regimen that is based on low calorie intake. "Low" can be defined relative to the subject's previous intake before intentionally restricting calories, or relative to an average person of similar body type. Calorie restriction without malnutrition has been shown to work in a variety of species, among them yeast, fish, rodents and dogs to decelerate the biological aging process, resulting in longer maintenance of youthful health and an increase in both median and maximum lifespan. The life-extending effect of calorie restriction is not universal. Wild mice, for instance, do not live longer when on a calorie restricted diet. In humans the long-term health effects of moderate CR with sufficient nutrients are unknown. Nutrition has long been recognized as an important factor for influencing both the health span and lifespan in a variety of animals, including humans (Weindruch, 1982; Walford and Spindler, 1997). Thus, within the field of aging research, use of known nutritional interventions that act as anti-aging therapies are employed as a tool to better understand the biology of aging. One such intervention is Dietary Restriction (DR), a robust method for extending lifespan and promoting vitality which is applicable through a broad range of taxa from yeast to mammals.

Here, we demonstrate a system that allows measure DR in two allopatric races of *Drosophila* namely *Drosophila albomicans* ($2n = 6$) and *D. nasuta* ($2n = 8$) are 2 sibling species with indistinguishable morphology; but distinct karyotypes. *Drosophila albomicans* and *D. nasuta* belong to the *D. nasuta* subgroup of the *D. immigrans* species group. During the past years, numerous studies have shown that *D. nasuta* and *D. albomicans* have different chromosomal configurations (Wilson *et al.*, 1969, Nirmala and Krishnamurthy, 1972).

In the present study an attempt has been made to understand the DR regimes of three different species of *Drosophila* namely *Drosophila melanogaster, Drosophila nasuta nasuta* and *Drosophila nasuta albomicans*. to record whether synergistic effect is seen in food intake during their survival period and also to tease apart the differences between the various dietary restriction paradigms with respect to lifespan in three species of *Drosophila* and also to test whether DR is independent of species.

MATERIALS AND METHOD

Fly Stock

Drosophila culture was maintained using wheat cream agar media. The control stocks were cultured at 22 ± 1°C at 70% humidity in 12hr/12hr dark and light laboratory conditions. The experimental stocks were *Drosophila melanogaster, Drosophila nasuta nasuta and Drosophila nasuta albomicans*. The regular media was standardized with different doses of carbohydrates, proteins and amino acids (Min *et al.*, 2006). Tryptaphan and casein were dissolved in 0.1N NaOH. The standard culture was being used and the appropriate concentration of nutritional composition is as shown in Table 9.1 to Table 9.3. The flies exposed to variable diets were used to assess for longevity.

Table 9.1: The Regular Media was Standardized with Different Doses of Sucrose

Diet → Comp ↓	Control media ↓	Sucrose		
		Low dose	Mid dose	High dose
Distilled water	1000 ml	1000 ml	1000 ml	1000 ml
Agar agar	10 g	10 g	10 g	10 g
Soji	100 g	100 g	100 g	100 g
Sucrose	—	20 g	40 g	80 g
Jaggary	100 g	100 g	100 g	100 g
Propionic acid	7.5ml	7.5ml	7.5ml	7.5ml

Table 9.2: The Regular Media was Standardized with Different Doses of Tryptophan

Diet → Comp ↓	Control media ↓	Sucrose		
		Low dose	Mid dose	High dose
Distilled water	1000 ml	1000 ml	1000 ml	1000 ml
Agar agar	10 g	10 g	10 g	10 g
Soji	100 g	100 g	100 g	100 g
Tryptophane	—	250 mg	500 mg	750 mg
Jaggary	100 g	100 g	100 g	100 g
Propionic acid	7.5 ml	7.5 ml	7.5 ml	7.5 ml

Table 9.3: The Regular Media was Standardized with Different Doses of Casein

Diet → Comp ↓	Control media ↓	Sucrose		
		Low dose	Mid dose	High dose
Distilled water	1000 ml	1000 ml	1000 ml	1000 ml
Agar agar	10 g	10g	10 g	10 g
Soji	100 g	100 g	100g	100 g
Casein	—	2.5 g	5.0 g	7.5 g
Jaggary	100 g	100 g	100g	100 g
Propionic acid	7.5 ml	7.5 ml	7.5 ml	7.5 ml

DESCRIPTIONS OF THE SELECTED DIETS ARE GIVEN BELOW

Sucrose

Sucrose is most well known as a sweetener in any cooked, uncooked or baked preparation of food and beverages. It is also used to produce an edible substance's look, texture, preservation and "mouth feel" or the chemical and physical effect to the mouth. It is extensively used as a main ingredient in many confectionery ingredients and desserts. A lot of people and experts have recognized that sugar provides humans with a sudden boost of energy once consumed.

Sucrose has both good and bad implications to human health. Adequate supply will provide the body just the right amount of energy. However, too much intake has very detrimental consequences including obesity and tooth decay. Too much sucrose also increases blood glucose levels. When there are prolonged elevated glucose levels, a person may suffer from diabetes or glucose metabolism imbalance that leads to complications in the vein and nerve systems of the body.

- Sucrose or common table sugar is a sweet white crystalline solid often used as a food additive.
- The molecular formula for sucrose is $C_{12}H_{22}O_{11}$ and its molecular mass is 342.30 g/mol.
- The solubility in water at 20°C is 211.5 grams/100 mls.
- The structural formula for sucrose is represented by the following diagram.

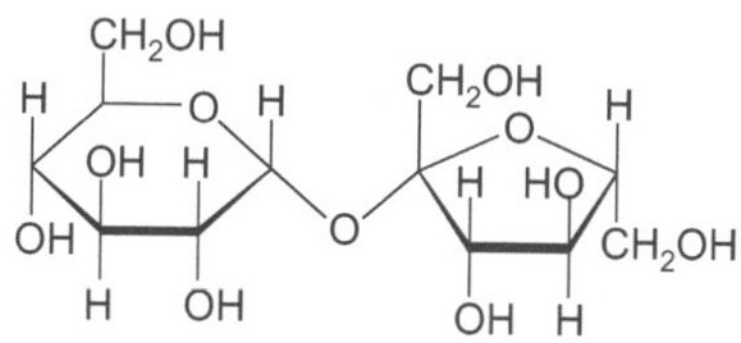

Casein

Commonly casein proteins came from the insoluble portion of cow's milk which is purified in a unique chemical process in order to make it more digestible. This common chemical is subjected to an old urban myth where a person may alleviate the spicy affects of chilli peppers by simply drinking milk. Therefore the active ingredient capsaicin, which causes burning hot sensation found in spicy foods to be eliminated by the calcium caseinate proteins.

The word hydrolysate literally translates in to the product of hydrolysis. Hydrolysis pertains to the breaking down of a chemical or substances in to smaller units. In this case protein is broken down in to its hydrolysate state in a mixture of amino acids and the splitting of proteins with acids, alkali, or different enzymes during the chemical process.

In nutritional terms, hydrolyzed proteins can be linked to equivalent of the original proteins they are derived from in terms of amino acid composition, but are now broken down in to a more readily digested form which is more easily absorbed. This means in layman terms, that casein hydrolysates are easier to digest in the stomach, this making them absorb faster in to a person's muscles and blood stream. Traditional casein supplements are known to be slow acting, but casein hydrolysate will not be present in the stomach for long causing the typical bloated feeling of common casein supplements.

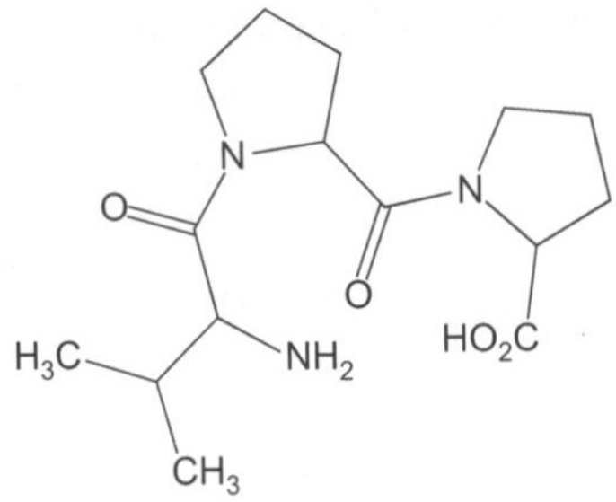

Tryptophan

(IUPAC-IUBMB abbreviation: Trp or W; IUPAC abbreviation: L-Trp or D-Trp; sold for medical use as Tryptan) is one of the 20 standard amino acids, as well as an essential amino acid in the human diet. It is encoded in the standard genetic code as the codon UGG. Only the L-stereoisomer of tryptophan is used in structural or enzyme proteins, but the D-stereoisomer is occasionally found in naturally produced peptides (for example, the marine venom peptide contryphan). The distinguishing structural characteristic of tryptophan is that it contains an indole functional group. It is an essential amino acid as demonstrated by its growth effects on rats. The isolation of tryptophan was first reported by Frederick Hopkins in 1901 through hydrolysis of casein. From 600 grams of crude casein one obtains 4-8 grams of tryptophan. Plants and microorganisms commonly synthesize tryptophan from shikimic acid oranthranilate Serotonin (a neurotransmitter), synthesized via tryptophan hydroxylase.

- Serotonin, in turn, can be converted to melatonin (a neurohormone), via 5-hydroxyindole-O-methyltransferase activities.
- Niacin is synthesized from tryptophan via kynurenine and quinolinic acids as key biosynthetic intermediates.
- Auxin (a phytohormone) when sieve tube elements undergo apoptosis tryptophan is converted to auxins.

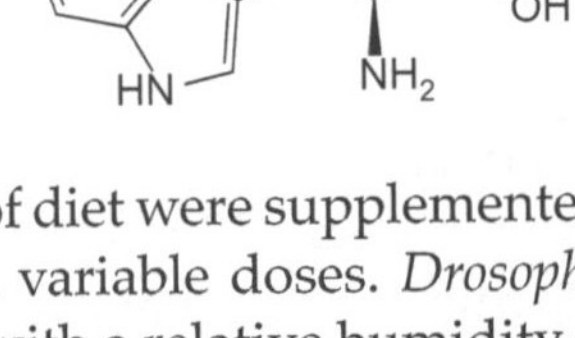

Different combinations of diet were supplemented along with the standard wheat cream agar media in variable doses. *Drosophila* will be maintained at room temperature 22 ± 1°C with a relative humidity of 70%. Further following assessments were carried out.

In this study, dietary restrictions (essential amino acids, proteins and carbohydrates) were evaluated for Lifespan in *Drosophila* species.

To Record the Role of Diet on Longevity

Longevity was assessed using the modified protocol of Luckinbill and Clare (1985). Simultaneously along with the lifetime fecundity and fertility the same set of flies were continued to assess the longevity. Each vial was observed daily from day of emergence to record the lifespan.

RESULTS

To record the role of diet on longevity in *Drosophila melanogaster, Drosophila nasuta nasuta and Drosophila nasuta albomicans*

Drosophila Melanogaster

Table 9.4a reveals the mean longevity of *Drosophila melanogaster* on exposure to different diet with varied concentrations of sucrose, casein and tryptophan. The mean longevity of *D.melanogaster* male and female fed with different concentrations of sucrose have shown significant increased longevity high dose 35±2.09 and 41±2.18 respectively. While in the males have shown significantly decreased has shown significantly decreased longevity (30±2.43) than the other concentrations.

Similarly the mean longevity of both males and females fed with high dose of casein have shown significantly increased longevity with the mean of 41±2.09 and 44±2.12 respectively. While the control flies have shown significantly decreased longevity than the other concentrations.

Interestingly even in the tryptophan diet also the longevity was increased in high dose than the other concentrations and the control flies have shown decreased longevity. The differences between control and LD of tryptophan diet are insignificant (Figure 9.1a)

Drosophila Nasuta Nasuta

Table 9.4b evidence that the mean longevity of *Drosophila nasuta nasuta* fed with different diets in varied concentrations of sucrose, casein and tryptophan. The mean longevity of *Drosophila nasuta nasuta* fed with different concentrations of sucrose has revealed that the Male (42±2.12) and female (45±2.09) fed with high dose have shown significantly increased longevity than the flies fed with control, LD, MD respectively. While the control of male (35±1.98) and female (40±2.31). have shown significantly decreased longevity than the other concentrations.

In addition to this in the casein diet also the mean longevity of males (45±2.18) and females (51±2.09) have shown significantly increased longevity with increased dose concentration.

Subsequently the tryptophan fed flies have shown increased longevity in male (40±2.18) and female (43±2.09) at higher dose, and in the control male and LD females have shown decreased longevity (Figure 9.1b).

Drosophila Nasuta Albomicans

Table 9.4c accounts for the mean longevity of *D.N. albomicans* on exposure to different diet with varied concentrations of sucrose, casein and tryptophan. The mean longevity of *Drosophila nasuta albomicans* fed with different concentrations of sucrose, casein and tryptophan have revealed that the higher dose fed flies have showed significantly increased longevity. While the control have shown significantly decreased longevity in both males and females (Figure 9.1c).

Specieswise Comparison

Figure 9.2 reveals the overall mean longevity of all the species fed with varied concentration diets. *D.n.nasuta* has shown increased longevity (45±2.43) followed by *D.n.albomicans* and *D.melanogaster* with df=2; F=23.56; P<0.05 (Table 4d).

Diet wise Comparison

Figure 9.3 indicates the mean longevity of males and females of three species fed with three different dietary media. In general the females of all the species irrespective of the diet have shown increased longevity than males. The flies fed with casein diet have shown increased longevity followed by tryptophan and sucrose, but the differences between tryptophan and sucrose in both males and females are insignificant with $df = 2$; F = 101.97; $p < 0.05$ (Table 9.4d).

Concentration of the Diet

Figure 9.4 The overall mean longevity with respect to concentration have shown increased longevity with increased concentration of all the experimental diets, while the control has decreased longevity, but the differences are insignificant between control and LD with $df = 3$; $F = 212.19$; $P < 0.05$. (Table 9.4d).

Species vs Diet Wise Comparison

Figure 9.5 provides the overall mean longevity of three different species of *Drosophila* fed with different diets. *D.n.nasuta* has shown increased longevity followed by *D.n.albomicans* and *D.melanogaster*. in addition to this the flies fed with tryptophan have shown decreased longevity in compilation with the other diets with $df = 4$; $F = 45.16$; $P < 0.05$ (Table 9.8D).

Species vs Concentration wise Comparison

Figure 9.6 reveals that the increase concentration is directly proportional to increased longevity in all the species of the present study with $df = 6$ $F = 30.14$; $P < 0.05$ (Table 9.8D)

Diet vs Concentrations

Figure 9.7 denotes that longevity has shown to increase in HD with respect all the diets and found to be decreased in control with $df = 6$, $F = 14.06$; $P < 0.05$ (Table 9.8D).

Diet Vs Species Vs Concentration

Figure 9.7 reveals that the multiple concentrations between diet, species and concentration. Irrespective of the species the casein fed flies have shown increased longevity than sucrose and tryptophan. In case sucrose fed flies of *D.melanogaster* has shown decreased longevity than the other two species. While the differences are insignificant between *D.N. nasuta* and *D.N. albomicans* which have shown increased longevity with $df = 12$ $F = 7.85$ $P < 0.05$ (Table 9.8D).

Table 9.4a: Mean (±SE) Longevity of *Drosophila melanogasters* Fed with Different Concentrations of Sucrose, Casein and Tryptophan

Concen-tration	*Drosophila melanogaster*					
	Sucrose		Casein		Tryptophan	
	Male	Female	Male	Female	Male	Female
Control	33.1 ± 2.31 a	36 ± 2.56 a	33.1 ± 2.31 a	36 ± 1.98 a	33.1 ± 2.31 a	36 ± 2.56 a
LD	30 ± 2.43 b	37 ± 2.35 ab	36 ± 2.43 b	41 ± 2.01 b	32 ± 2.43 a	38 ± 2.35 b
MD	34 ± 1.98 ac	38 ± 2.63 cb	39 ± 1.98 c	42 ± 2.56 b	35 ± 1.98 b	40 ± 2.63 c
HD	35 ± 2.09 dc	41 ± 2.18 d	41 ± 2.09 d	44 ± 2.12 c	38 ± 2.09 c	41 ± 2.18 c
ANOVA	F = 87, df = 198 P < 0.05	F = 34, df = 58 P < 0.05	F = 58, df = 231 P < 0.05	F = 42, df = 176 P < 0.05	F = 112, df = 213 P < 0.05	F = 61, df = 190 P < 0.05

Note: Means in each column followed by different alphabetical letter with in the same life stage were significantly different by Tukey HSD (P<0.05)

Table 9.4b: Mean (±SE) Longevity of *Drosophila nasuta nasuta* Flies Fed with Different Concentrations of Sucrose, Casein and Tryptophan

Concen-tration	*Drosophila nasuta nasuta*					
	Sucrose		Casein		Tryptophan	
	Male	Female	Male	Female	Male	Female
Control	35 ± 1.98 a	40 ± 2.31 a	35 ± 2.56 a	40 ± 2.31 a	35 ± 2.56 a	40 ± 2.31 a
LD	38 ± 2.01 b	42 ± 2.43 b	41 ± 2.35 b	43 ± 2.43 b	37 ± 2.35 b	38 ± 2.43 b
MD	39 ± 2.56 b	44 ± 1.98 c	43 ± 2.63 c	45 ± 1.98 c	36 ± 2.63 b	39±1.98 b
HD	42 ± 2.12 c	45 ± 2.09 c	45 ± 2.18 d	51 ± 2.09 d	40 ± 2.18 c	43 ± 2.09 c
ANOVA	F = 71, df = 156 P < 0.05	F = 58, df = 185 P < 0.05	F = 49, df = 214P < 0.05	F = 38, df = 163P < 0.05	F = 75, df = 181 P < 0.05	F = 56, df = 254P < 0.05

Note: Means in each column followed by different alphabetical letter with in the same life stage were significantly different by Tukey HSD (P<0.05)

Table 9.4c: Mean (±SE) Longevity of *Drosophila nasuta albomicans* Flies Fed with Different Concentrations of Sucrose, Casein and Tryptophan.

Concen-tration	*Drosophila nasuta albomicans*					
	Sucrose		Casein		Tryptophan	
	Male	Female	Male	Female	Male	Female
Control	32 ± 1.98 a	38 ± 2.31 a	32 ± 2.56 a	38 ± 1.98 a	32 ± 2.31 a	38 ± 2.56 a
LD	35 ± 2.01 b	37 ± 2.43 a	41 ± 2.35 b	43 ± 2.01 b	34 ± 2.43 b	39 ± 2.35 ab
MD	37 ± 2.56 c	40 ± 1.98 b	42 ± 2.63 b	45 ± 2.56 c	38 ± 1.98 c	40±2.63 ba
HD	39 ± 2.12 d	41 ± 2.09 b	44 ± 2.18 c	46 ± 2.12 c	41±2.09 d	42 ± 2.18 c
ANOVA	F = 32, df = 168 P < 0.05	F = 48, df = 175 P < 0.05	F = 72, df = 112 P < 0.05	F = 57, df = 198P < 0.05	F = 176, df = 320P<0.05	F = 123,df = 234P<0.05

Note: Means in each column followed by different alphabetical letter with in the same life stage were significantly different by Tukey HSD ($P < 0.05$)

Table 9.4d: Three-way ANOVA of Longevity of Three Species, Three Diets and Three Concentrations Along with Control

Source	Type III Sum of Squares	df	Mean Square	F	Sig.
Corrected Model	50179.837[a]	71	706.758	29.868	.000
Intercept	3549422.963	1	3549422.963	150002.331	.000
Species	1115.093	2	557.546	23.562	.000
Diet	4825.701	2	2412.850	101.970	.000
Concentration	15063.441	3	5021.147	212.199	.000
Species * Diet	4274.735	4	1068.684	45.164	.000
Species * Concentration	4279.381	6	713.230	30.142	.000
Diet * Concentration	1996.440	6	332.740	14.062	.000
Species * Diet * Concentration	2230.880	12	185.907	7.857	.000
Error	49407.200	2088	23.662		
Total	3649010.000	2160			
Corrected Total	99587.037	2159			

DISCUSSION

Dietary restriction (DR), the extension of life span by reduction of nutrient intake without malnutrition is often used as a benchmark comparison for interventions that extend life span (Masoro, 2002). Since McCay's pioneering experiments in rats 70 years ago (McCay *et al.*, 1935), some form of food restriction has been shown to increase life span in commonly used model organisms such

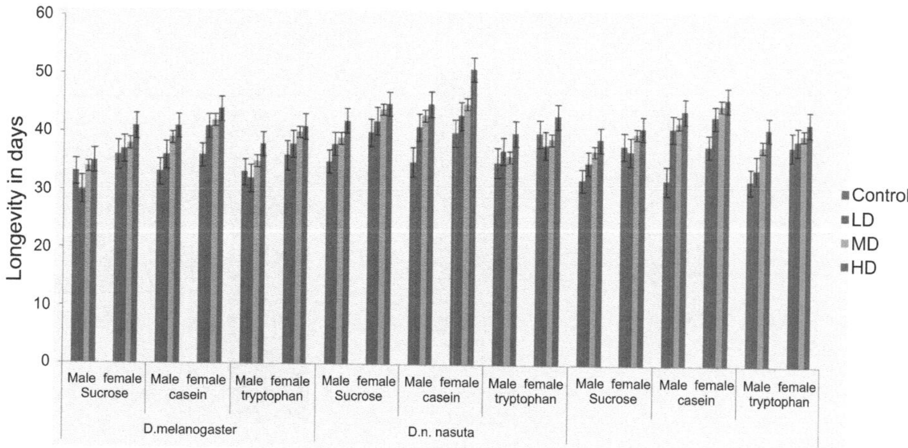

Fig. 9.1a: Mean (±SE) Longevity of *D.melanogaster, D.N. nasuta* and *D.N. albomicans* flies fed with different concentrations of Sucrose, casein and tryptophan.

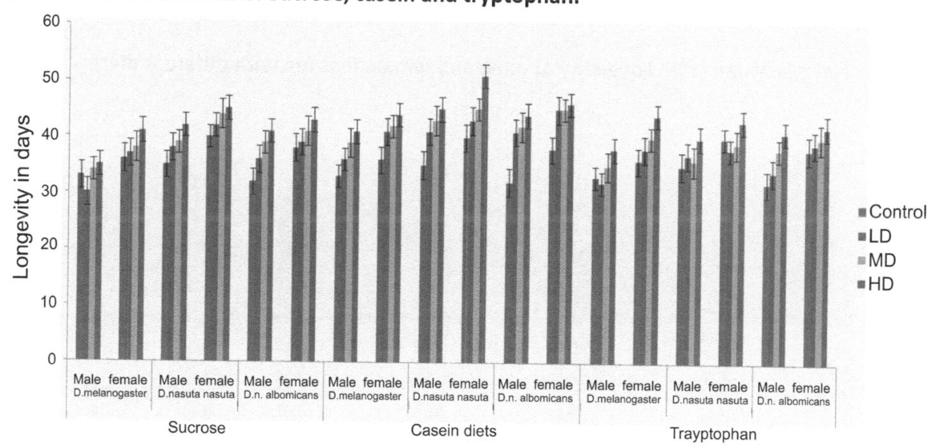

Fig. 9.1b: Mean (±SE) Longevity of *D.melanogaster, D.n.nasuta* and *D.N. albomicans* flies fed with different diet

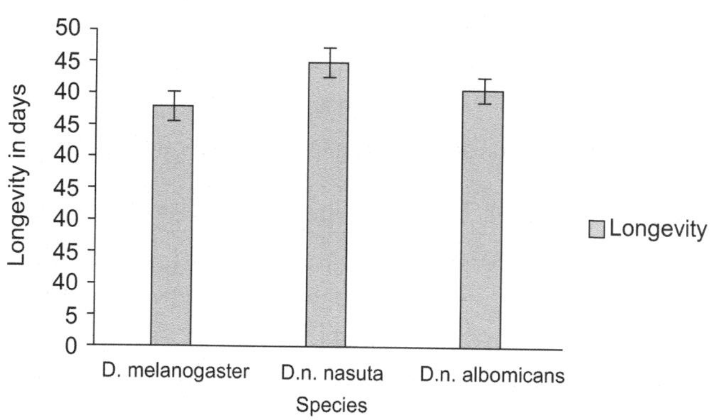

Fig. 9.2: Mean (±SE) Longevity of *D. melanogaster, D.N. nasuta and D.N. albomicans*

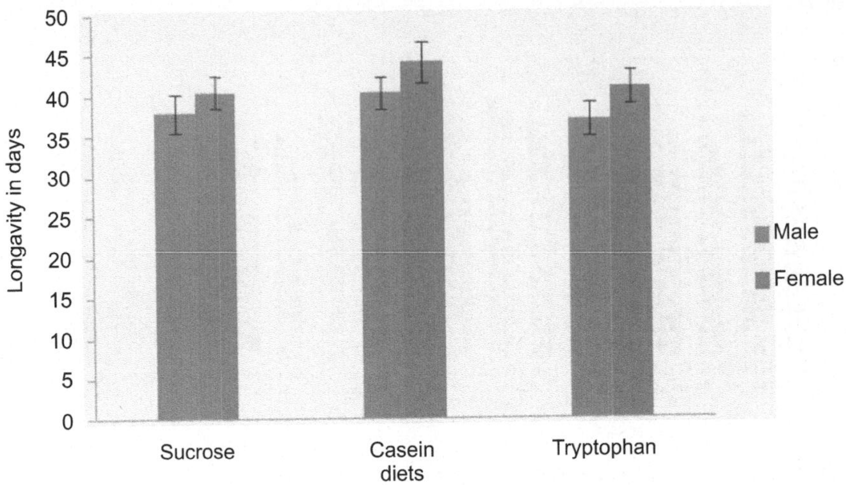

50

Fig. 9.3: Mean (±SE) Longevity of male and female flies fed with different diets

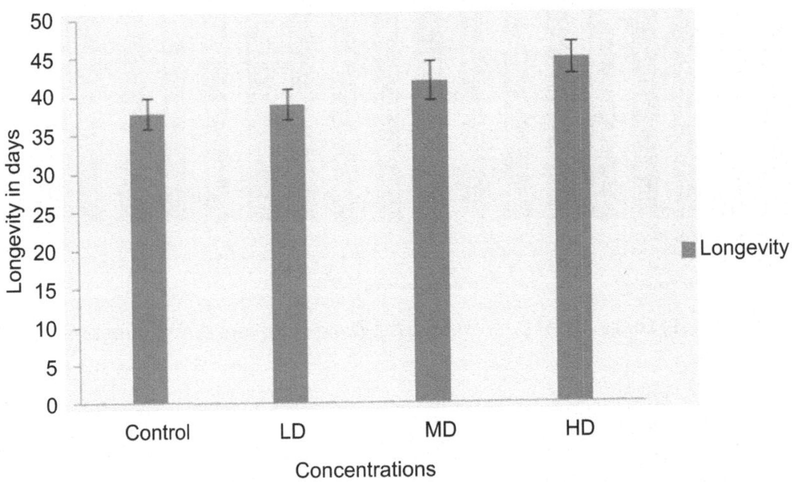

Fig. 9.4: Mean (±SE) Longevity of flies fed with different concentrations

as nematodes (Klass, 1977), fruit flies (Chippindale *et al.*, 1993; Chapman and Partridge, 1996), and mice (Weindruch and Walford, 1982), along with many species less often used for laboratory research such as water fleas, spiders, fish (Weindruch and Walford, 1988). Although it is fairly well-established that dietary restriction (DR) can affect longevity in many animals (Fontana *et al.*, 2010), methods used to implement DR vary greatly across model organisms.

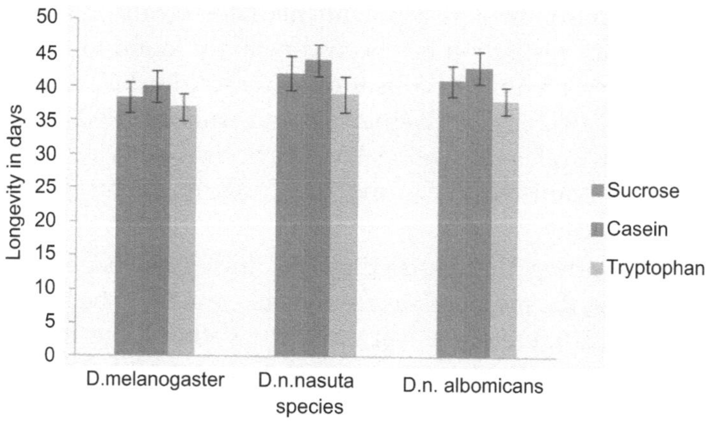

Fig. 9.5: Average mean (±SE) Longevity of three species of flies fed with different diets

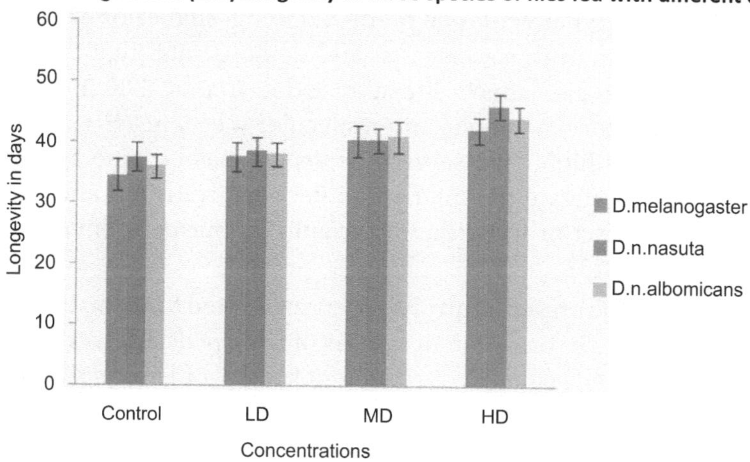

Fig. 9.6: Mean (±SE) Longevity of flies fed with different concentrations

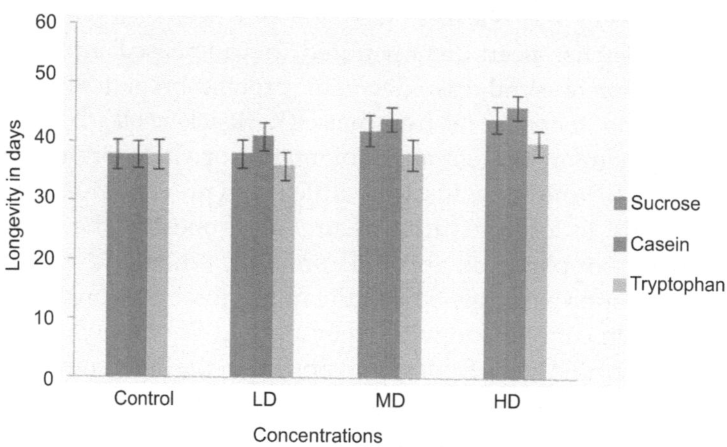

Fig. 9.7: Mean (±SE) Longevity of flies fed with different concentration with varied diets

Nutritional environment is a potent mediator of an organism lifespan, in particular dietary restriction has been constantly found to extend lifespan across a vast range of animal taxa including Yeast (Lin *et al.*, 2002), Fruit flies (Chippidale *et al.*, 1993), Mice (Weindruch and walford, 1982). The influence of distinct carbohydrates on ageing has previously been tested for several different model organisms, including the fruit fly *Drosophila melanogaster* (Diptera: *Drosophilidae*).

Despite the finding that restricting diet increases longevity in such a diversity of species, the mechanisms responsible remain to be fully elucidated in any of them. It is therefore as yet unclear whether these mechanisms are evolutionarily conserved across taxa or if instead life extension during DR is an example of convergent evolution. Flies fed food media with very similar caloric content showed marked differences in their life spans. This finding is in direct contrast to what would be predicted if ingested calories were the key mediator of life span in *D. melanogaster* and demonstrates that the nutritional composition of the diet affects life-span extension by DR in this species. Since many of the core metabolic and molecular mechanisms involved in the response to DR are highly conserved, *Drosophila* has become an extensively used model to investigate the interaction between nutrition and lifespan. In the fruit fly, the effect of individual nutrients on lifespan remains less clear (Kimberley *et al.*, 2013).

In view of this the present study has been structured to access the interaction between diet influences on different species of *Drosophila*. Dietary restriction as immense impact on life span across different species of *Drosophila* taxa, but the key nutritional components driving this process and their interaction remains indecisive. In the present study different species of *Drosophila* have shown substantial affects on the longevity with the allocated dietary component such as sucrose, casein and tryptophan.

Several studies has been demonstrated that increased intake of protein may increase protein synthesis, decrease protein breakdown, reduce fat accumulation, and increase fat-free mass (Kerksick *et al.*, 2006) has been demonstrated. Therefore protein supplementation or a high-protein diet (HPD) is recommended to build the muscle in athletes, to prevent muscle wasting in severe illness, and to lose the fat in treatment of obesity. The most popular forms of protein supplements are milk proteins, whey and casein. Casein, which makes up approximately 80% of the milk protein, is considered "slow" protein because, in comparison with whey protein, is emptied from stomach more slowly and amino acids from casein appear in the blood more slowly, and the response lasts longer. It is believed that while whey protein affects protein balance mostly by stimulation of protein synthesis, casein works to decrease protein breakdown (Boirie *et al.*, 1997).

Fig. 9.3 reveals that the multiple concentrations between diet, species and concentration. Irrespective of the species the casein fed flies have shown increased longevity than sucrose and tryptophan. In case sucrose fed flies of *D.melanogaster* has shown decreased longevity than the other two species. While the differences are insignificant between *D.N. nasuta* and *D.n.albomicans* which have shown increased longevity with $df = 12$ $F = 7.85$ $P < 0.05$ (Table 9.4d).

However, the effect of carbohydrate diets, and particularly the type of carbohydrate, as well as the protein-to-carbohydrate ratio on reproduction and life span are poorly investigated and generally studied in comparatively simple organisms like *Drosophila melanogaster*, which is intensively used as a model for nutritional studies. Over the last decade, several studies explored the effect of diet on life span, reproduction, behaviour, and adaptation of fruit flies (Vigne and Frelin, 2010).

Casein contains high proportions of all essential amino acids and high amounts of glutamine and proline but, in comparison with blood meal, provides relatively low amounts of glycine and cysteine (Li *et al.*, 2011). Therefore, it may be suggested that chronic intake of high amounts of casein may induce the imbalance in amino acid concentration in body fluids. This may affect a number of biochemical pathways, susceptibility to oxidative damage, and the response of the body to different physiological and pathological conditions, such as starvation or illness. There is scarce information available on how nutrition affects life history traits in *Drosophila*. The importance of diet is often underestimated in experimental design (Prasad *et al.*, 2003).

Studies have revealed that Carbohydrates are important dietary components for many omnivorous and herbivorous animals, including both humans and livestock. Carbohydrates provide energy for many reactions and processes flowing inside cells. Most organisms can tightly adjust their metabolism according to the availability of dietary components, including carbohydrates. Physiological effects of carbohydrates depend on their type and dosage, as well as on the physiological state of an organism (Wheeler and Pi-Sunver, 2008). Very low carbohydrate intake restricts an organism's available energy and may slow down growth and regeneration, thereby altering survival and health. However, low carbohydrate intake has been proposed as a possible intervention to decrease the risk of, and complications related to, metabolic diseases such as obesity and metabolic syndrome (Giugliano *et al.*, 2008).

The present investigation claims that protein (casein) plays a central role followed by carbohydrates (sucrose) and amino acid (tryptophan). Carbohydrate and amino acid are also found to be equivocal in determining the lifespan of *Drosophila melanogaster, D.nasuta nasuta* and *Drosophila nasuta albomicans*. For further clarification a series of diets with varying sucrose, casein and tryptophan content were fed to record how nutritional factors influence longevity. But one cannot always expect increased dietary protein, carbohydrate or amino acid concentration does not always result in increased longevity. Henceforth, as there is a decrease in longevity of control flies, one can assume that the additional dietary nutrients have a role on extending lifespan.

Newly evolved allopatric races namely *D.nasuta nasuta* and *Drosophila nasuta albomicans* have shown increased longevity than *D.melanogaster.* The ancestral species ie *D.melanogaster* as decreased longevity when compared to the newly evolved races, which imbibes that the newly evolved species flourish well with extended lifespan on consuming varied nutritional diets rather than the regular food media. Thereby the "Dietary stress is a factor causing a change in the biological system, which is potentially detrimental". Lifespan is resolute largely by the stressful conditions, the severity of the stress and the organism's ability to cope with it is very important for its survival.

CONCLUSION

The present investigation claims that protein plays a essential role than carbohydrates or amino acid in determining the lifespan of *Drosophila* species. It is also proven by the study that longevity is decreased in control flies compared to additional nutrient fed flies, thus supplementary dietary nutrients have an impact on extending lifespan. In addition to this irrespective of diet and concentrations the females have revealed augmented lifespan than males.

However the relation between physiological and evolutionary trade-offs are not similar, and physiological trade-offs might not translate into trade-off at the population level. When the expression of the physiological trade-off is genetically variable among individuals in the population, it may contribute to an evolutionary trade-off and thus explicate varied response to reproductive and lifespan in different species of *Drosophila*.

In light of this, we apparently emphasize the importance of protein intake for optimal life history trade-offs for improved survivability in different species of *Drosophila*.

REFERENCES

Barrett E.L.B, Moore A.J and Moore P.J. 2009. Diet and Social Conditions During Sexual Maturation have Unpredictable Influences on Female Life History Trade-offs. *Journal of Evolutionary Biology*. 22:571–581.

Carey J.R, Harshman L.G and Liedo P. 2005. Longevity-Fertility Trade-offs in the Tephritid Fruit Fly, *Anastrepha ludens,* Across Dietary-restriction Gradients. *Aging Cell*. 7:470–477.

Chapman T and Partridge L. 1996. Female fitness in *Drosophila melanogaster:* An Interaction Between the Effect of Nutrition and of Encounter Rate with Males. *Proc R Soc Lond B Biol Sci.* 263: 755–59.

Chippindale A.K, Leroi A.M, Kim S.B and Rose M.R. 1993. Phenotypic Plasticity and Selection in *Drosophila* Life-history Evolution, Nutrition and the Cost of Reproduction. *J. Evol. Biol.* 6:171–193.

Fontana A.L, Partridge L, Valter D. and Longo R. 2010. Extending Healthy Life Span—from Yeast to Humans. *Science,* 328(5976) : 321-326.

Giugliano D, Cereiello A and Esposito K. 2008. Are there Specific Treatments for the Metabolic Syndrome? *American Journal of Clinical Nutrition.* 87:8-11.

Jiang J.C, Jaruga E, Repnevskaya M.V and Jazwinski S.M. 2000. An Intervention Resembling Caloric Restriction Prolongs Lifespan and Retards Aging in Yeast. *FASEB J.* 14: 2135-2137.

Joshua P.M.P., Shinichi N, Malgorzata L and Craig A.W. 2016. The Effect of Dietary Restriction on Reproduction: A Meta-analytic Perspective. *BMC Evolutionary Biology* 16:181-199.

Kealy R.D, Lawler D.F, Ballam J.M, Mantz S.L and Biery D.N. 2002. Effect of Diet Restriction on Lifespan and Age-related Changes in Dogs. *J Amer. Vet Med. Assoc.* 220:1315-1320.

Kerksick C.M, Rasmussen C.J, Lancaster S.L, Magu B, Smith P, Melton C, Greenwood M, Almada A.L, Earnest C.P and Kreider R.B. 2006. The Effects of Protein and Amino Acid Supplementation on Performance and Training Adaptations During Ten Weeks of Resistance Training. *J of Srength and Conditioning Research.* 20: 643-653.

Kimberley D.B, Sany Hoxha, Gil B.C, Ryuichi y, Horng D.W, Paul K, Shan H, Ted B, Pankaj K and William W.J. 2013. High Carbohydrate-Lowprotein Consumption Maximizes *Drosophila* Lifespan. *Experimental Gerontology.* 48: 1129-1135.

Klass M.R 1977. Ageing in the Nematode *Caenorhabditis elegans*: Major Biological and Environmental Factors Influencing Life Span. *Mech Ageing Dev.* 6:413–429.

Li H, Dong Y, Yin H, Wang N, Yang J, Liu X, Wang Y, Wu J and Li. 2011. Characterization of the Stress Associated Micro RNAs in Glycine Max by Deep Sequencing. *BMC Plant Biol.* doi: 10.1186/1471-2229-11-170.

Luckinbill L.S and Clare M.J. 1985. Selection for Life Span in *Drosophila melanogaster. Heredity* **55:** 9-18.

Magwere T, Chapman T and Partridge L. 2004. Sex Differences in the Effect of Dietary Restriction on Life Span and Mortality Rates in Female and Male *Drosophila melanogaster. The Journals of Gerontology Series A: Biological Sciences and Medical Sciences.* 59:B3–B9.

Masoro E.J. 2003. Subfield History: Caloric Restriction, Slowing Aging, and Extending Life. *Sci. Aging Knowl. Environ.* 328:63 – 68.

McCay C.M, Crowell M.F and Maynard L.A. 1935. The Effect of Retarded Growth Upon the Length of Life Span and Upon the Ultimate Body Size. *Nutrition.* 5(3):155-171.

Min K.J and Tatar M. 2006. Restriction of Amino Acids Extends Lifespan in *Drosophila melanogaster. Mech. Ageing Dev.* 127: 643–646.

Morehouse N.I, Nakazawa T, Booher C.M, Jeyasingh P.D and Hall M.D. 2010. Sex in a Material World: Why the Study of Sexual Reproduction and Sex-specific Traits Should Become More Nutritionally-Explicit. *Oikos.* 119; 766–778.

Nirmala S.S. and Krishnamurthy N.B. 1973. *Drosophila neonasuta,* A New Species of *Drosophila* from Mysore. (Diptera: *Drosophilidae*). *Oriental Insects.* 7 (2):267-270.

Partridge L, Piper M.D and Mair W. 2005. Dietary Restriction in *Drosophila. Mech. Ageing Dev.* 126(9):938-950.

Prasad N.G, Shakarad M, Rajamani M and Joshi A. 2003. Interaction Between the Effect of Maternal Larval Nutrition Levels on Pre-adult Survival in *Drosophila Melanogaster. Evolutionary Ecology Research.* 5:903-911.

Raubenheimer D, Simpson S.J and Mayntz D. 2009. Nutrition, Ecology and Nutritional Ecology: Toward an Integrated Framework. *Functional Ecology.* 23:4–16.

Schneider D. 2000. Using *Drosophila* as a Model Insect. *Nat Rev Genet.* 1:218-226.

Vigne P and Ferlin C. 2010. Food Presentation Modifies Longevity and Beneficial Action of Dietary Restriction in *Drosophila. Experimental Gerontology.* 45: 113-118.

Walford R.L and Spindler S.R. 1997. The Response to Calorie Restriction in Mammals Shows Features also Common to Hibernation—A Cross-adaptation Hypothesis. *Journal of Gerontology.* 52:179 –183.

Weindruch R and Walford R.L. 1982. Dietary Restriction in Mice Begining at One Year of Age: Effect on Life Span and Spontaneous Cancer Incidence. *Science.* 215:1415–1421.

Weindruch R and Walford R.L. 1988. The Retardation of Aging and Disease by Dietary Restriction *Journal of Gerontology.* 241:324-328.

Weithoff G. 2007 Dietary Restriction in Two Rotifer Species: The Effect of the Length of Food Deprivation on Life Span and Reproduction. *Oecologia.* 153:303–308.

Wheeler M.L and Pi-Sunyer F.X. 2008. Carbohydrate Issues: Type and Amount. *J of the Amer. Diet. Assoc.* 108: 34-39.

Wilson F.D, Wheeler M.R, Harget M and Kambysellis. 1969. Cytogenetics Relations in the *Drosophila nasuta* Subgroup of Species. *Univ. Texas Publ.* 6918:207-254.

Analytical Techniques in Chemical and Biological Sciences **Page: 107-138**
Edited by: Dr. Deep Mala and Dr. Pawan Kumar 'Bharti'
ISBN: 978-93-86841-59-9
Edition: 2018
Published by: Discovery Publishing House Pvt. Ltd., New Delhi (India)

10

Mitotic Images Morpho-Variation Characteristics of *Allium* Species from Nagaland (India)

Sanjay Kumar[1] and Tsipila Thonger

ABSTRACT

The *Allium* species (*A. chinense, A. tuberosum, A. hookeri, A. ascalonicum* and *A. sativum*) were collected from the different regions of the Nagaland (India). The species were maintained in the departmental garden and root tips were processed according to the conventional root tip squash technique for the collection of different mitotic stages for 24 h under the microscope. The recorded stages and their variations with their characteristics were reported in the present paper.

Keywords: Mitosis, Mitotic stages, variations, cell cycle.

INTRODUCTION

There are two important requirements for successful long term cell propagation. The first requirement is the steps of the chromosome replication and division cycle must occur in a correct and fixed order. The replication of DNA (S phase) always precedes chromosome segregation (mitosis or M phase), followed by cell division (cytokinesis). The second requirement is that the sequence of chromosomal events repeats with a period equal to the mass doubling time (the time required to double cytoplasmic mass). The chromosome replication and division cycle is necessary to maintain the integrity of the genome while chromosome segregation (mitosis or M phase) and cell division (cytokinesis) necessary to maintain the cell's nucleocytoplasmic ratio within feasible limits (Bakhoum *et al.*, 2009).

The correct sequence of events [resting nucleus (G_0, G_1, S and G_2), karyokinesis {Mitosis (PMAT)} and cytokinesis (cell or cytoplasm division)] is a vigorous characteristic of the chromosome cycle. If an early event (DNA replication or Mitosis or Cell growth) is blocked, then usually none of the following events (Mitosis and Cytokinesis or cell division and S phase or G1 and G2) takes place respectively, suggesting that cell cycle events form a dependent sequence (Khodjakov and Rieder, 2009).

[1] Department of Botany, Nagaland University, Lumami, Nagaland (India)

The G1, S, and G2 phases comprise interphase, which accounts for most of the time in each cell cycle.

The M phase or mitosis is relatively short (approximately 1 hour of a 24 hour cell cycle) and divided into several steps. At the very beginning of M phase or prophase, the chromosomes condense while the cytoplasmic microtubules are being reorganized to build a bipolar mitotic spindle. Its purpose is to accurately segregate the two sister chromatids to opposite poles of the cell (Konvicka and Levan, 1972).

The nuclear envelope then breaks down, allowing the sister chromatids, which are attached to each other through sister chromatid cohesion, to become linked to the microtubules via attachment sites on each chromatid called kinetochores (Pinsky and Biggins, 2005). Kinetochores are protein-DNA complexes in which proteins that can capture microtubules are held tightly by DNA sequences at the centromere on each sister chromatid pair. The other end of a spindle microtubule is attached to microtubule organizing centers, MTOCs (plants), centrosome (animals) and spindle pole body (yeast), which has duplicated by this time to form the two spindle poles (Yang *et al.*, 2009). Because the two kinetochores on each pair of sister chromatids are attached to opposite spindle poles, they are under tension due to pulling forces that are attempting to move them to opposite poles. Eventually, the balance between these forces causes each chromosome to line up near the center of the spindle, which marks the metaphase stage of mitosis.

After all the chromosomes achieve bipolar attachment to spindle microtubules in metaphase, sister chromatid cohesion is rapidly dissolved. As a result, the pulling forces of the microtubules cause the two sister chromatids to move rapidly to the opposite poles at anaphase (Levan, 1935).

After sister chromatids segregate to opposite poles, cells physically divide into two daughter cells through a process that involves pinching in the plasma membrane called cytokinesis (Verma and Mittal, 1978).

The present chapter is an attempt to identify different mitotic stages, sequence of mitotic stages, and variations available at each mitotic stage during the cell division cycle for five *Allium* species (*A. chinense, A. tuberosum, A. hookeri, A. ascalonicum* and *A. sativum*). The study has been taken in consideration to most the students who involved in the cytological studies are not aware of the different phases of the cell division cycle or not able to identify proper stages during the mitosis or meiotic studies. Therefore, we tried to present the different variations in the mitotic stages during mitosis and hope it may be useful to the students and other new aspirant for cytological studies.

MATERIALS AND METHOD

The species of *Allium* (*A. chinense, A. tuberosum, A. hookeri, A. ascalonicum* and *A. sativum*) were collected from the different parts of the Nagaland and maintained in the Department for root tips. The chromosomal analysis was done according to the conventional root tip squash method (Sharma and Sharma, 1980). The root tips were pretreated with saturated PDB for 3 h then fixed in carnoy's 1 (3:1 ethanol: glacial acetic acid) solution for 24 h and stored in preservative (70% v/v ethanol) at 4°C for further use.

Preparation of slides: Each root tip was washed with distilled water (5 min) and then treated with 1N HCl (15 min). The hydrolysed root tips washed repeatedly with distilled water and stained (5 min) with acetocarmin (2% w/v) and then squashed. The slides were analyzed and observed for number, size and morphology of the chromosomes. The different mitotic stages (interphase, prophase, metaphase, anaphase, telophase and cytokinesis) were observed for 24 h cell division cycle and variations among the mitotic images were recorded.

RESULTS

The observed variations in the structures of different mitotic stages (interphase, prophase, metaphase, anaphase, telophase and cytokinesis) for *Allium* species (*A. chinense, A. tuberosum, A. hookeri, A. ascalonicum* and *A. sativum*) recorded and presented (Figure 9.1-9.32).

DISCUSSION

The variations in the structure of different mitotic stages (interphase, prophase, metaphase, anaphase, telophase and cytokinesis) were observed for 24 h cell division cycle in the *Allium* species (*A. chinense, A. tuberosum, A. hookeri, A. ascalonicum* and *A. sativum*). The varied mitotic structures involved in the mitosis and yield two daughter mitotic cells at the end of cell division cycle. The production of daughter cells involved in the development and growth of the plant. The plant species showed their growth fast or slow depends upon the division of mitotic cells (also environmental factors may affect) during mitosis of a cell division cycle. The variations were observed at each identified stages and recorded.

Interphase

The interphase is a stage between telophase and the beginning of the rapidly dividing cells of prophase. The term 'resting stage' was used to denote the interphase stage, where necessary, in less actively dividing cells especially in older portions of the root-tip. The quiescent period of interphase leads to maximum extension of the chromonemata. The distinguishing feature of interphase is the spherical nucleolus (highly stained, lightly stained or unstained), nuclear net or reticulum, intertwined threads of the chromosomes, chromatic dots, spiral or coiled threads, faintly stained threads, chromatic threads with dots or minute beads. The identity of the chromosome has not been lost in interphase nuclei but it is masked into the reticulum, nuclear membrane and cell wall clearly marked.

The morphological variation and characteristics of mitotic image interphase were recorded in *A. chinenseas* chromatic dots (Figure 10.1A), chromatic threads and beads (Figure 10.1B), spherical nucleoli (Figure 10.1C) and spiral chromatic threads (Figure 10.1D), *A. tuberosumas* chromatic dots (Figure 10.7D), chromatic threads and beads (Figure 10.7E), intertwined and spiral threads (Figure 10.107F), *A. hookeri* as chromatic dots (Figure 12F), chromatin extension (Figure 10.13A), intertwined threads (Figure 13B) and chromatin net (Figure 10.13C), Nucleolus (Figure 10.13D), Spiral form (Figure 10.13 E), Chromatin threads and beads (Figure 13 F),*A. ascalonicum* as chromatic threads and minute beads (Figure 10.18D), extension of chromonemata (Figure 18E), spherical nucleolus faintly stained chromatin threads (Figure 10.18 F), spherical nucleolus chromatic threads and minute beads (Figure 10.19 A) and spiral chromatic threads (Figure 10.19B) and *A. sativum* as intertwined chromatic threads (Figure 25A), chromatin net (Figure 10.25B), nucleoli dots (Figure 10.25C) and spiral threads and dots (Figure 10.25D) and threads and dots (Figure 10.25E).

Prophase

After a period of 'rest' the nucleus again prepares for the division, the earliest prophase is marked as an enlarging nucleus. The chromatic threads are tangled, smooth, and slender ribbon, dark stained nodules or small masses of chromatin, chromere or minor loops in the chromonemata.

The single thread is double may be revealed by clear loops along the thread (but generally the swelling of the thread by acetic acid in the fixative serves to conceal the duality). The coiled chromonemata are definitely forming into recognizable chromosomes. Prophase may be considered as the chromosomes assemble on the equatorial plate at their greatest contraction, swollen (due to the action of acetic acid in fixative) with accumulations of chromatic material. When fully formed they move to the equatorial plate as the ensuing metaphase approaches. The nucleoli and nuclear membrane disappear. The prophase is the most common phase on any slide so it is presumed to be of rather long duration.

The morphological variation and characteristics of mitotic image prophase were recorded in *A. chinense* as enlarged nucleus (Figure 10.1E), entangled chromatin threads (Figure 10.1F), smooth and long chromatin threads (Figure 10.2A), looped chromatin thread (Figure 10.2B), chromatids near to equatorial plate (Figure 10.2C), swollen and recognizable chromosomes (Figure 10.2D), small mass aggregation of chromatids (Figure 10.2E), chromatids in nodule form (Figure 10.2F), chromatids in ribbon form (Figure 10.3A), looped form (Figure 3B), entangled (Figure 10.3C) and entangled and bridges (Figure 10.3D), *A. tuberosum* as entangled chromatic threads (Figure 10.D), long and smooth chromatids (Figure 10.8E), long ribbon like structure (Figure 10.8F), looped form (Figure 10.9A), minor loops form (Figure 10.9B), nodule form (Figure 10.9C), ribbon form (Figure 10.9D) and towards equatorial plate (Figure 10.9E), *A. hookeri* as chromomere form (Figure 10.14A), entangled form (Figure 10.14B), long thread form (Figure 10.14C), long slender ribbon like structure (Figure 10.14D), recognizable chromosome structure (Figure 10.14E),ring or loop form (Figure 10.14F) and swollen and recognizable form (Figure 10.15A), *A. ascalonicum* as chromomere form (Figure 10.19C), dark nodule form (Figure 10.19D), enlarged nucleus and swollen chromatids (Figure 10.19E), entangled chromatid thread (Figure 10.19F), long smooth threads (Figure 10.20A), long smooth form (Figure 10.20B), minor loop formation (Figure 10.20C), minor loop and chromatic threads (Figure 10.20D), recognizable chromosomes (Figure 10.20E) and slender long ribbon form (Figure 10.20F), *A. sativum* as chromomere form (Figure 10.25F), entangled form (Figure 10.26A), entangled (Figure 10.26B), long and smooth chromosomes (Figure 10.26C), long entangled ribbons (Figure 10.26D), loops (Figure 10.26E), nodule form (Figure 10.26F), recognizable chromosomes (Figure 10.27A), ribbons (Figure 10.27B) and towards equator (Figure 10.27C).

Metaphase

Metaphase begins as the chromosomes assemble on the equatorial plate. The kinetochore is observed to be attracted to the equatorial plate and held there to lie in the equatorial plane but the arms of the chromosomes point out at various angles. The chromosomes that are double and composed of two chromatids is unmistakable is a c-mitosis metaphase. Similarly each chromatid is composed of two apparently interwining chromonemata or moniliform appearance. Chromosomes of late metaphase are remarkable in that there is but little matrix. Metaphase terminates with separation of sister chromatids. Separation may begin at the kinetochore but not always, in c-mitosis the ends may separate first. If the chromosomes are sticky, separation may bring about the formation of chromosome bridges. Metaphase thus sees the assembling of the double chromosomes at the equatorial plate followed by the separation of the sister chromatids as they move along the spindle toward the poles.

The morphological variation and characteristics of mitotic image metaphase were recorded in *A. chinense* as chromosome arms at various angles (Figure 10.3E), c-mitosis (Figure 10.3F), chromosomes at equatorial plate (Figure 10.4A), thick chromosomes and less matrix (Figure 10.4B), intertwined (Figure 10.4C), metaphase less matrix (Figure 10.4D), metaphase and nucleus (Figure 10.4E), multipolar axis (Figure 10.4F) and separation from kinetochore (Figure 10.5A), *A. tuberosum* as bridge and sticky (Figure 10.9F), at equator (Figure 10.10A), kinetochore towards plate (Figure 10.10B) and late metaphase less matrix (Figure 10.10C), *A. hookeri* as arms differently angled (Figure 10.15B), arms differently angled (Figure 10.15C), C-mitosis (Figure 10.15D), double or paired chromosome (Figure 10.15E), kinetochore towards plate (Figure 10.15F) and metaphase less matrix (Figure 10.16A), *A. ascalonicum* as bridge and separation (Figure 10.21A), C-mitosis (Figure 10.21B), double or pair chromosome at plate (Figure 10.21C), arms differently angled at equator (Figure 10.21D), kinetochore attraction towards equator (Figure 10.21E), metaphase less matrix (Figure 10.21F), moniliform (Figure 10.22A) and various angled arms (Figure 10.22B), *A. sativum* as double or paired chromosome (Figure 10.27D), at equator and arms angled (Figure 10.27E), kinetochore at equatorial plate (Figure 10.27F), metaphase less matrix (Figure 10.28A), ring formation (Figure 10.28B), separation (Figure 10.28C) and at equator and sticky (Figure 10.27D).

Anaphase

The chromosomes have a truly individualized and independent existence at anaphase. The two darkely stained rod like chromatids lying parallel in a common but less chromatic matrix. The separation of the sister chromosomes is almost completed. Most of the chromosomes are assuming or have assumed U or V form, but a J or shepherd's crook man be also observed.

The chromosomes are more extended as the coils or interlacing chromonemata are loosened. Late anaphase chromosomes have reached the poles or more accurately the kinetochores have arrived there. The clear areas denote the re-forming nucleoli; the chromosomes are assembled in a hemisphere not unlike the ribs of an expended umbrella. The chromosome extremities appear to be turning inwards to form an apparent hollow cylinder. The completely formed cylinder may enclose the nucleoli which appear as clear unstained areas within the nucleus. With the completion of the cylinder the anaphase ends and the telophase begins. Anaphase is of short duration. Anaphase chromosomes is seen to a more or less cylindrical body, quite smooth in outline or undulating in outline or it may be moniliform which denote the coiling of chromonemal threads embedded in the chromosome. It composed of a pair of darkly stained chromatin, parallel, hooked rods called chromatids or half chromosomes.

The morphological variation and characteristics of mitotic image anaphase were recorded in *A. chinense* as coils and loose chromonemata (Figure 10.5B), interlacing and reforming nucleoli (Figure 10.5C), late anaphase at poles and hollow cylinder (Figure 10.5D) and UVJ shaped (Figure 10.5E), *A. tuberosum* as chromatids at poles (Figure 10.10D), coils or loose threads (Figure 10.10E), dark rod like structure of chromosome at two poles (Figure 10.10F), interlacing chromatids (Figure 10.11A) and UVJ shaped and sticky (Figure 10.11B), *A. hookeri* as chromatids at poles (Figure 10.16B), hemisphere interlacing (Figure 10.16C), loose chromatids at poles (Figure 10.16D), sticky and interlacing (Figure 10.16E) and star and UVJ shaped (Figure 10.16F), *A. ascalonicum* as chromatids at poles (Figure 10.22C), coil and loose chromonemata (Figure

10.22D), dark stained rods (Figure 10.22E), interlacing (Figure 10.22F) and UVJ shaped (Figure 10.23A) and *A. sativum* as chromatids at poles (Figure 10.28E), cylinder form (Figure 10.28F), cylinder form (Figure 10.29A), dark stained rod like structure (Figure 10.29B), interlacing (Figure 10.29C), ribs structure (Figure 10.29D) and UVJ shape (Figure 10.29E).

Telophase

Telophase begins with the anaphase chromosomes rolled into an apparent hollow cylinder. As telophase proceeds, the chromaticity is much lessened and the constituent chromonemata appear as a maze of emerging coils. Giant cells (very late telophase of giant cells) are found in the central cylinder of the root tips. The appearance of nuclear membrane rises; nucleoli reappear and steadily increase in size. It may believe that nucleolus arises from the chromosomal matrix, the disappearance of which reveals the chromonemata structure. The extended chromonemata appear as faintly staining ladder like structures.

The morphological variation and characteristics of mitotic image telophase were recorded in *A. chinense* as extended chromonemata (Figure 10.5F), loose chromatids (Figure 10.6A), nucleoli reappear (Figure 10.6B), nucleoli reappear (Figure 10.6C) and rolled hollow cylinder structure (Figure 10.6D), *A. tuberosum* as extended chromonemata (Figure 10.16C), loose chromaticity (Figure 10.11D), nucleoli reappear (Figure 10.11E) and rolled hollow cylinder (Figure 10.11F), *A. hookeri* as emerging coils (Figure 10.17A), extended chromatids (Figure 10.17B), loose chromaticity (Figure 10.17C) and rolled hollow cylinder (Figure 10.17D), *A. ascalonicum* as extended ladder like structure (Figure 10.23B), late telophase and emerging coils (Figure 10.23C), loose chromaticity (Figure 10.23D), nuclear membrane reappearance (Figure 10.23E), nucleoli reappear (Figure 10.23F) and rolled hollow cylinder (Figure 10.24A) and *A. sativum* as chromonemata (Figure 10.29F), emerging coils (Figure 10.30A), extended chromatids (Figure 30B), hollow cylinder (Figure 10.30C), ladder structure (Figure 10.30D), late telophase (Figure 10.30E), loose chromatids (Figure 10.30F) and nucleoli (Figure 10.31A).

Cytokinesis

The formation of cell plate is the most characteristic feature of the cytokinesis, also it indicates the approaching end of the telophase.

The morphological variation and characteristics of mitotic image cytokinesis were recorded in *A. chinense* as cell notch (Figure 10.6E), clumping and cell plate (Figure 10.6F), cylinder and cell plate (Figure 10.7A), nucleoli reappear (Figure 10.7B) and cell plate formation (Figure 10.7C), *A. tuberosum* as cell plate formation (Figure 10.12A), cell plate formation and division (Figure 10.12B), cylinder structure and cell plate (Figure 10.12C), notch, division and cylinder (Figure 10.12D) and nucleoli reappear and cell plate (Figure 10.12E),

A. hookeri as cell plate (Figure 10.17E), clumping and division (Figure 10.17F), cylinder and notch (Figure 10.18A), notch (Figure 10.18B) and nucleoli and cell plate (Figure 10.18C), *A. ascalonicum* as cell plate (Figure 10.24B), clumping (Figure 10.24C), cylindrical cell plate (Figure 10.24D), nucleoli reappear and cell plate (Figure 10.24E) and nucleoli and membrane reappear (Figure 10.24F) and *A. sativum* as cell plate (Figure 10.31B), cell plate (Figure 10.31C), clumping (Figure 10.31D), cylinder (Figure 10.31E), notch (Figure 10.31F), notch (Figure 10.32A) and nucleoli (Figure 10.32B).

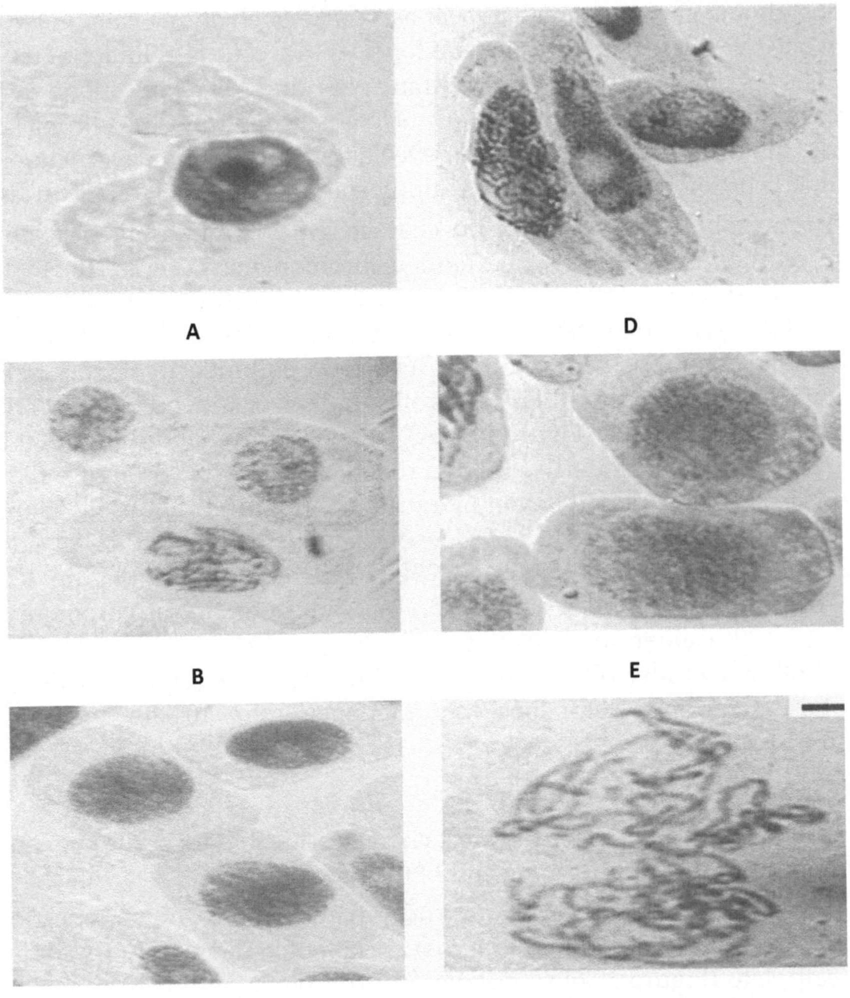

Fig. 10.1: *A. CHINENSE*, Mitotic Interphase, A. chromatic dots, B. chromatic threads beads, C. spherical nucleoli, D. spiral chromatic threads, Prophase, E. enlarging nucleus, and F. Entangled.

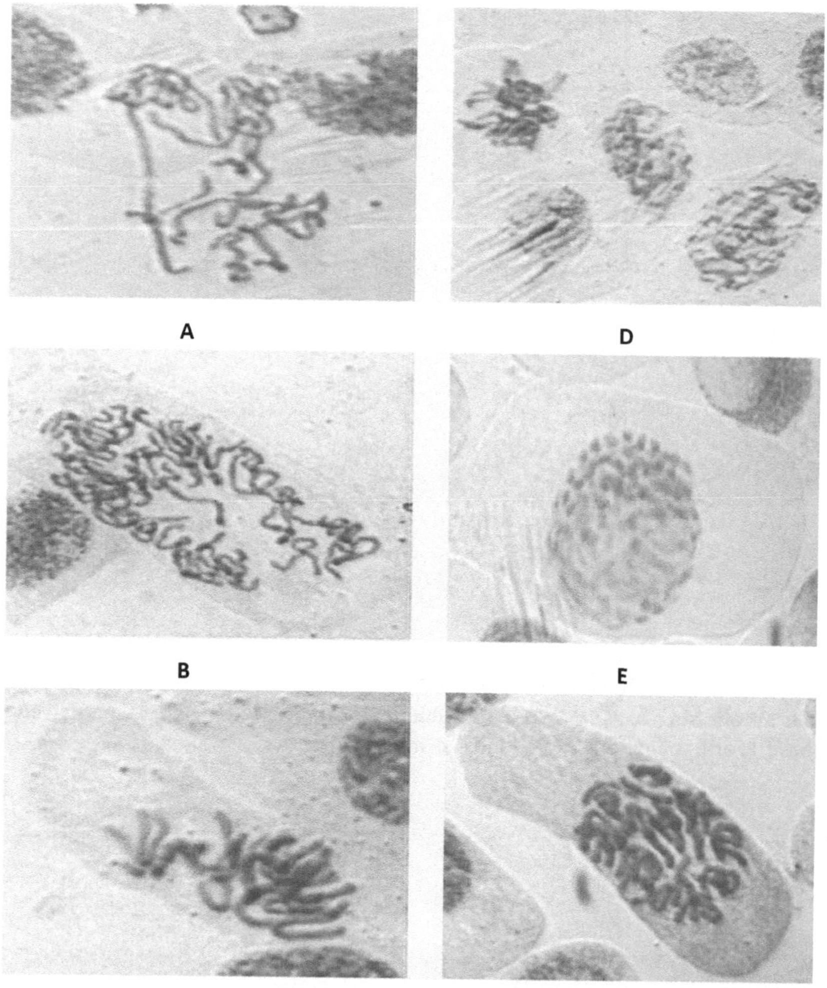

C F

Fig. 10.2: Mitotic stages, *A.CHINENSE*, A. Smooth, B. loop , C. equatorial plate, D. Swollen and recognizable, E. small masses, and F. Nodules.

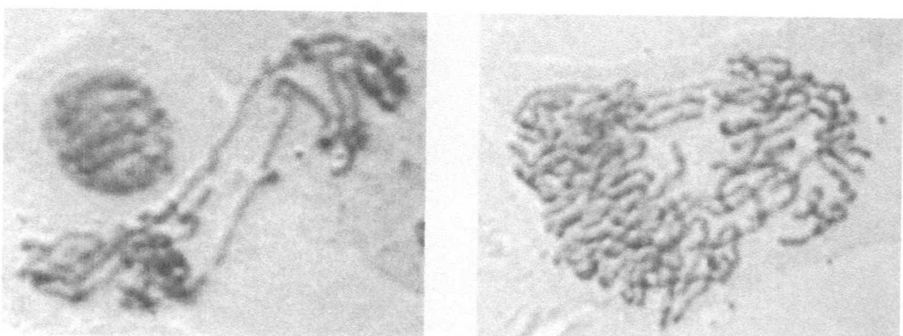

A D

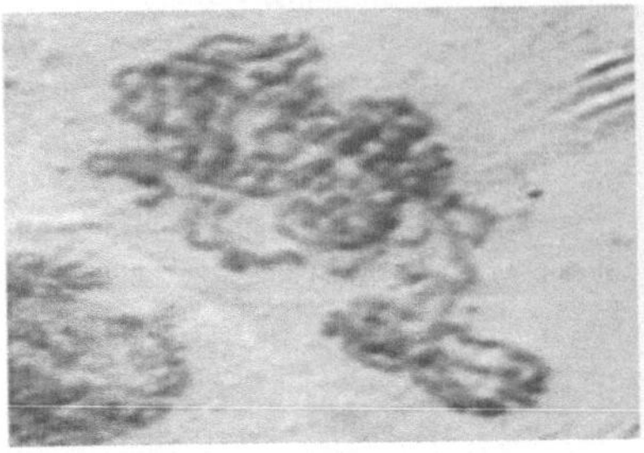

B

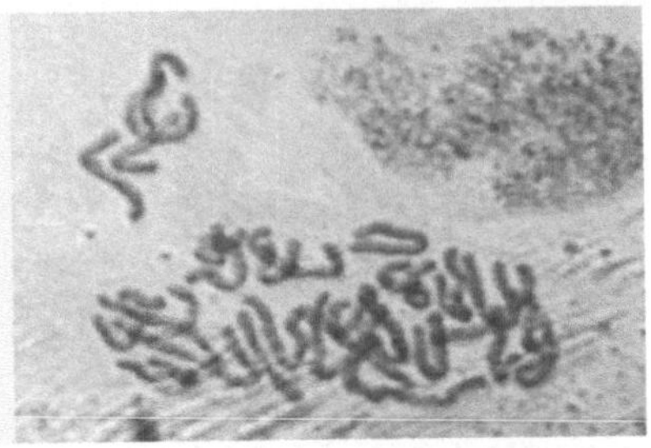

E

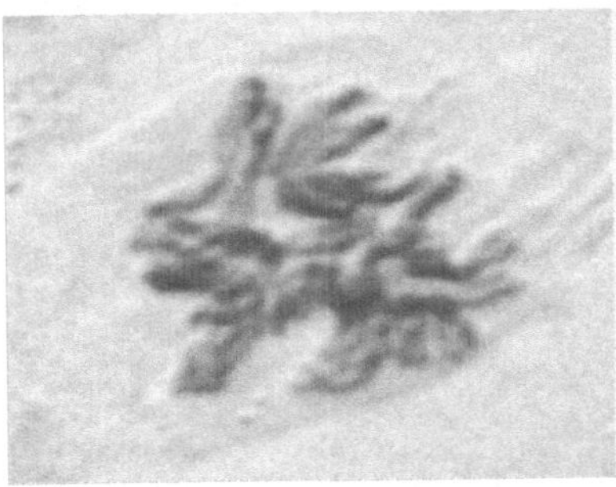

C

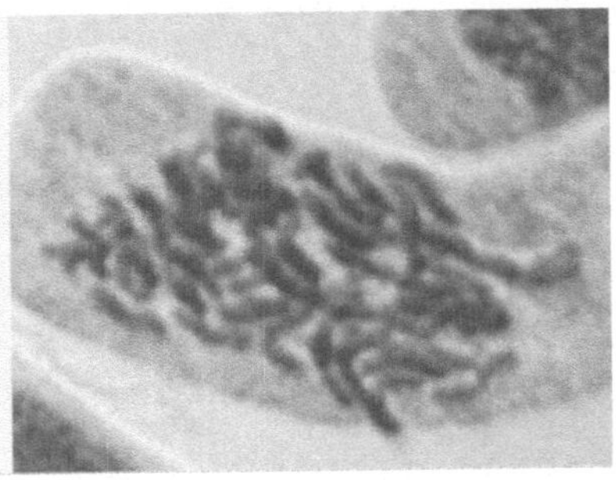

F

Fig. 10.3: Mitotic stages, *A.CHINENSE*, A. Ribbon, B. loop, C. entangled, D. entangled bridge, Metaphase, E. arms at various angles and F. c- mitosis.

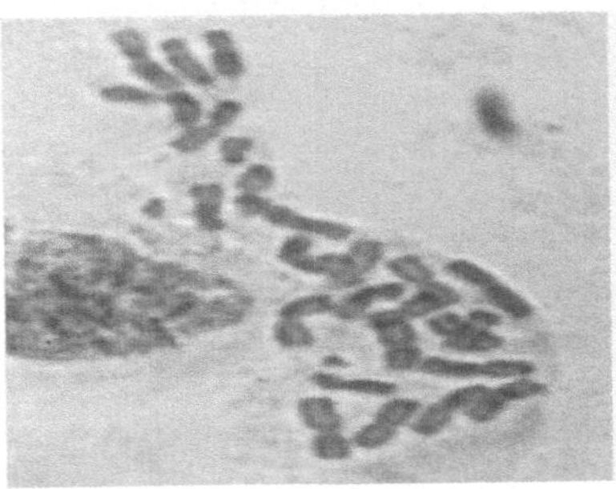

A

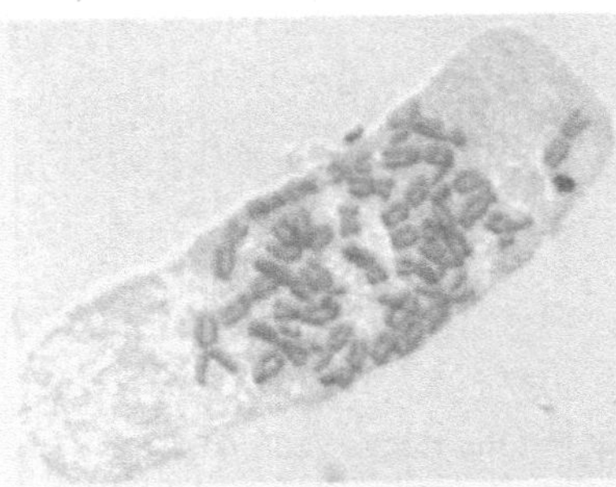

D

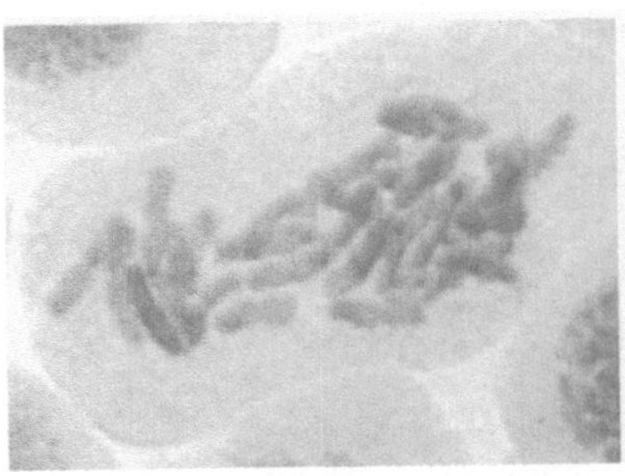

B

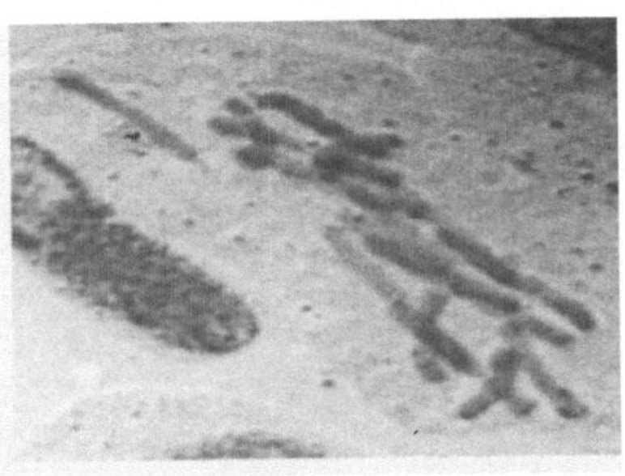

E

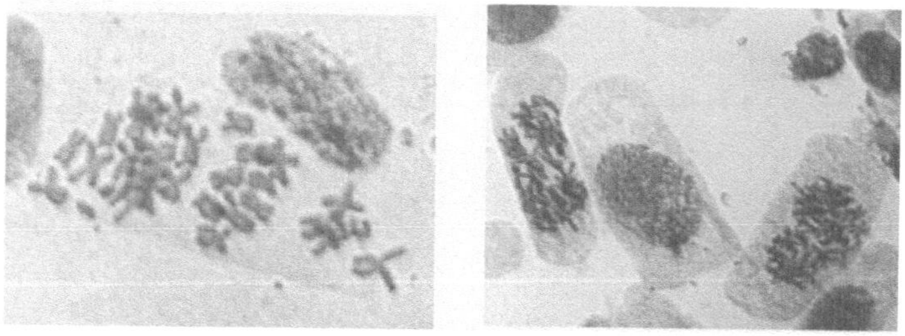

C F

Fig. 10.4: Mitotic stages, *A.CHINENSE*, A equatorial plate, B. less matrix , C. interwined, D. less matrix, E. metaphase with nucleus and F. multipolar axis.

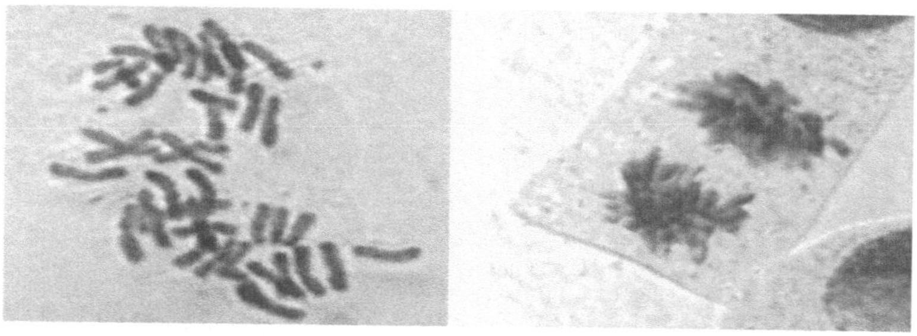

A D

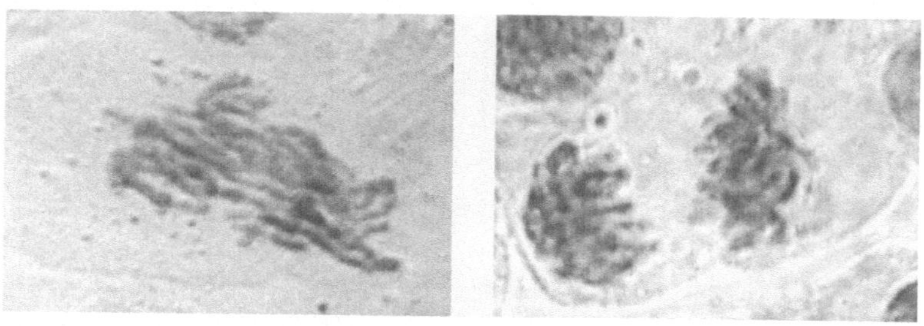

B E

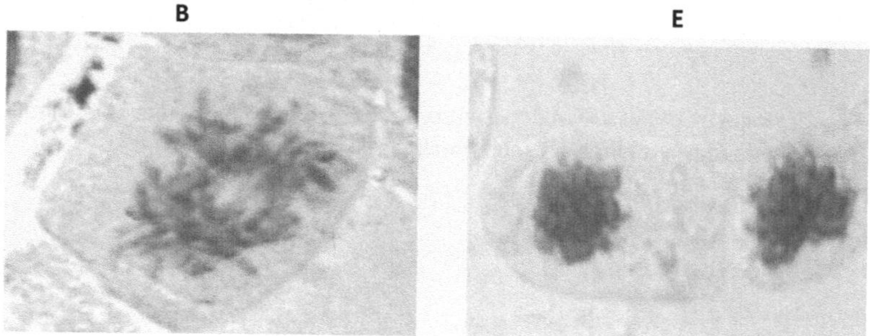

C F

Fig. 10.5: Mitotic stages, *A.CHINENSE*, A. separation from kinetochore, Anaphase, B coils or loose chromanemata, C. interlacing and reforming nucleoli, D. late anaphase at poles and hollow cylinder, E. UVJ shaped, Telophase, F. extended chromonemata.

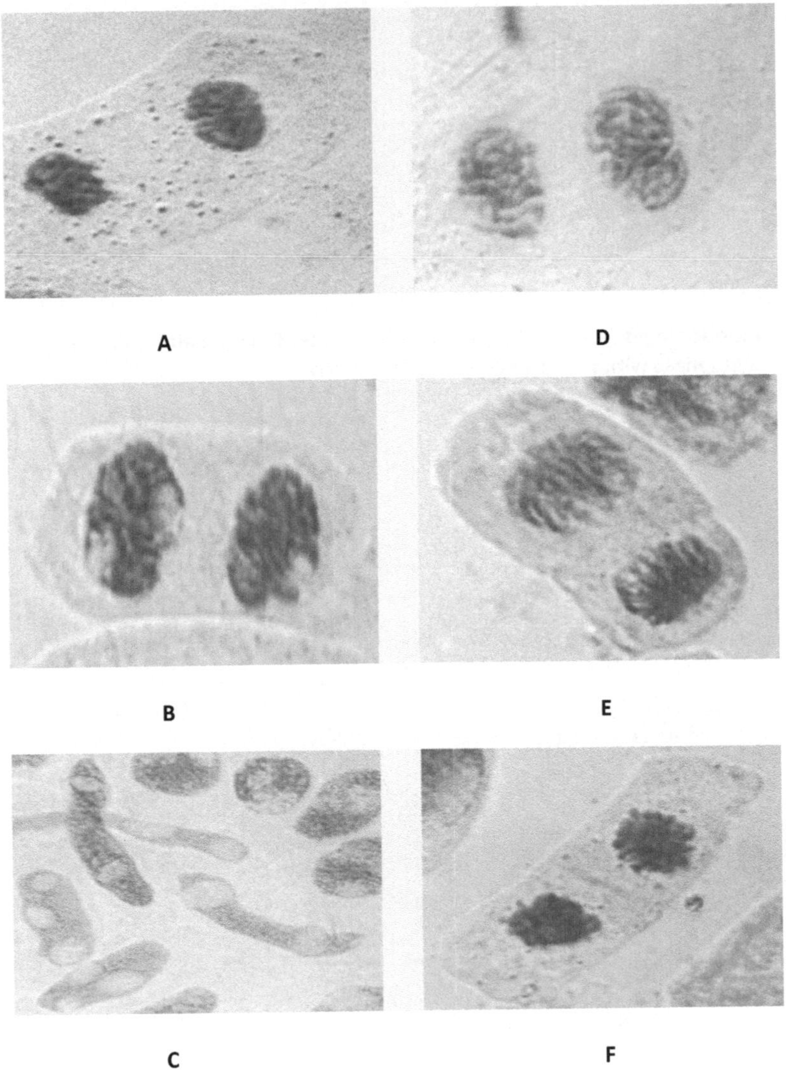

Fig. 10.6: Mitotic stages, *A.CHINENSE*, A. loose chromatids, B. nucleoli reappear , C.nucleoli reappear, D. rolled hollow cylinder, Cytokinesis, E. cell notch, and F. Clumping.

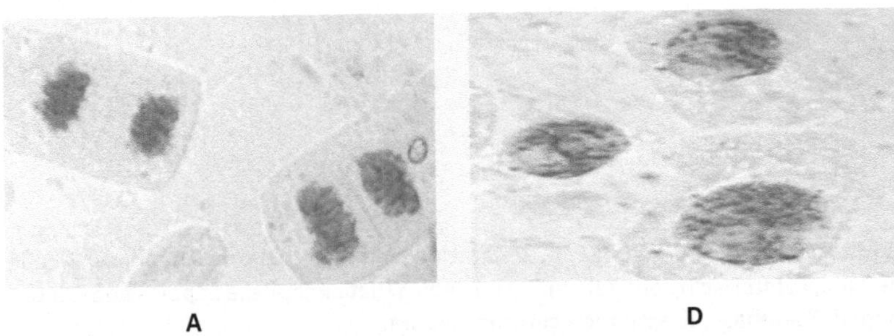

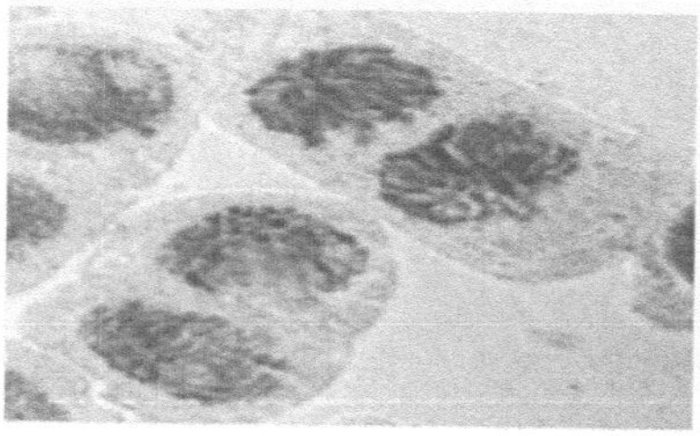

B

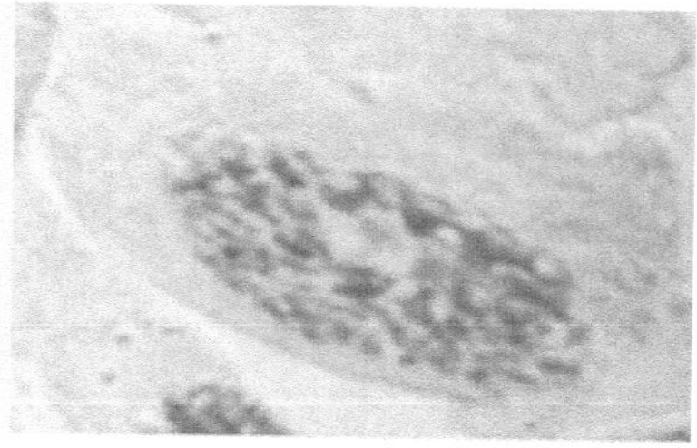

E

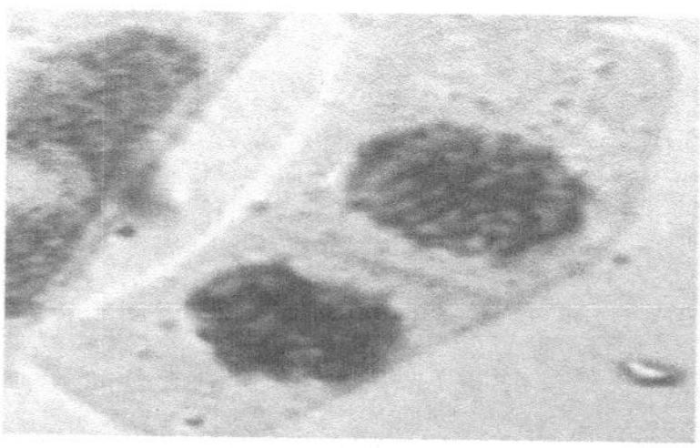

C

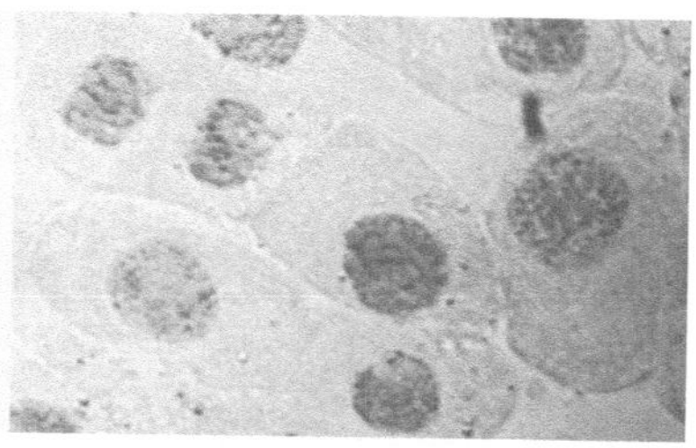

F

Fig. 10.7: Mitotic stages, *A.CHINENSEE,* A. Cylindrical, B. nucleoli reappear, C. plate formation. Mitotic images, Interphase, *A. TUBEROSUM,* interphase. D. chromatic dots, E. chromatic threads and beads, F. interwined and spiral threads.

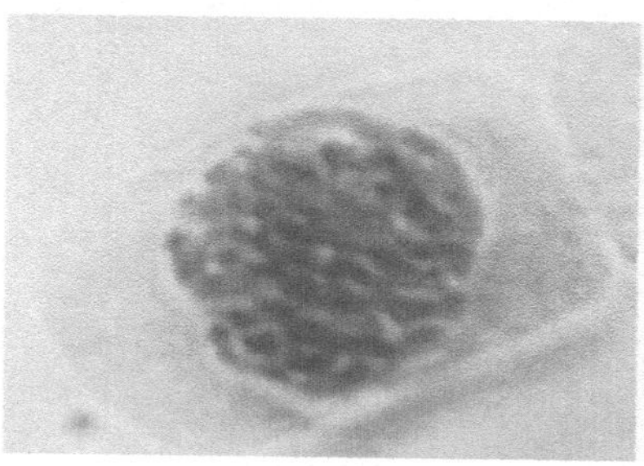

A

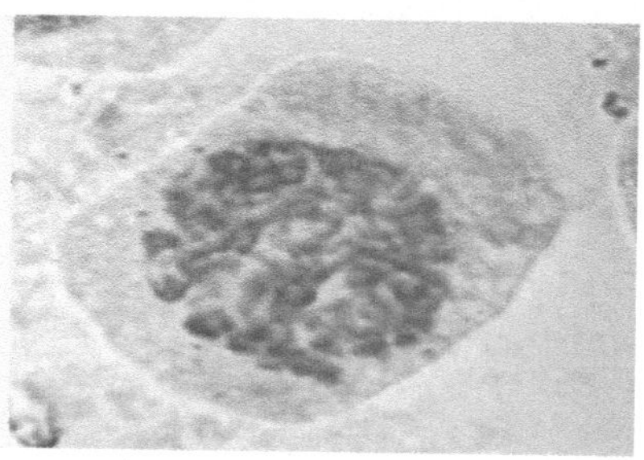

D

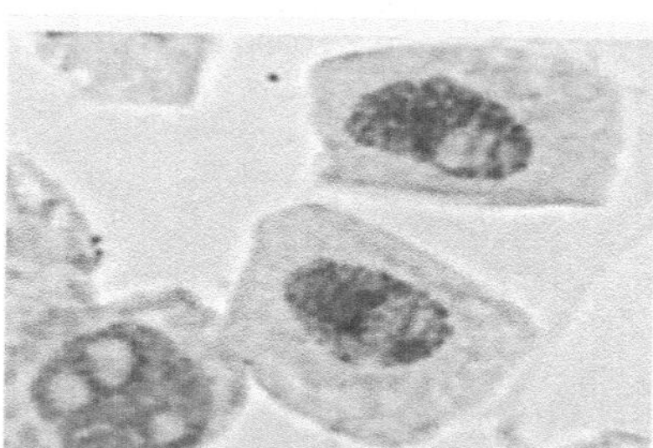

B

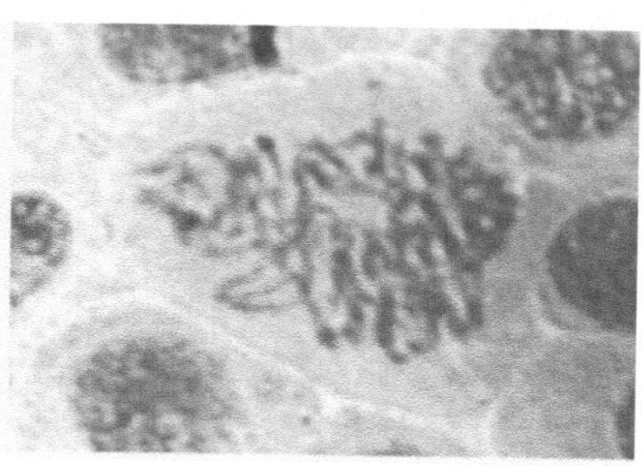

E

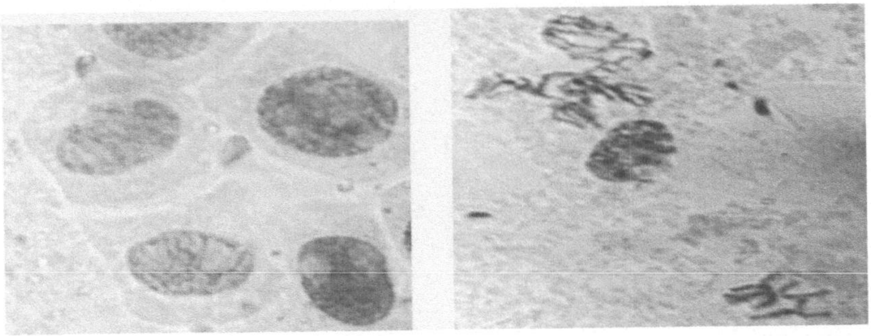

C F

Fig. 10.8: Mitotic stages, *A.TUBEROSUM*. A. nuclear net ,B. spherical nucleolus C spiral chromatic threads, Prophase, D. entangled chromosome threads, E. long and smooth, F. long ribbon.

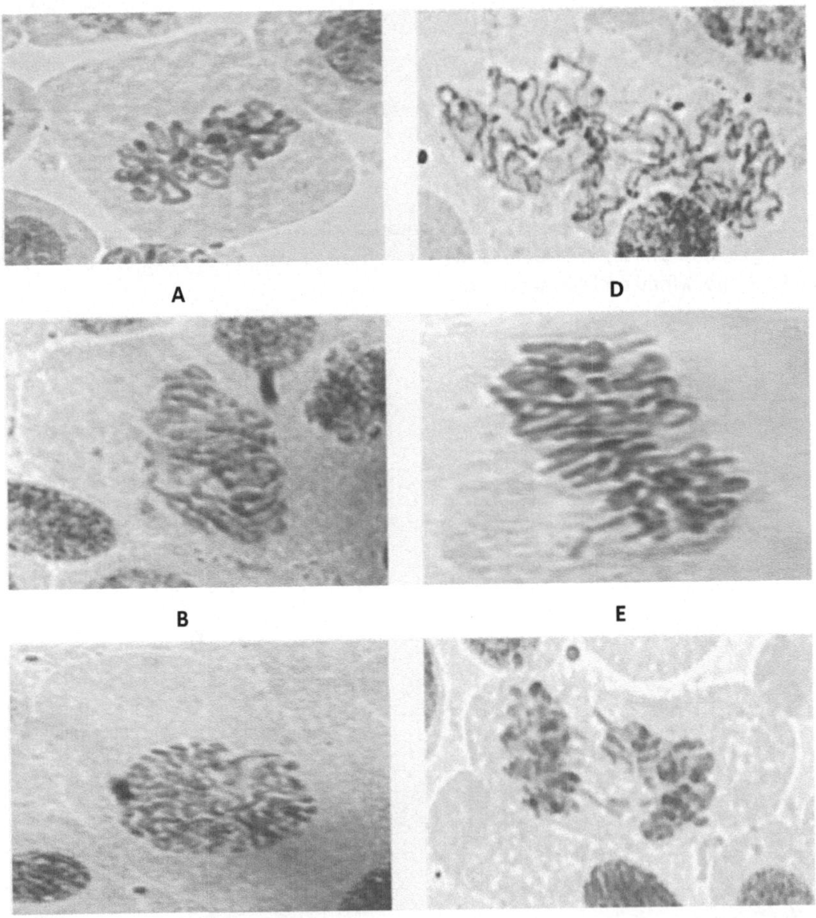

C F

Fig. 10.9: Mitotic stages, *A.TUBEROSUM,* A. loops, B. minor loops, C. Nodules, D ribbon, E.towards equatorial plate, Metaphase, F. bridge sticky.

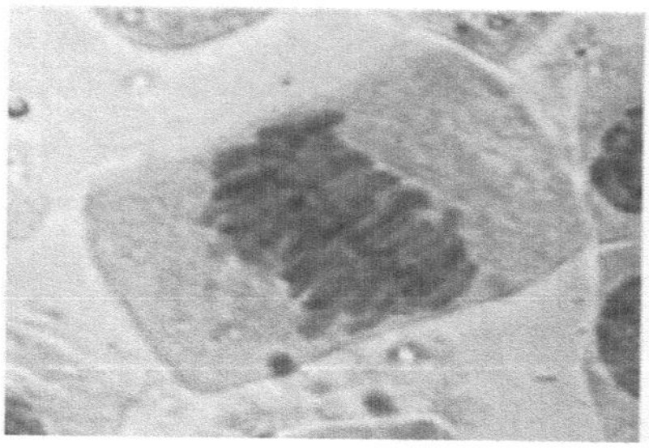

A

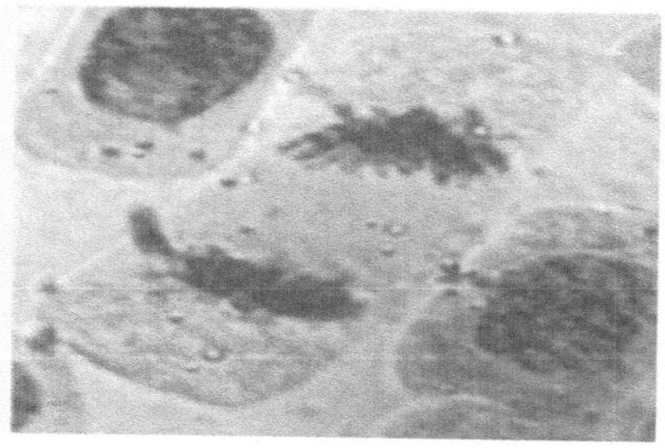

D

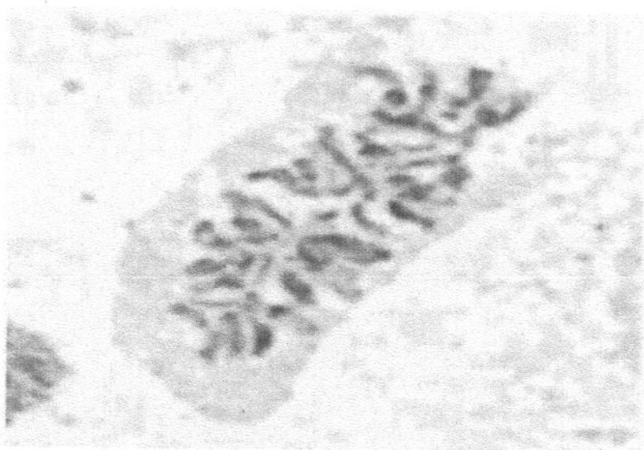

B

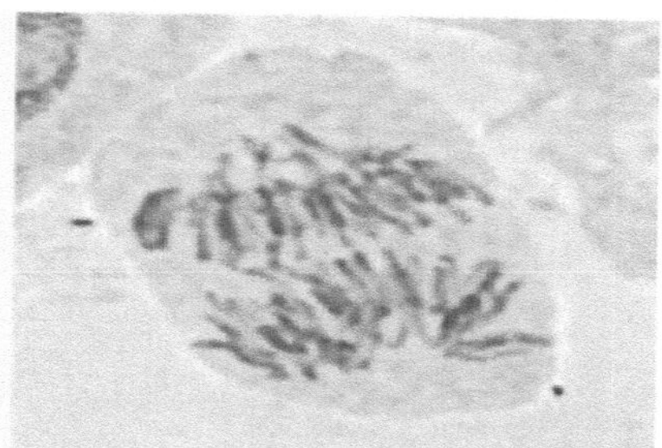

E

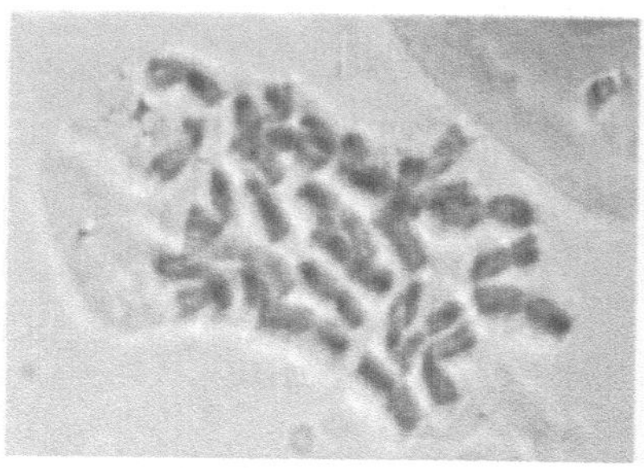

C

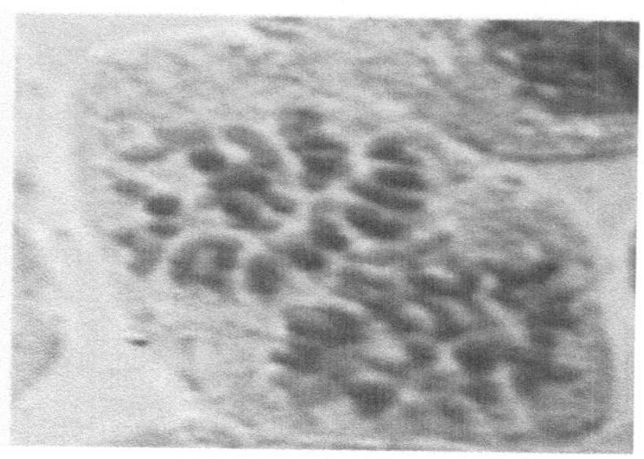

F

Fig. 10.10: Mitotic stages, *A.TUBEROSUM*, A. equatorial, B. kinetochore towards plate and C. late metaphase little matrix, Anaphase, D. at poles, E. coils or loose, and F. dark rod like.

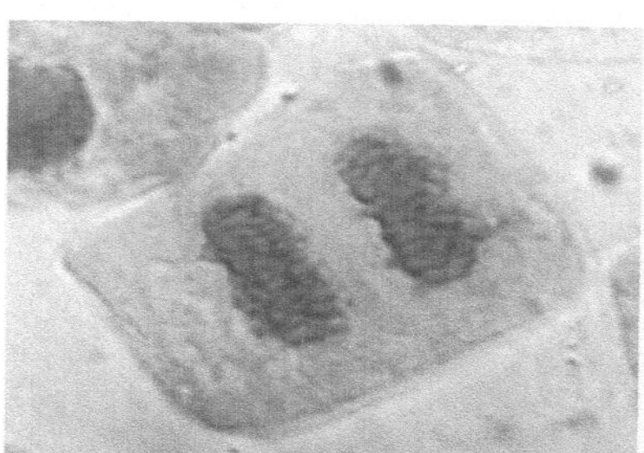

A

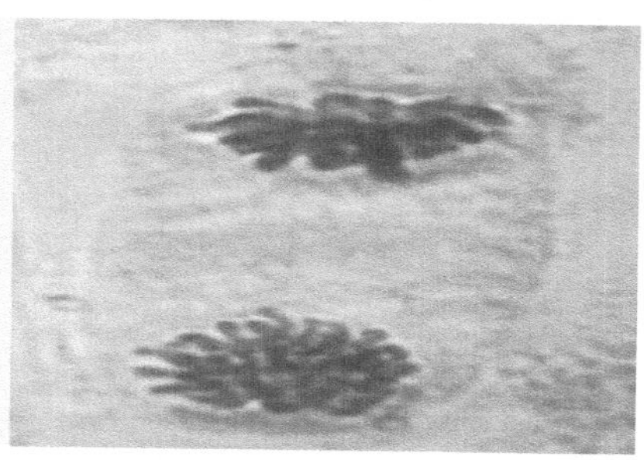

D

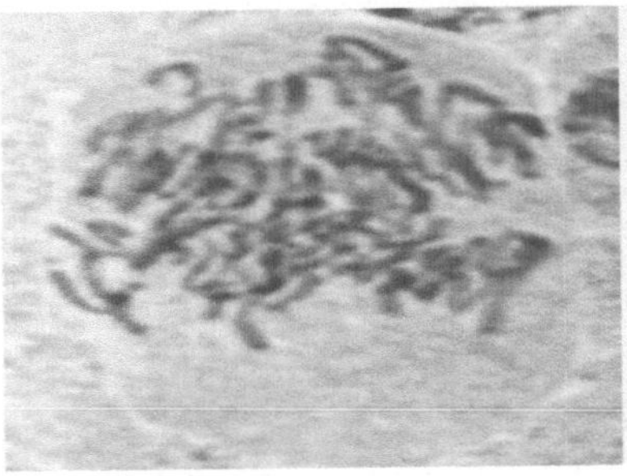 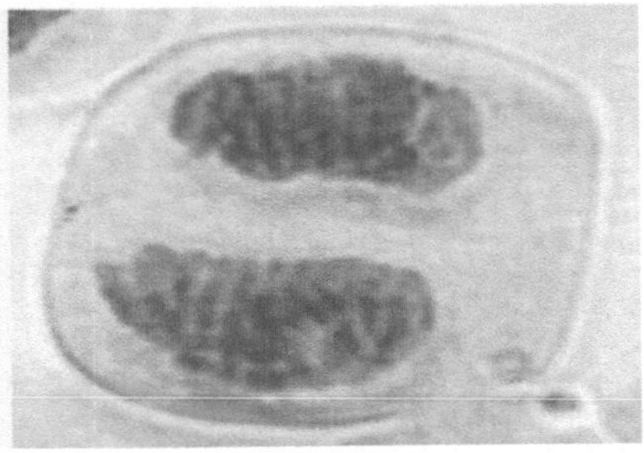

B E

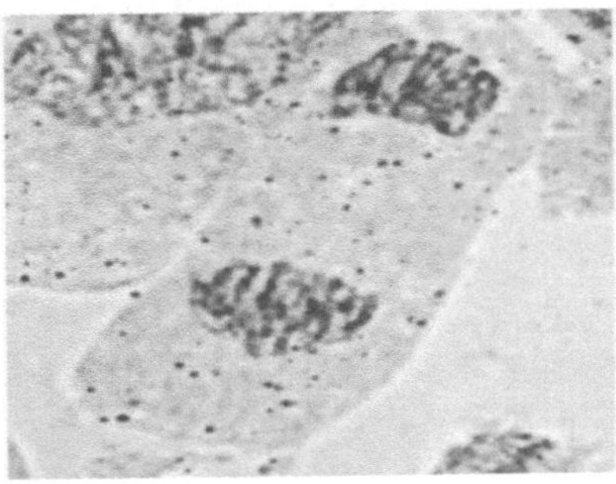 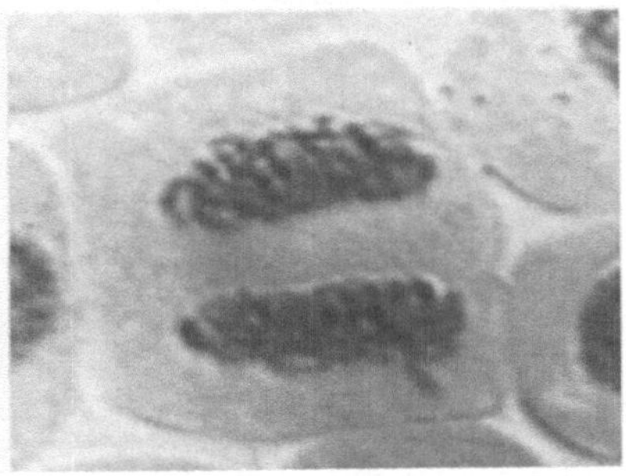

C F

Fig. 10.11: Mitotic stages, *A.TUBEROSUM*, A. interlacing B. sticky UVJ shape, Telophase, C. extended chromonemata. D. loose chromaticity E. nucleoli reappear, and F. rolled hollow cylinder.

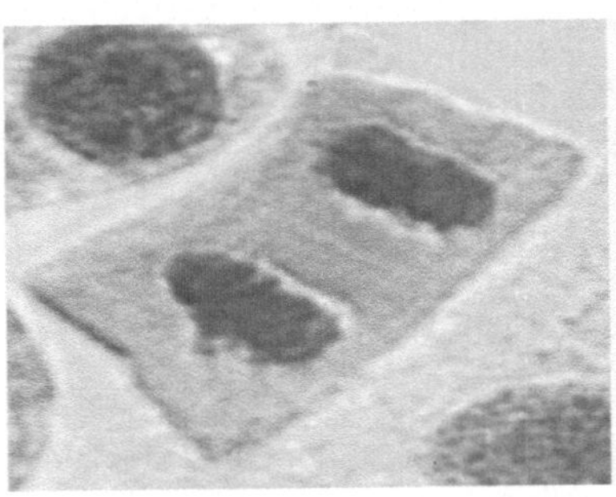 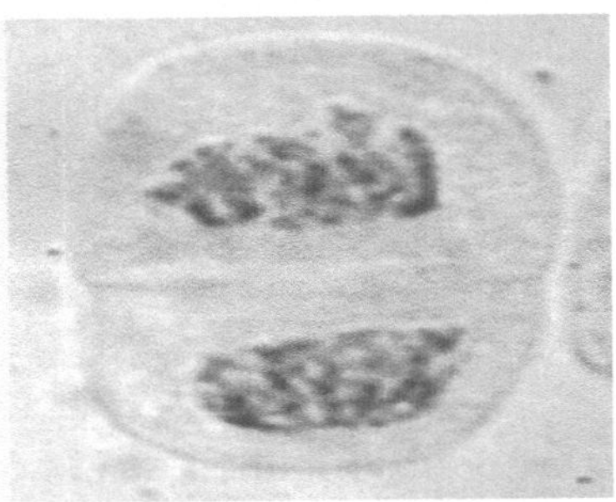

A D

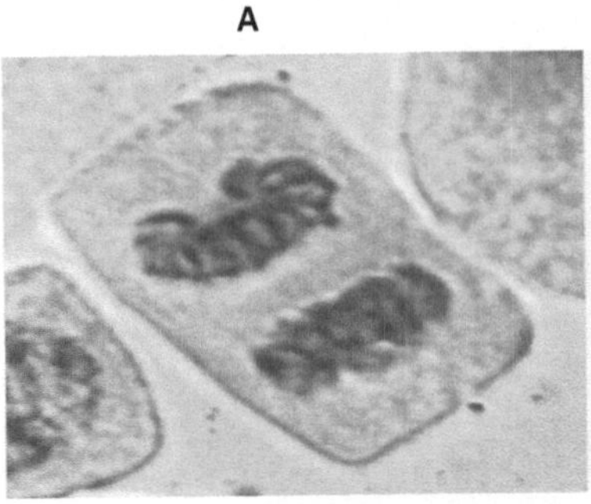 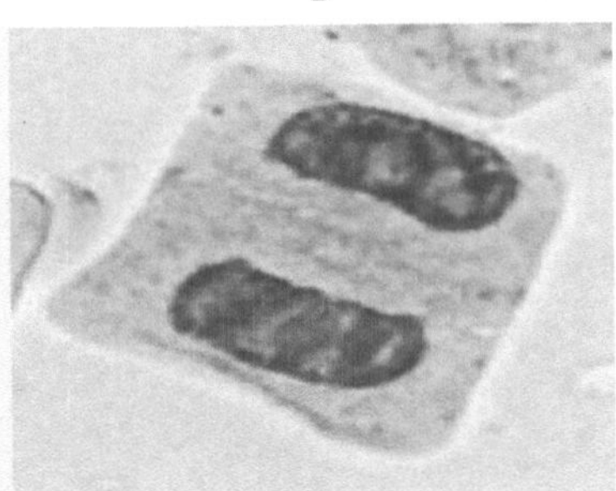

B E

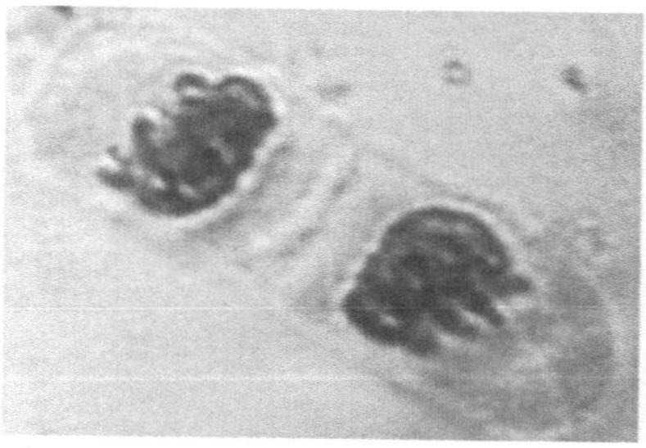

C

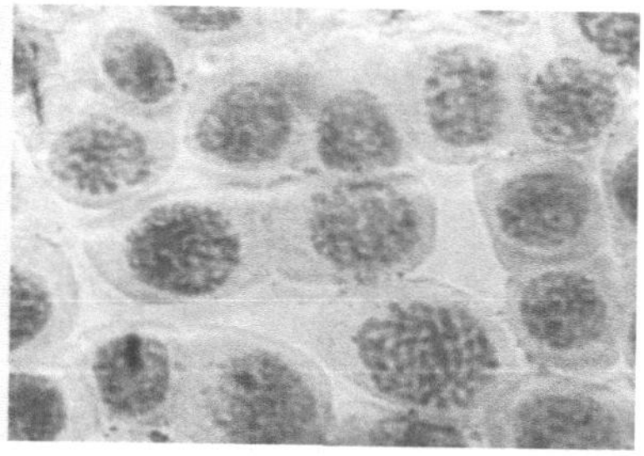

F

Fig. 10.12: Mitotic stages, *A.TUBEROSUM*, Cytokinesis,A. cell plate, B. cell plate and C Cylinder, D. notch and cylinder,E. nucleoli reappear. *ALLIUM HOOKERI*, Interphase, F. Dots.

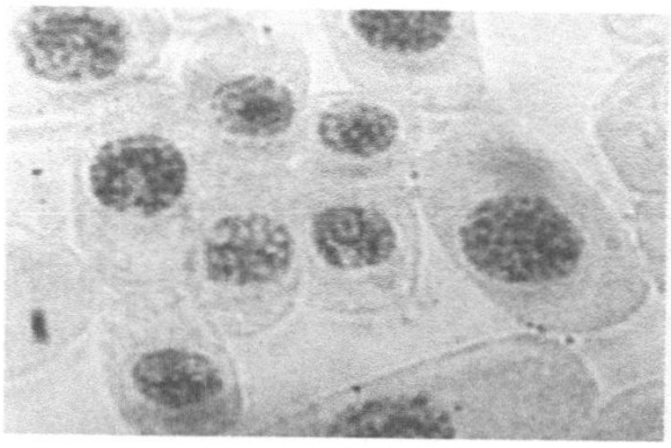

A

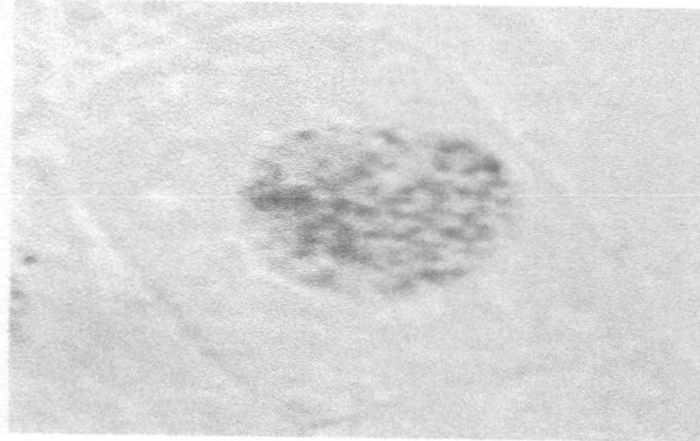

D

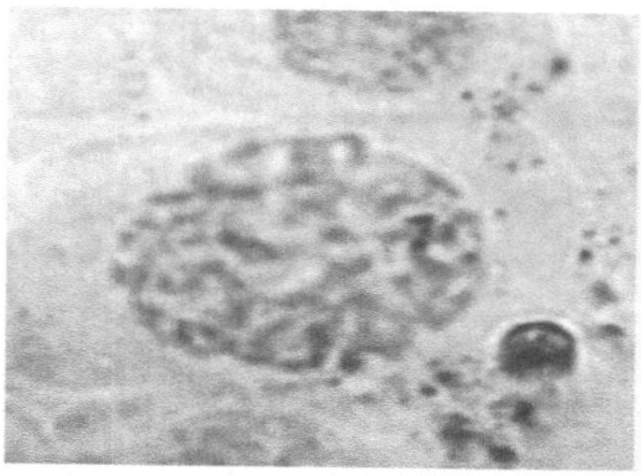

B

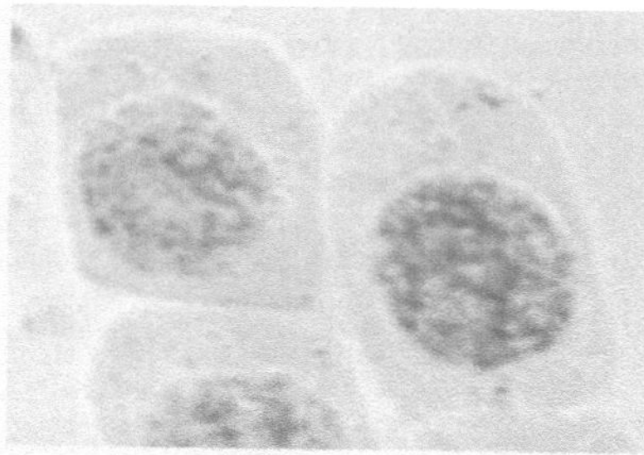

E

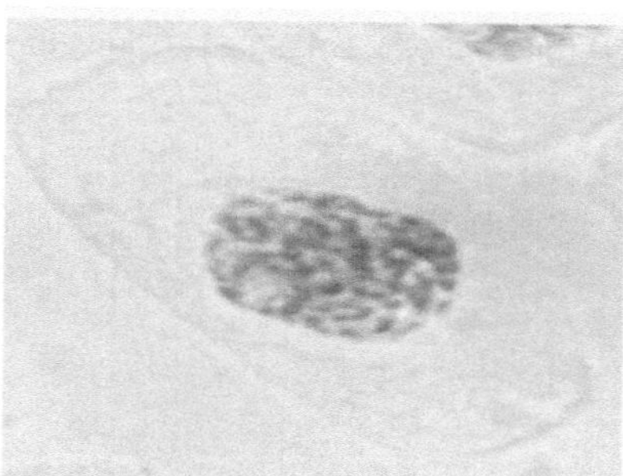

C

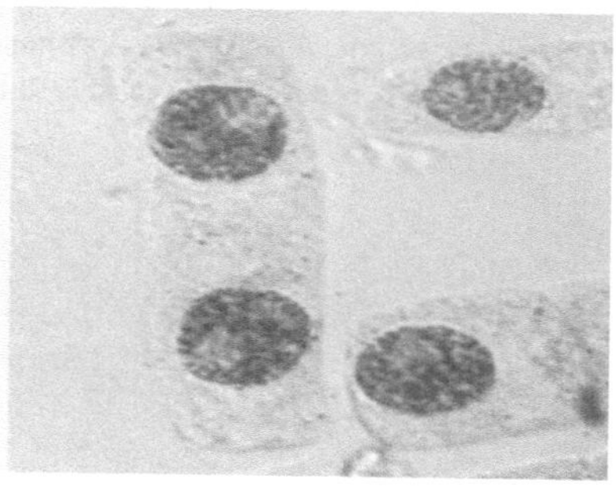

F

Fig. 10.13: Mitotic stages, *A.HOOKERI*, A. extension, and B. Interwined, C. net, D. nucleolus, E. spiral, and F. thread beads.

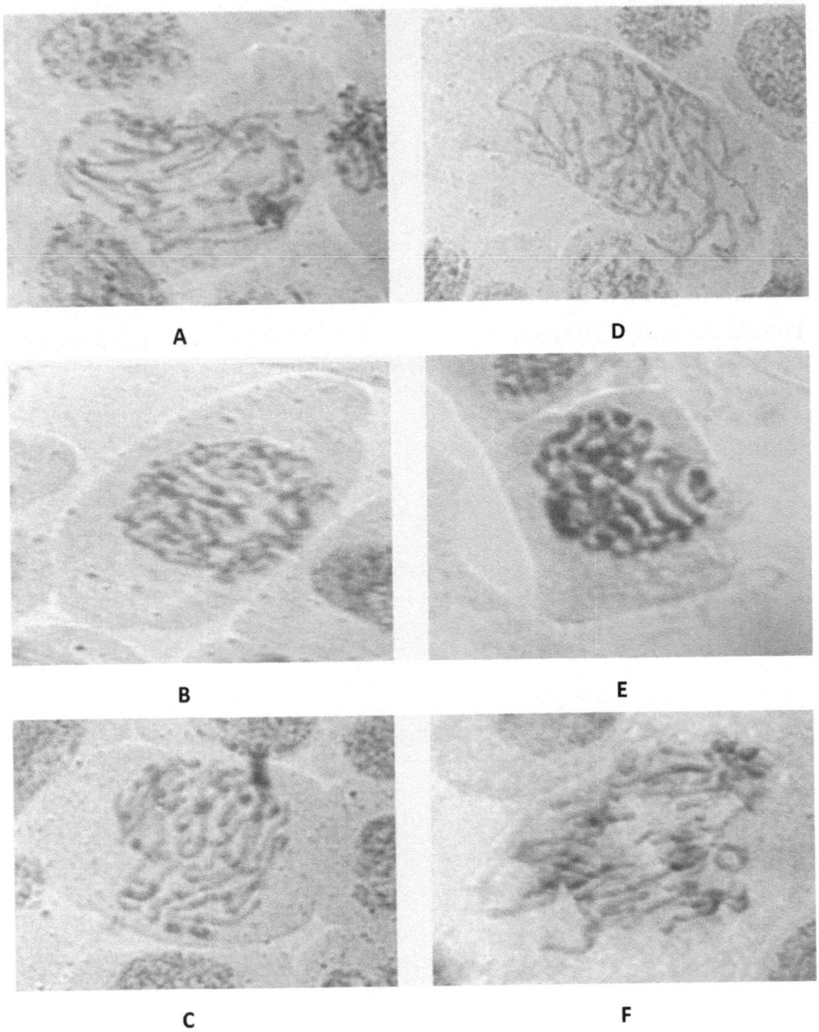

Fig. 10.14: Mitotic stages, *A.HOOKERI,* Prophase A. chromomere, B. entangled , C. long threads,D. long slender ribbon, E. recognisable, and F. Ring.

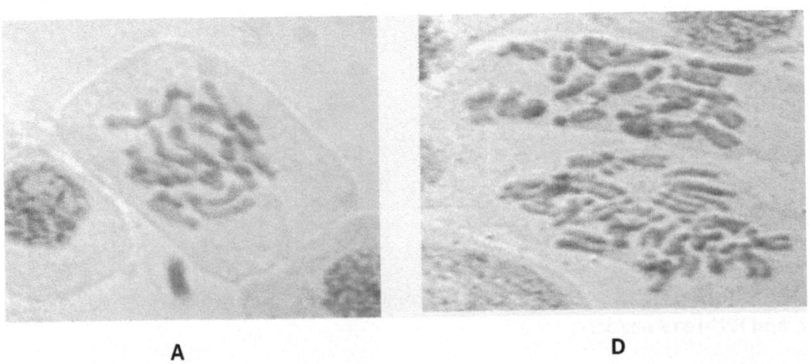

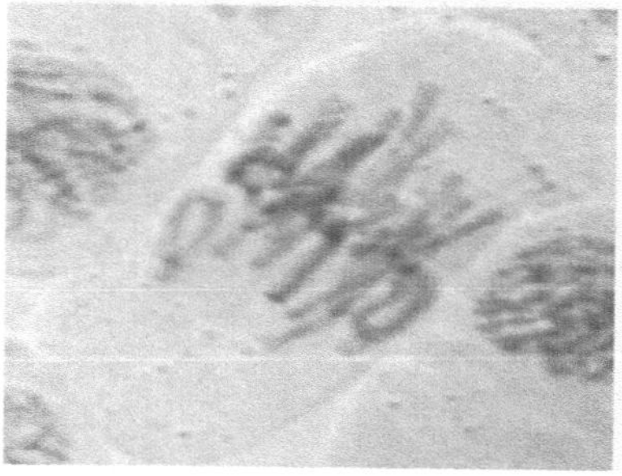

B

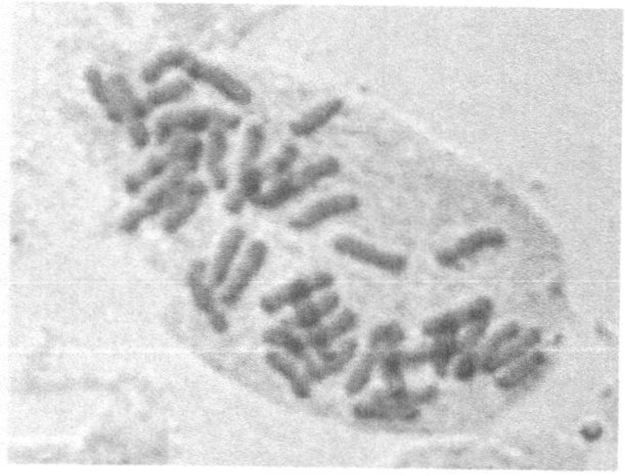

E

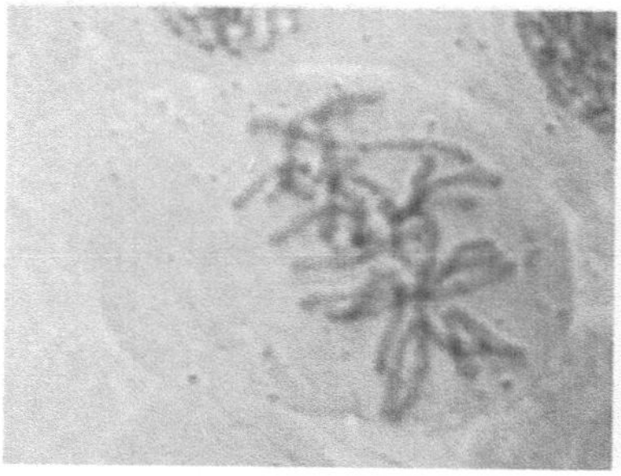

C

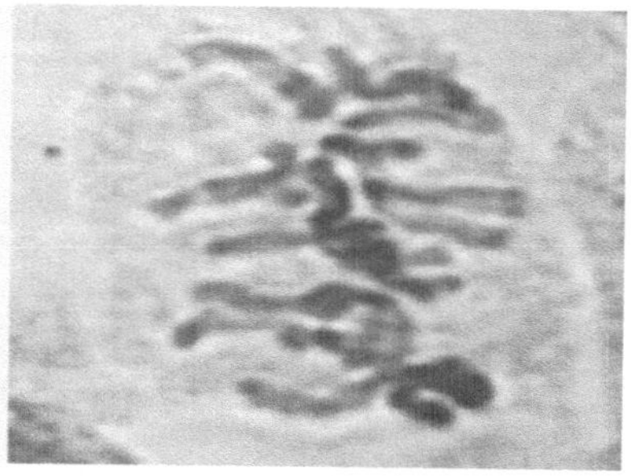

F

Fig. 10.15: Mitotic stages, *A.HOOKERI,* A. Swollen, Metaphase, B. arms angles, C. arms angles, D. C- mitosis, E. double chromosome, and F. kinetochore towards plate.

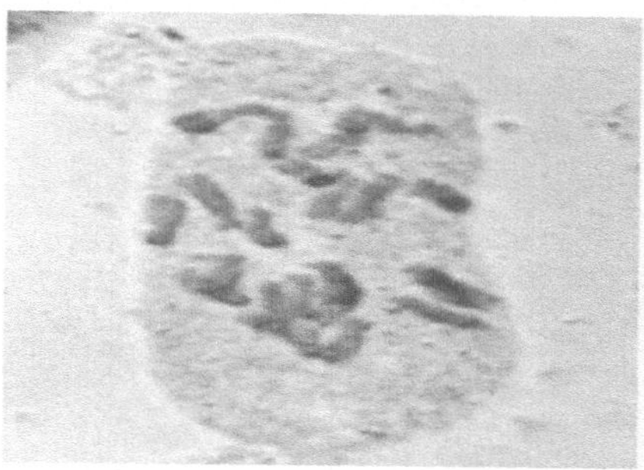

A

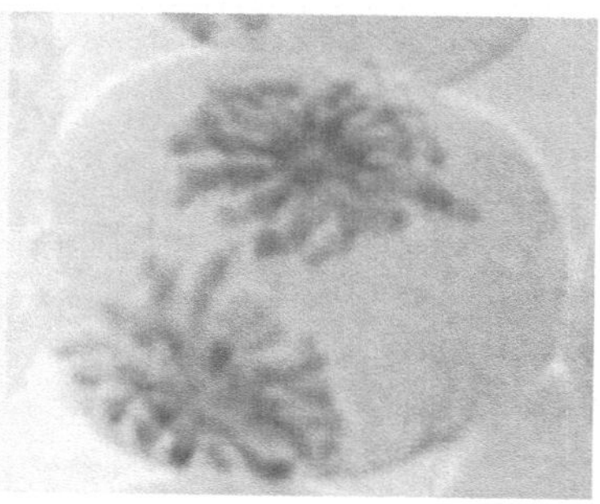

D

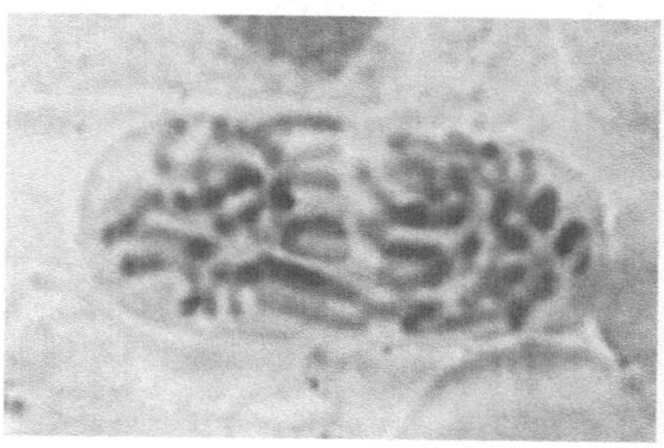

B

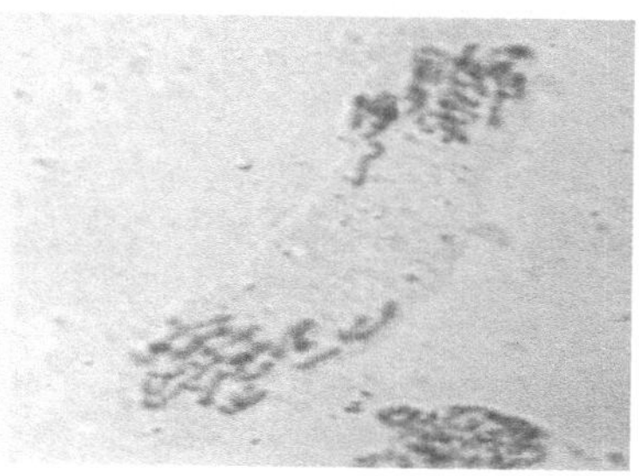

E

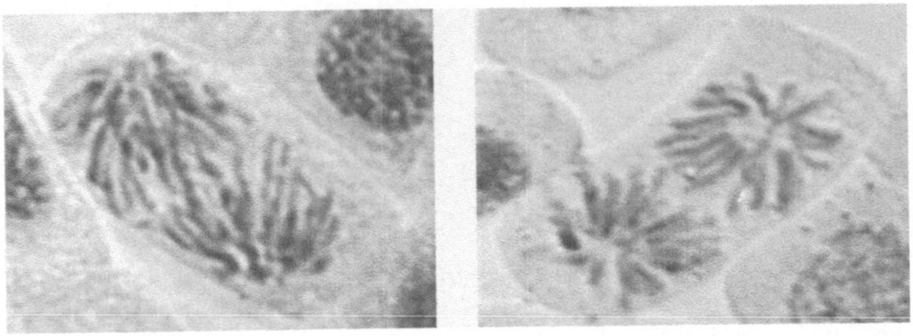

C F

Fig. 10.16: Mitotic stages, *A.HOOKERI,* A less matrix, Anaphase, B. at poles, C. hemisphere interlacing, D. loose, E. sticky interlacing, and F. UVJ shaped.

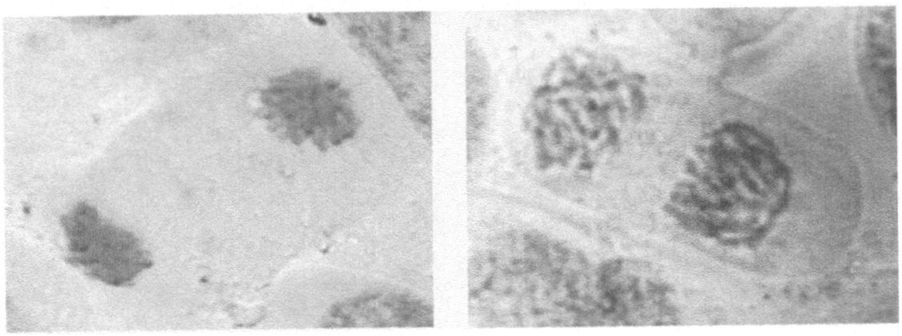

A D

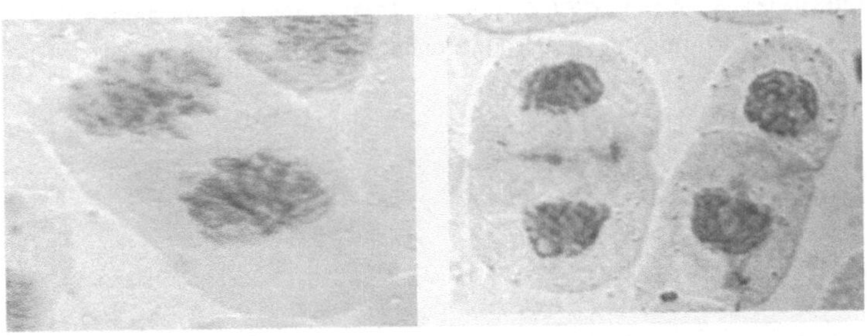

B F

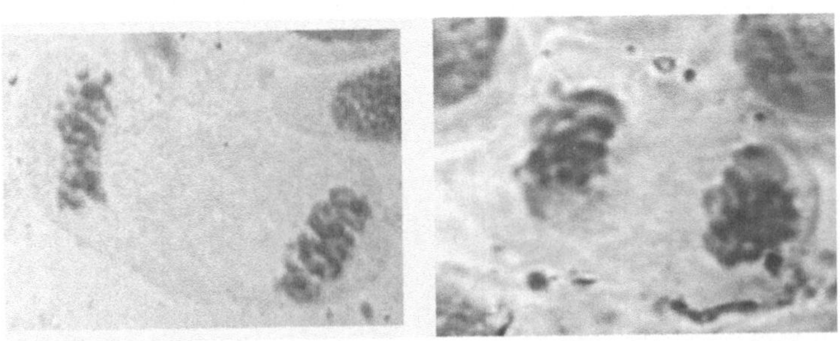

C F

Fig. 10.17: Mitotic stages, *A.HOOKERI,* Telophase A. emerging coils, and B. Extended. C. loose chromaticity, D. rolled hollow cylinder, Cytokinesis, E. cell plate, and F. Clumping.

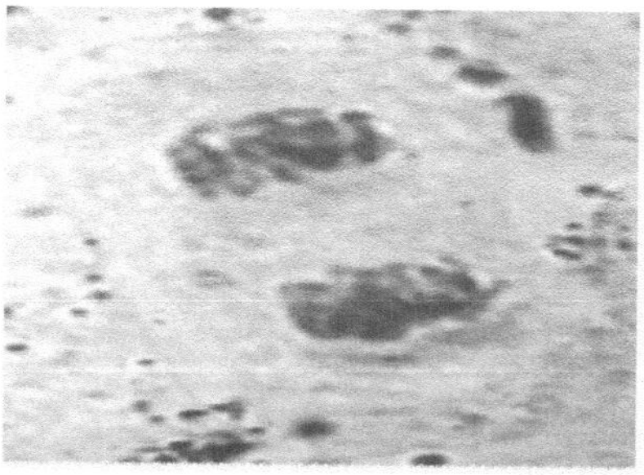

A

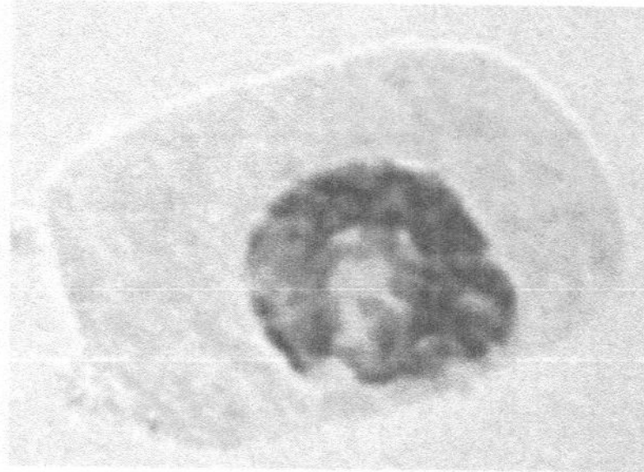

D

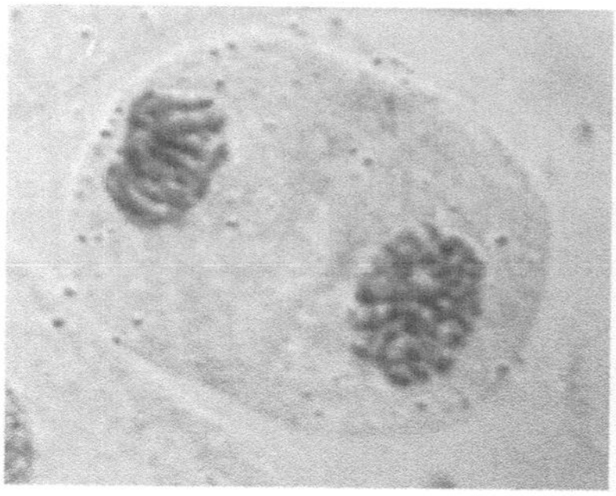

B

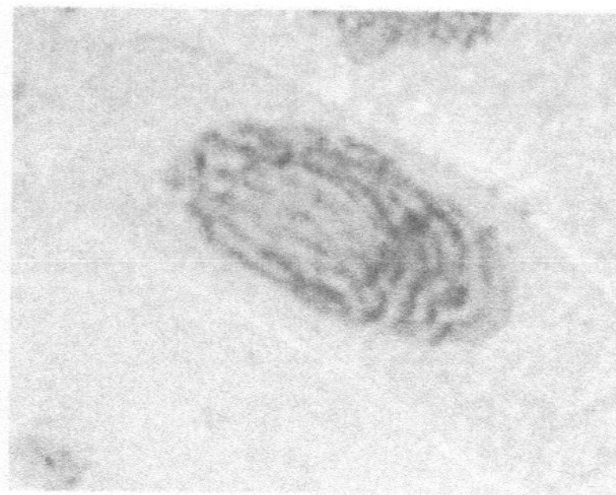

F

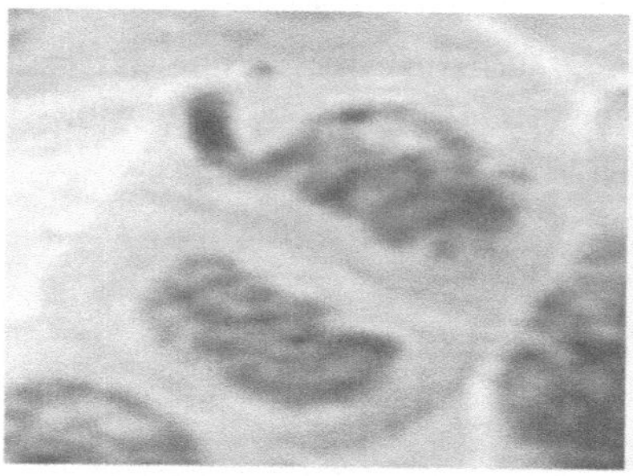

C

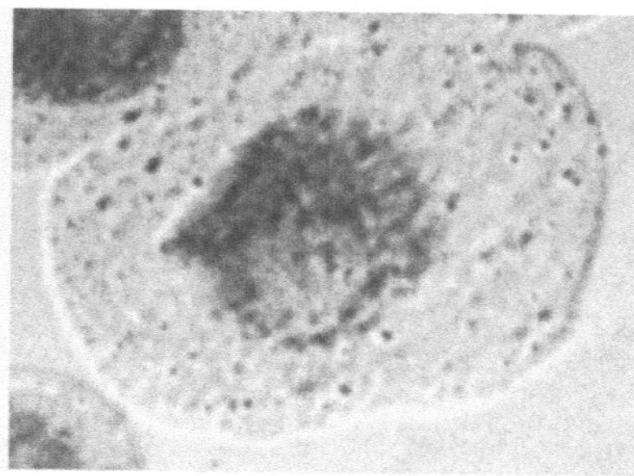

F

Fig. 10.18: Mitotic stages, *A.HOOKERI,* A cylinder, and B. Notch, C. nucleoli. *A.ASCALONICUM* Interphase, D. chromatic threads minute beads, E. extension chromanemata, and F. spherical nucleolus faintly stained chromatin threads.

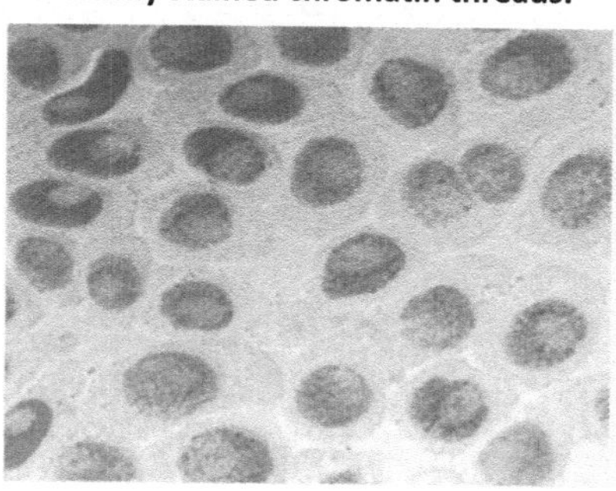

A

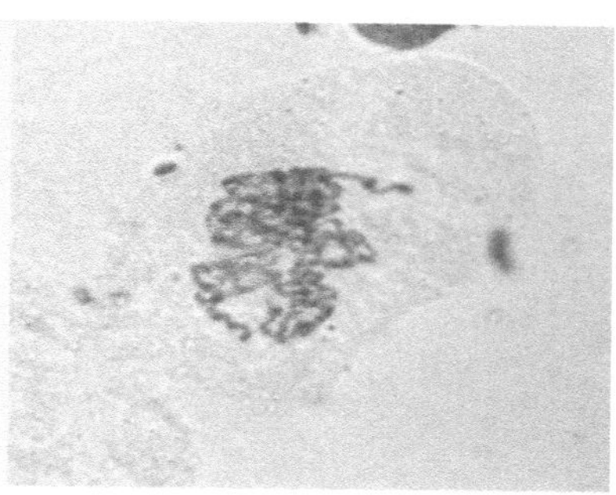

D

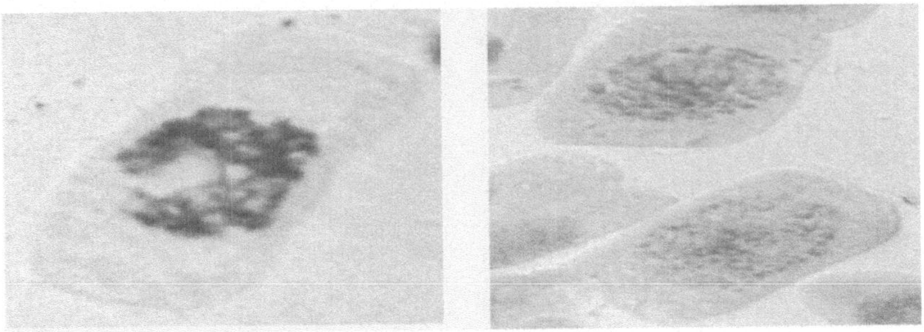

B E

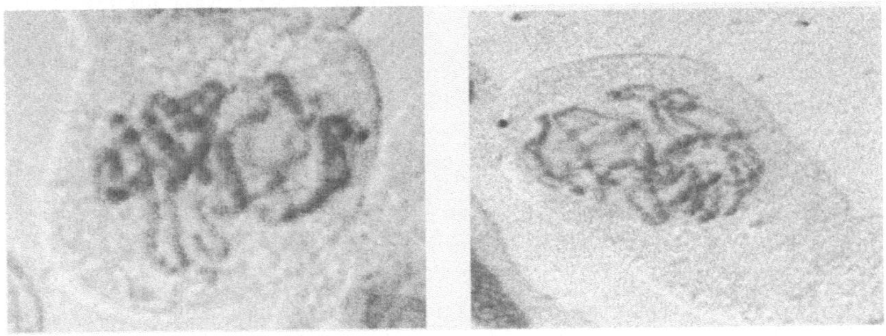

C F

Fig. 10.19: Mitotic stages, *A.ASCALONICUM,* A. spherical nucleolus chromatic threads minute beads and B spiral chromatic threads. Prophase, C. Chromomere, D. dark nodules, E. enlarged nucleus and swollen chromatids, and F. entangled chromatid thread.

A D

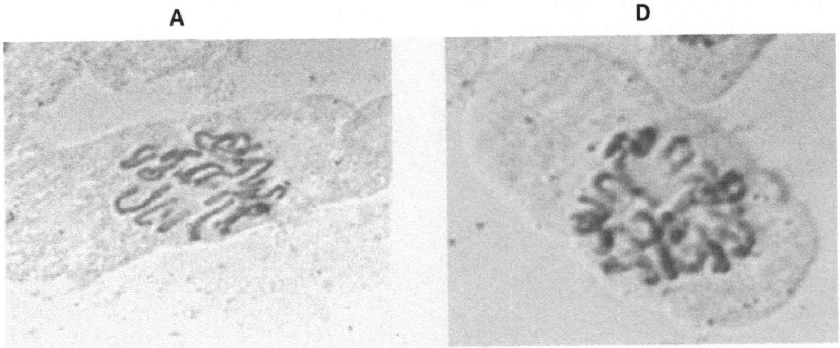

B E

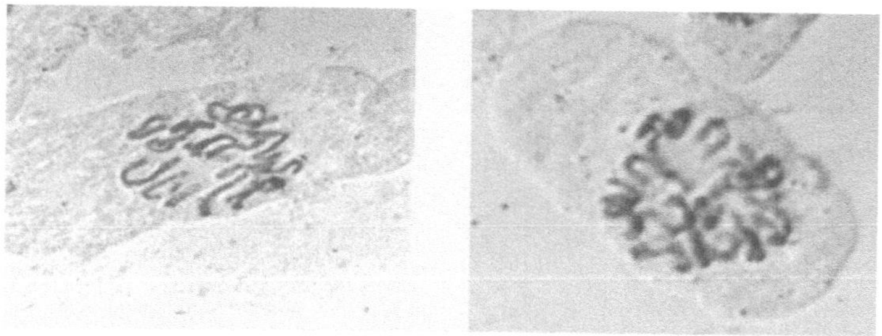

C F

Fig. 10.20: Mitotic stages, *A.ASCALONICUM,* A. long smooth, B. long smooth, C minor loops, D. minor loops chromatid threads, E. Recognizable, and F. slender long ribbon.

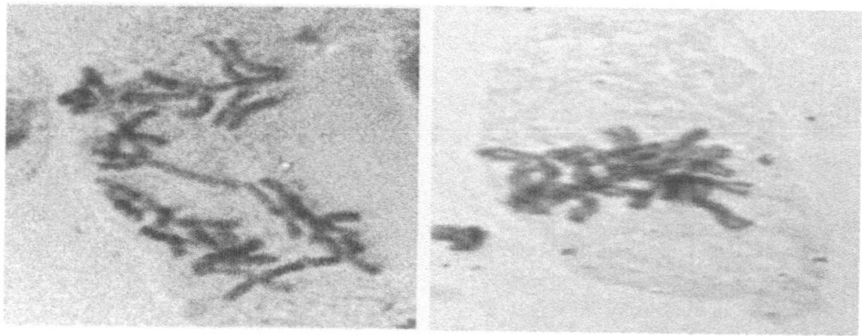

A D

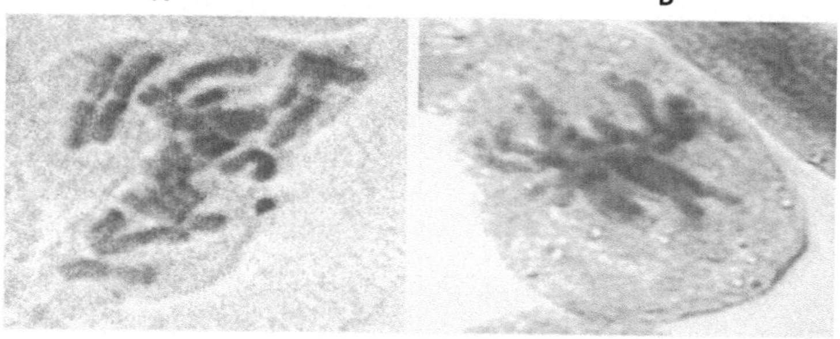

B E

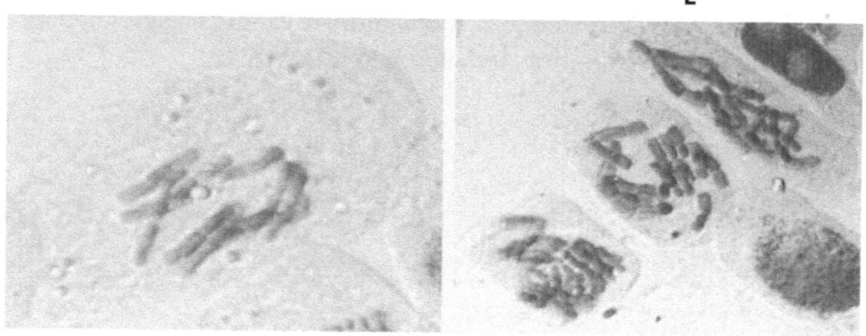

C F

Fig. 10.21: Mitotic stages, *A.ASCALONICUM,* Metaphase, A. bridge and separation, B. C- mitosis. C. double chromosome at plate, D. equator arms various angles, E. Kinetochore attraction, and F. less matrix metaphase.

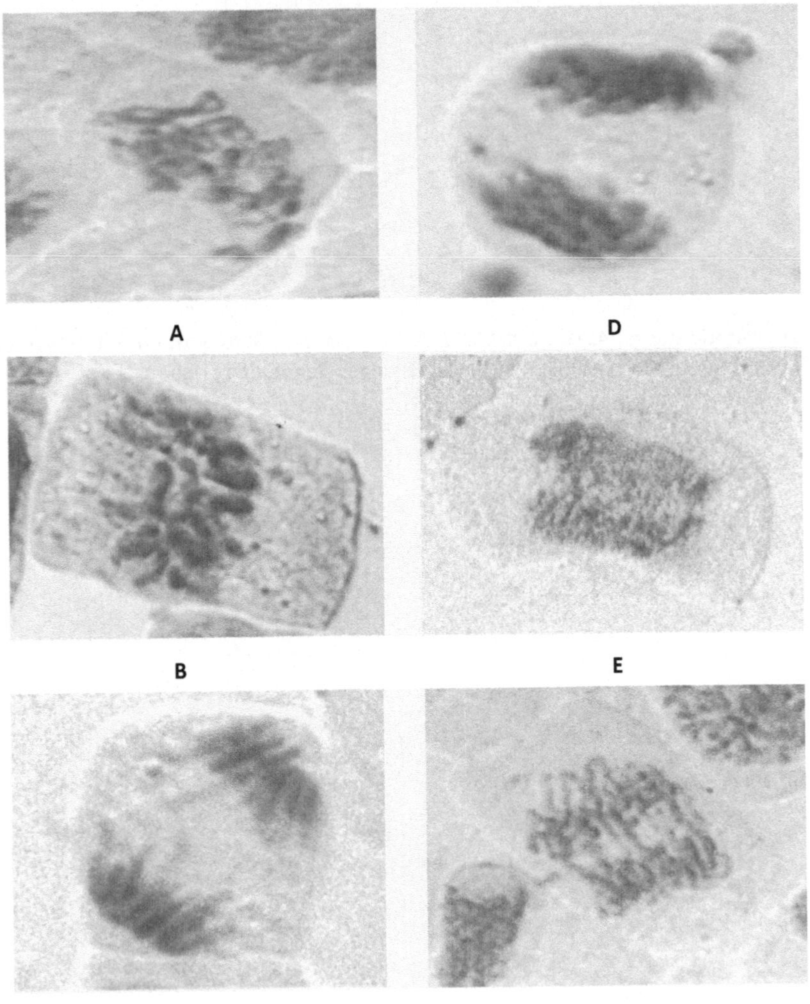

Fig. 10.22: Mitotic stages, *A.ASCALONICUM,* A. moniliform, B. various angles, Anaphase, C. at poles, D. coil loose chromanemata, E. dark stain rod, and F. Interlacing.

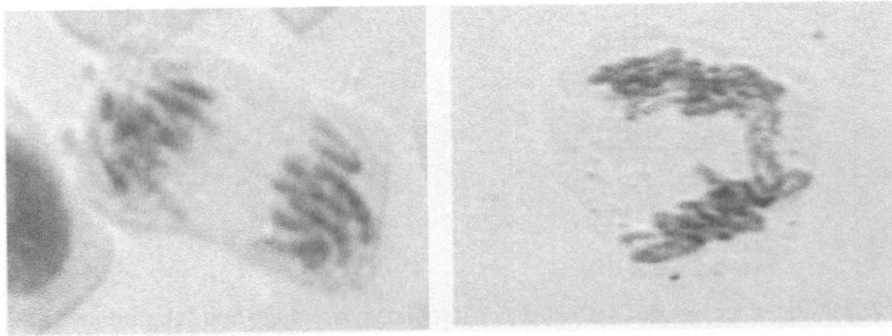

A D

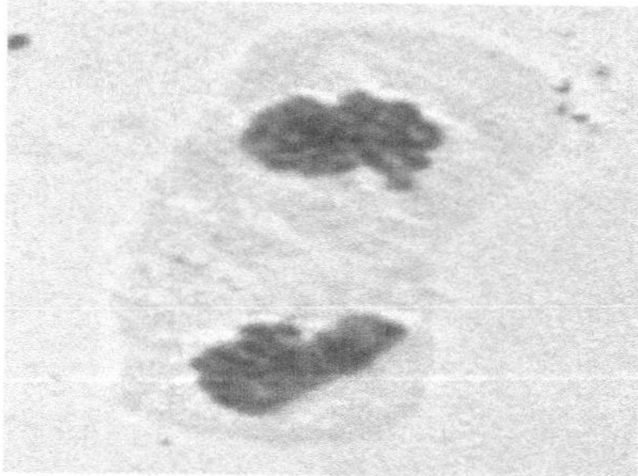

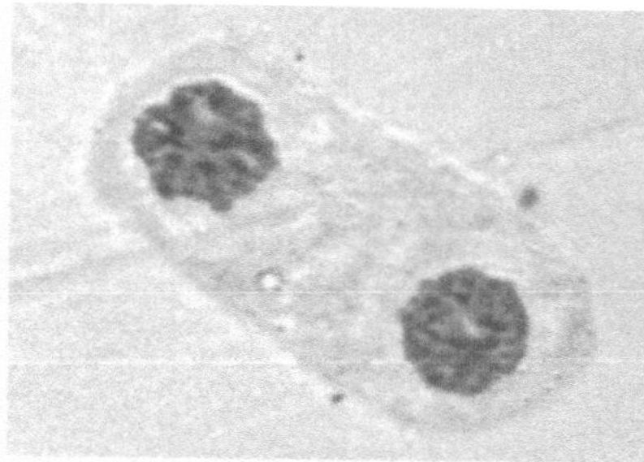

B E

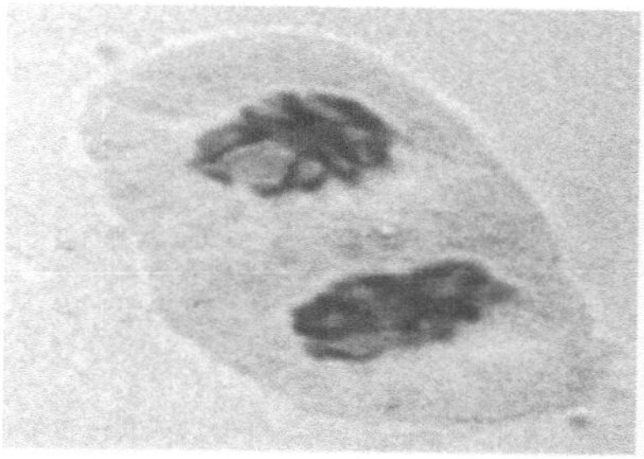

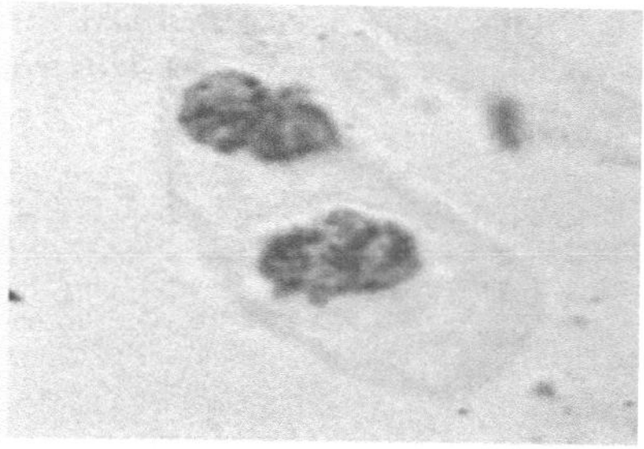

C F

Fig. 10.23: Mitotic stages, *A.ASCALONICUM,* A. UVJ shaped, Telophase, B. extended ladder like, C. late telophase emerging coils, D. loose chromaticity, E. nuclear membrane reappearance, and F. nucleoli reappear.

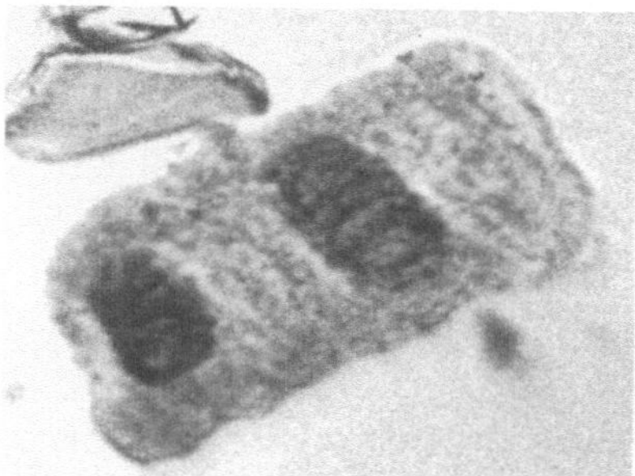

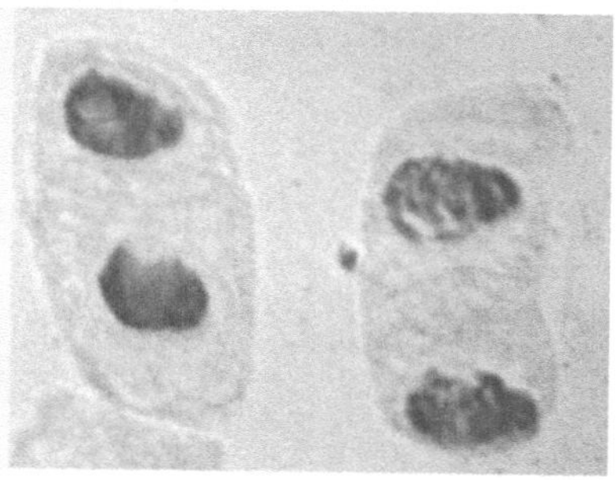

A D

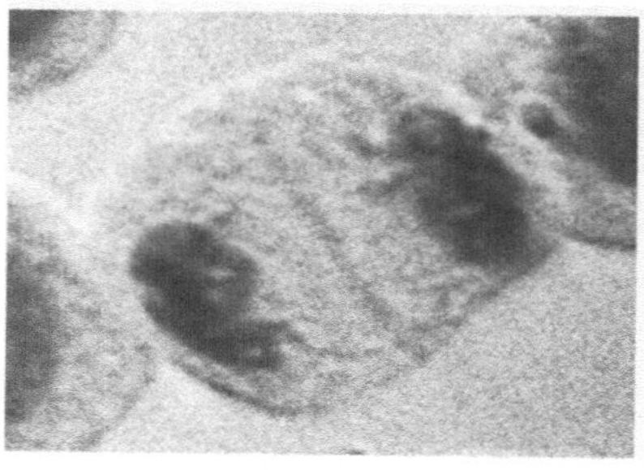

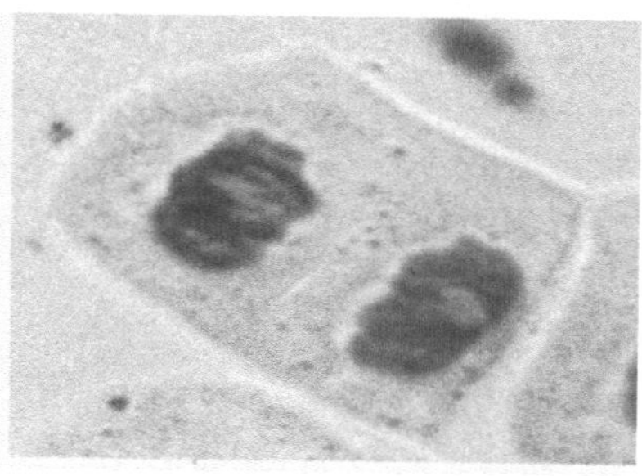

B E

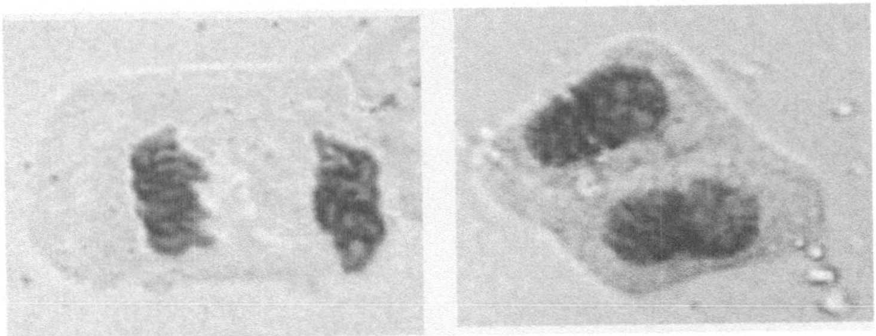

C F

Fig. 10.24: Mitotic stages, *A.ASCALONICUM,* A. rolled hollow cylinder, Cytokinesis, B. cell plate, C. Clumping, D. cylindrical cell plate, E. nucleoli reappear and cell plate and F. nucleus and membrane reappear.

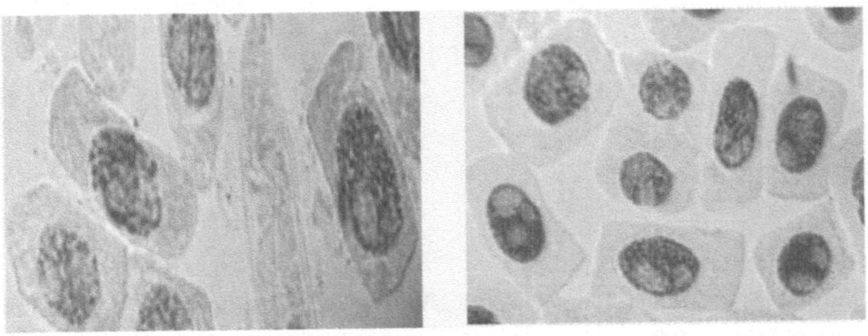

A D

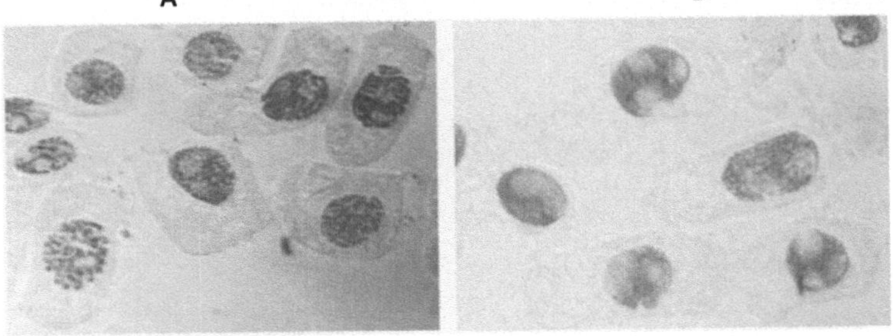

B E

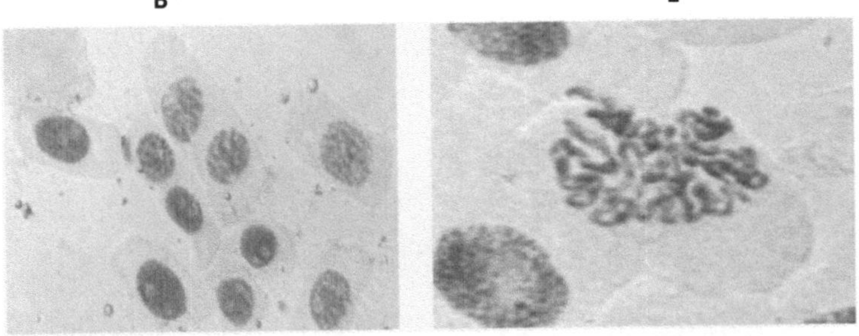

C F

Fig. 10.25: Mitotic stages, *A. SATIVUM,* Interphase, A. interwine, B. Net. C. nucleoli dots, D. spiral thread, E. threads and dots, Prophase, F. Chromomere.

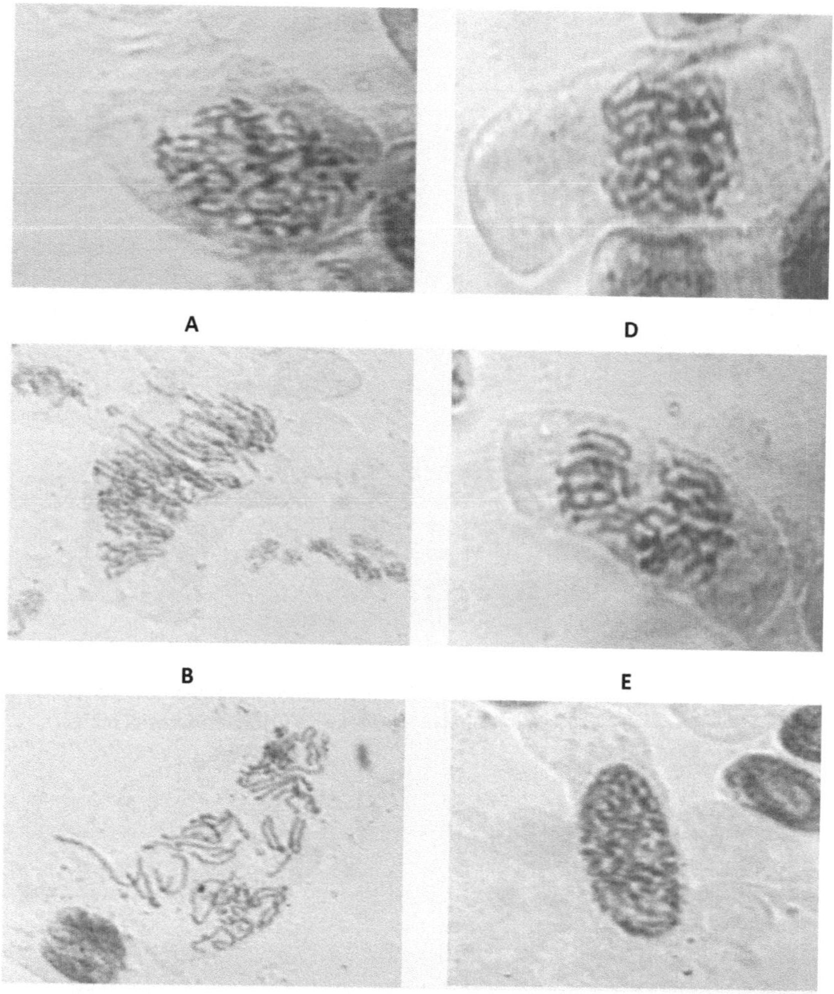

Fig. 10.26: Mitotic stages, *A.SATIVUM,* A.entangled, B. Entangled, C. long and smooth chromosome, D. long entangled ribbon, E. loops, and F. Nodules.

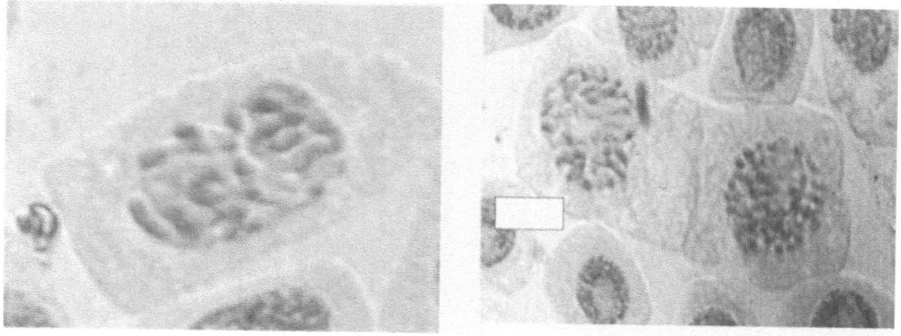

A **D**

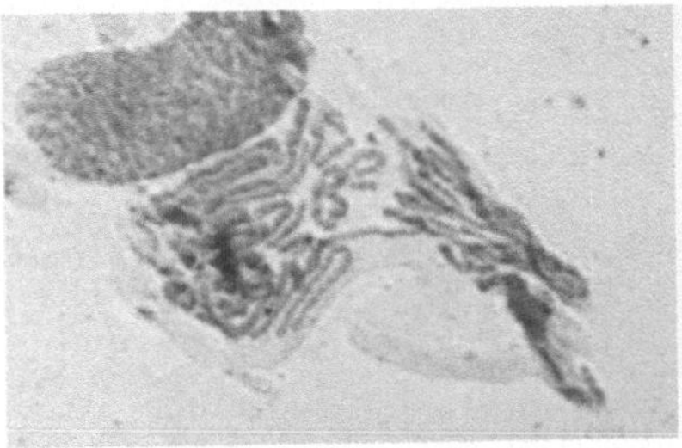

B

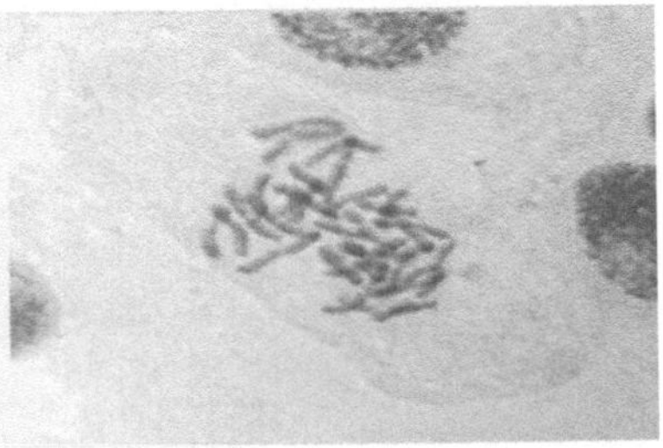

E

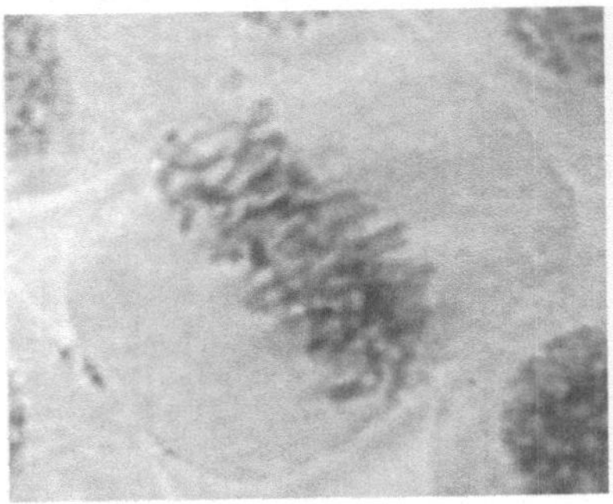

C

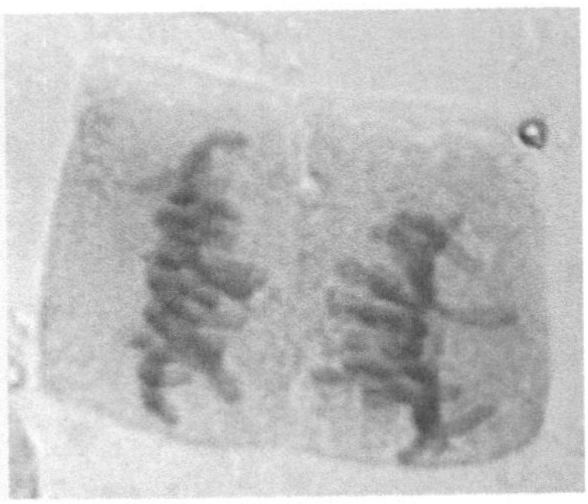

F

Fig. 10.27: Mitotic stages, *A.SATIVUM,* A. Recognizable, B. Ribbons. C. towards equator, Metaphase, D. double chromosome, E. equator arms angles, and F. kinetochore equatorial plate.

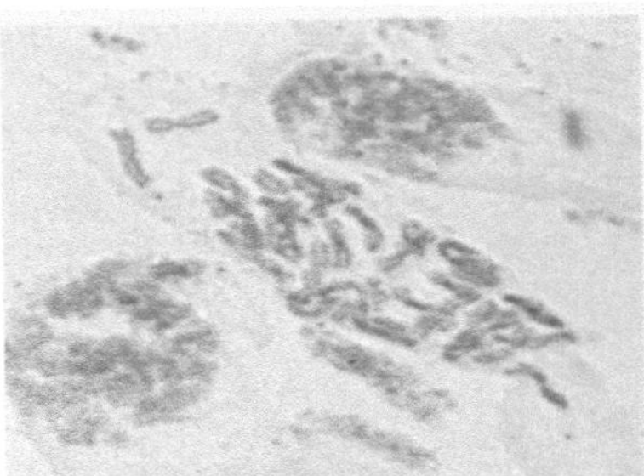

A

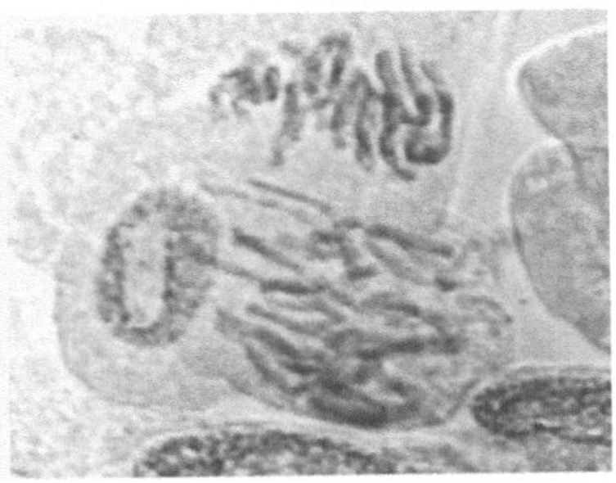

D

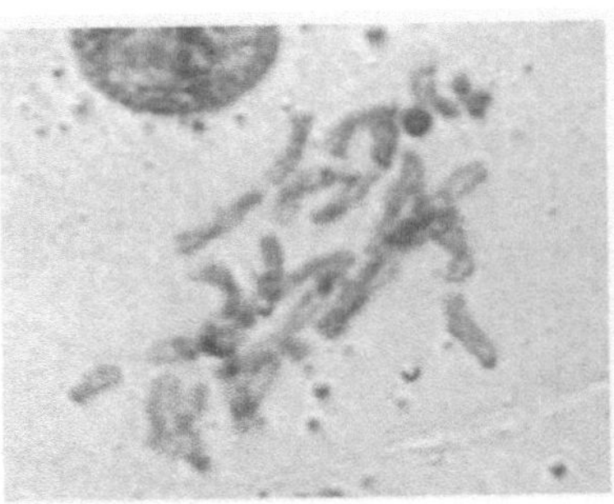

B

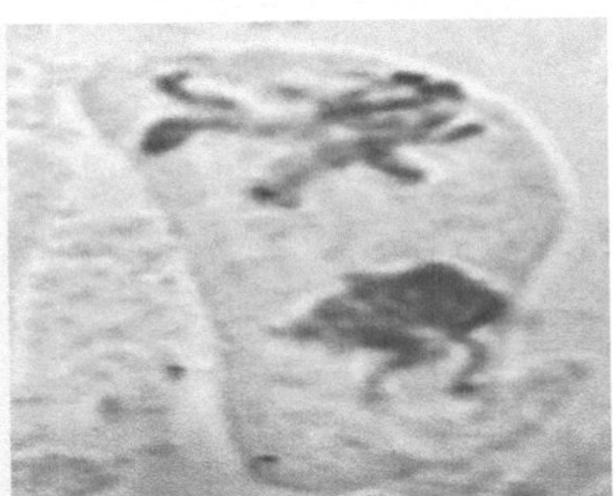

E

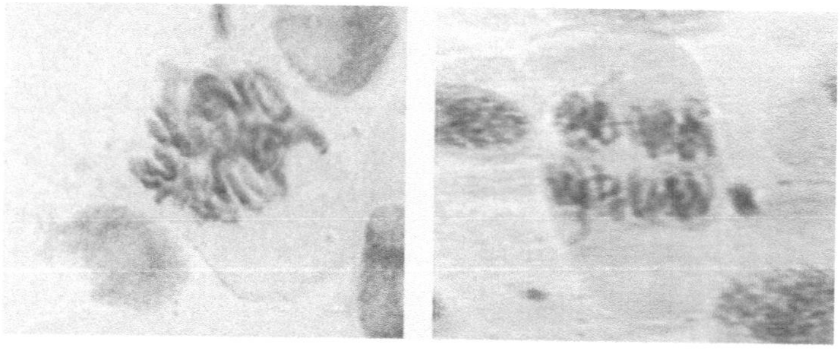

C F

Fig. 10.28: Mitotic stages, *A.SATIVUM,* A. less matrix, B. Ring, C. separation, D. sticky bridge, Anaphase, E. at poles, and F. Cylinder.

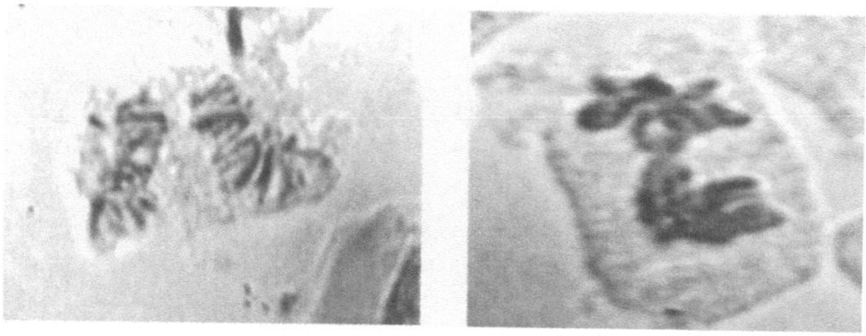

A D

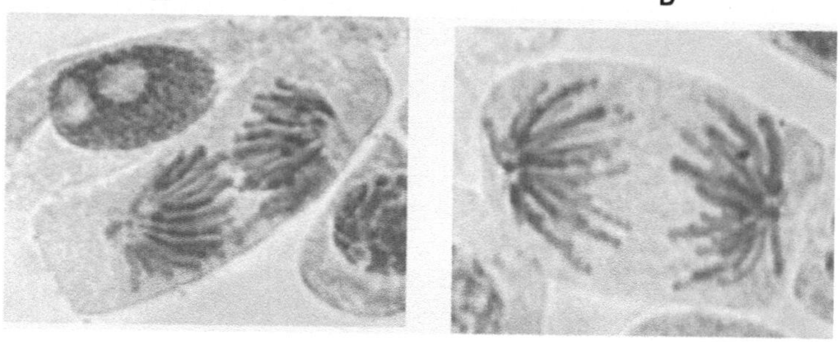

B E

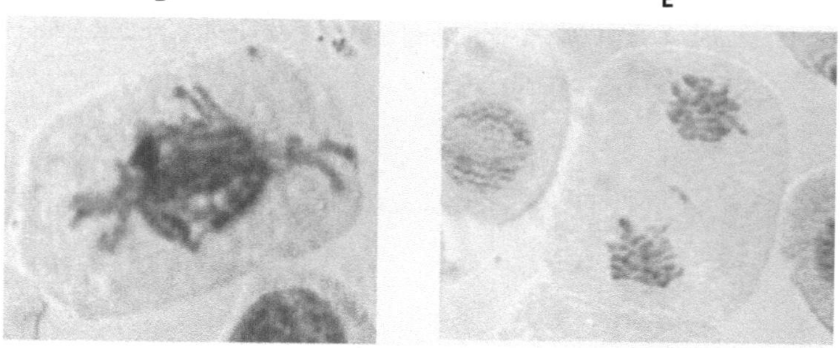

C F

Fig. 10.29: Mitotic stages, *A.SATIVUM,* A. cylinder, B. dark stain rods like, C. interlacing, D. ribs, E. UVJ shaped, and Telophase, F. Chromonemata.

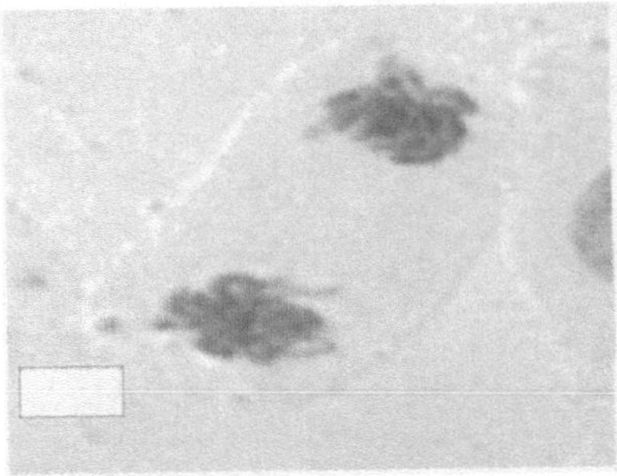

A

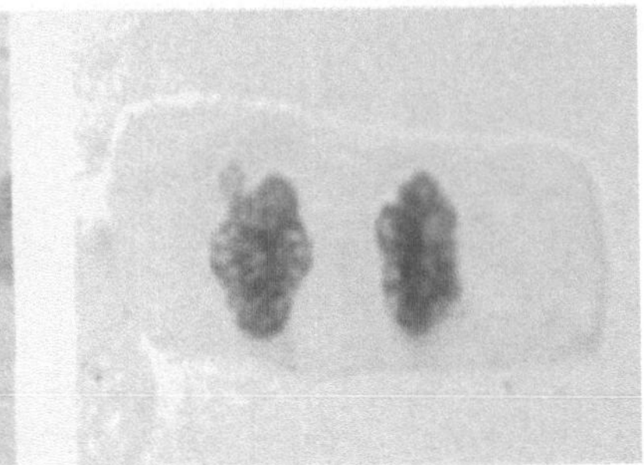

D

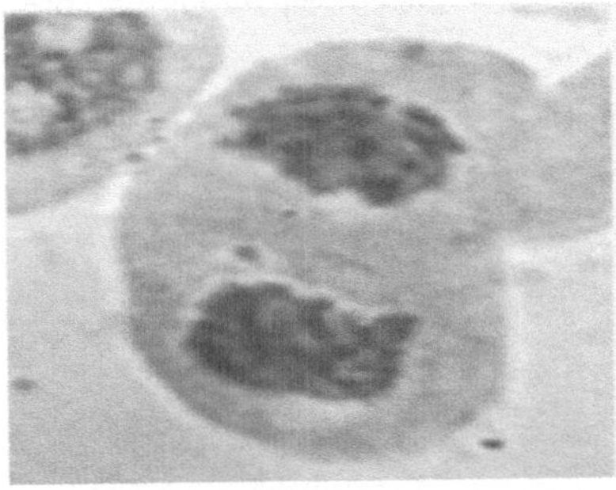

B

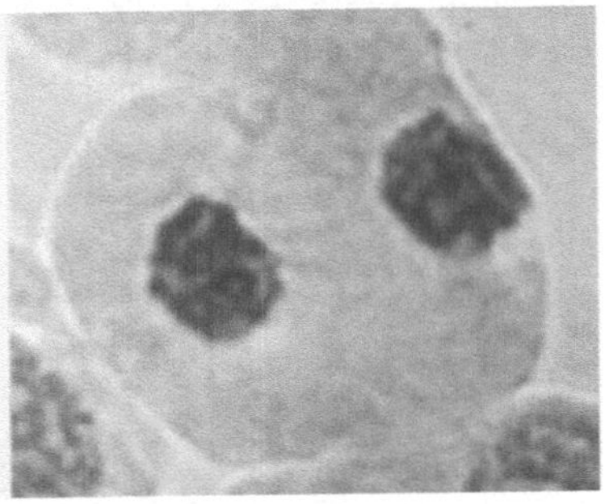

E

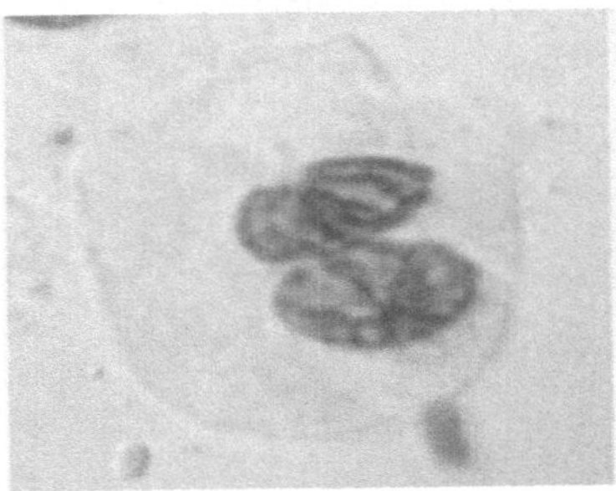

C

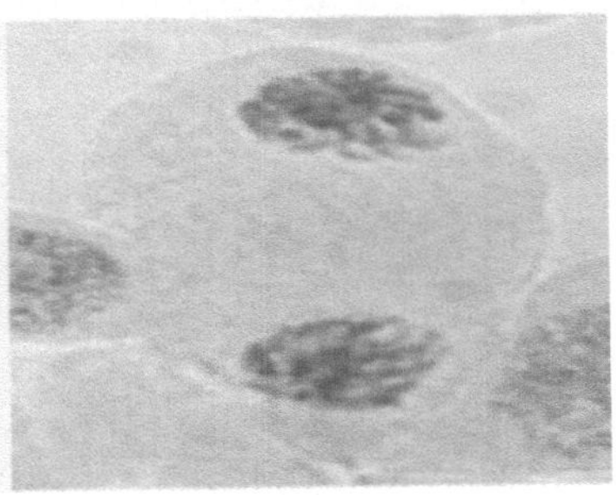

F

Fig. 10.30: Mitotic stages, *A.SATIVUM,* A. emerging coils, B. Extended, C. hollow cylinder, D. ladder, E. late telophase, and F. Loose.

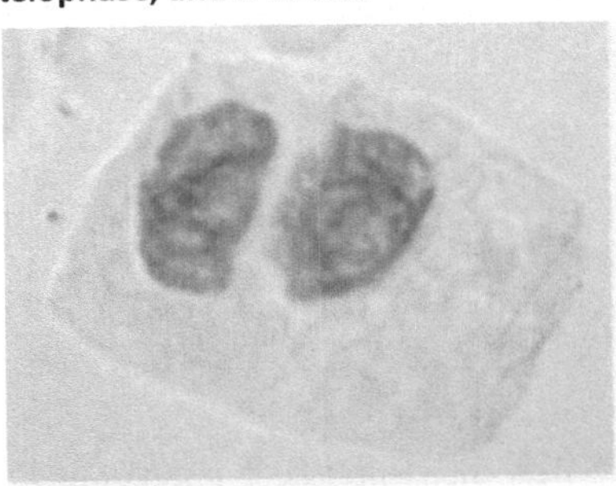

A

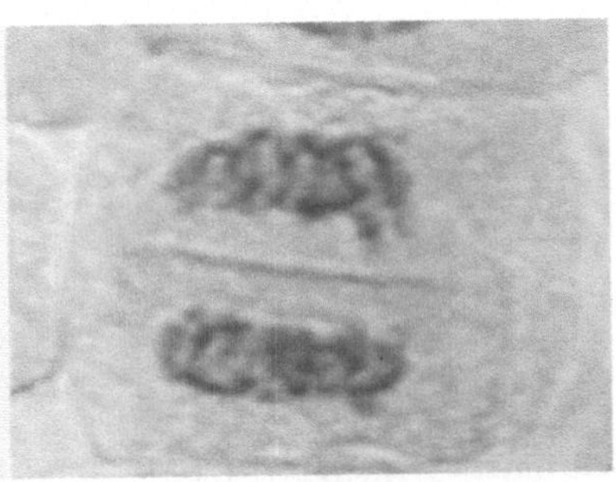

D

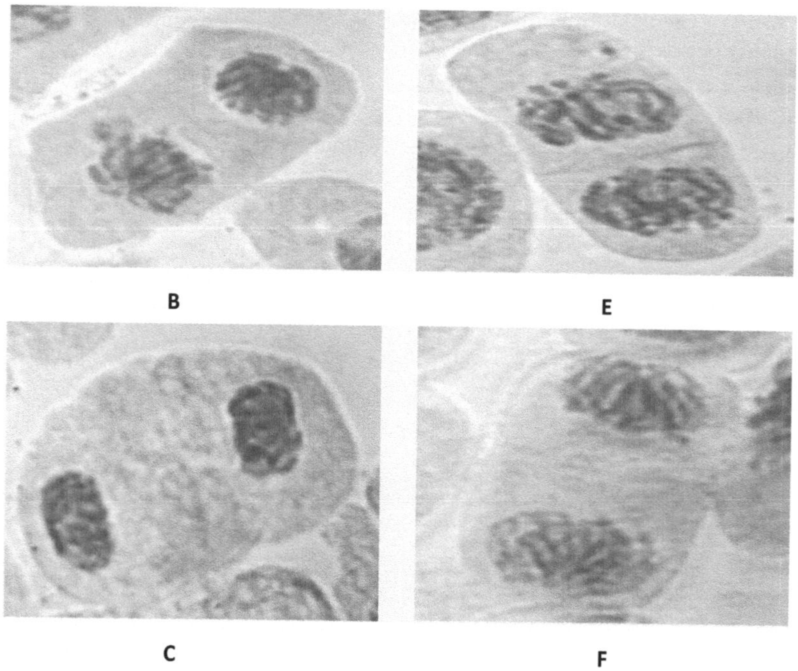

Fig. 10.31: Mitotic stages, *A.SATIVUM,* A. Nucleoli, Cytokinesis, B. cell plate, C. cell plate, D. clumping, E. cylinder, and F. Notch.

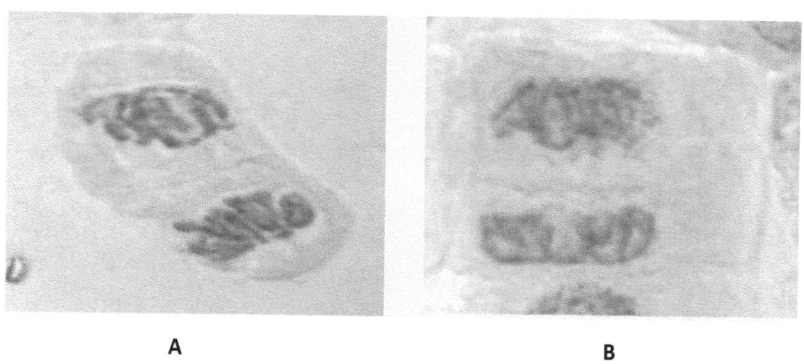

Fig. 10.32: Mitotic stages, *A.SATIVUM,* A. notch and B. Nucleoli

REFERENCES

Bakhoum, S.F., Thompson, S.L., Manning, A.L., Compton, D.A. 2009. Genome Stability is Ensured by Temporal Control of Kinetochore Microtubule Dynamics. *Nat Cell Biol.*; **11**: 27-35.

Khodjakov, A., Rieder, C.L. 2009. The Nature of Cell-cycle Checkpoints: Facts and Fallacies. *J Biol.*; **8**: 88.

Konvicka, O. and Levan, A. 1972. Chromosome Studies in *Allium sativum*. *Hereditas* **72**: 129 148.

Levan, A. 1935. Cytological Studies in *Allium,* VI. The Chromosome Morphology of Some Diploid Species of *Allium.* - *Hereditas* **20**: 289-330.

Pinsky, B.A. and Biggins, S. 2005. The Spindle Checkpoint: Tension versus Attachment. *Trends Cell Biol.* **15**: 486-493.

Sharma A. K., Sharma A. 1980. Chromosome Techniques. Theory and Practice. 3rd edition, Butterworths, London.

Verma, S.C. and Mittal, R.K. 1978.Chromosome Variation in the Common Garlic, *Allium sativum* L. *Carylogia* **43**: 383-396.

Yang, Z., Kenny, A., Brito, D., Rieder, C.L. 2009. Cells Satisfy the Mitotic Checkpoint in Taxol and Do so Faster in Concentrations that Stabilize Syntelic Attachments. *J Cell Biol.* **186**: 675-684.

Analytical Techniques in Chemical and Biological Sciences
Edited by: Dr. Deep Mala and Dr. Pawan Kumar 'Bharti'
ISBN: 978-93-86841-59-9
Edition: 2018
Published by: Discovery Publishing House Pvt. Ltd., New Delhi (India)

Page: 139-157

11

Evolution of Insect Flight, Mechanism and Behaviour

Mandla Rajashekhar[1], Nenavath Balram[2], Padala Vinod Kumar[3]
Vennampally Nataraj[4], Veeranna. D.[5]

ABSTRACT

Insects were the first flying animals on the planet and the modifications that led to flight probably occurred no later than 350 million years ago. During the course of insect evolution, all pterygote insects descended from a common ancestor. Flight was probably the most important evolutionary step in the insects, conferring significant advantages in finding food, locating mates, laying eggs in suitable places, colonizing new habitats, long range dispersal or migration and escaping predation. The flight makes the insects most successful in the world to survive and reproduce in wide range of locations. Insect flight involves two possible mechanisms *i.e.,* a direct or an indirect flight mechanism. Direct flight muscles attach to the wing joint and may power the wing or control wing rotation, deformation etc. Odonata and Blattodea use direct muscles for wing upstroke and down stroke movements. Many insects generate flight power using indirect flight muscles, whereas locusts use both, direct as well as indirect muscles to power the wings. On the basis of aerodynamics of flight, clap & fling mechanism and click mechanism are involved in wing movement. In most insects, the forewings and hind wings work in tandem. During flight, the front and rear wings usually remain locked together, and both move up and down at the same time. In some insect orders, most notably the Odonata, the wings move independently during flight, as the forewing lifts, the hind wing lowers.

Flight requires relatively large amount of energy, flight metabolism is a function of aerodynamic requirements, which in turn are determined primarily by the morphological characteristics of each insect. Insects use different types of fuels

[1,3&5]Division of Entomology, IARI, New Delhi, 110012.
[2] Division of Plant Pathology, IARI, New Delhi, 110012.
[4] ICAR-IISR, Indore.
As per email: Corres. Author:
N. Balram, Room No. 100, Vasanth Hostel, Indian Agricultural Research Institute (IARI), Pusa Campus, New Delhi-110012.
Mobile number: 9821492644

for flight *viz.*, carbohydrates (Diptera and Hymenoptera), lipids & carbohydrates (locusts), amino acids (*Glossina*) and triglycerols. Body temperature of insects is also dependent on insect flight behaviour. However, flight behaviour is often contrary to the reproductive development in insects. Female insects engaged in long distance flights produce less number of eggs as compared to non-flying females. In case of males, flight behaviour enhances mate finding behaviour but continuous flight adversly effect the longevity of the males.

Introduction to Insect Behaviour

Behaviour refers to what insect do. It can be defined more precisely as an internally directed system of adaptive activities that facilitate survival and reproduction. In general, behaviour may be classified as innate, learned and complex.

Flight Behaviour

Insects were the first animals on the planet to fly. The modifications that led to flight probably occurred no later than 350 million years ago and are believed to have happened only once during the course of insect evolution, with all pterygote insects descending from a common ancestor. Abiotic factors may have been different at the time and these differences may have promoted the acquisition of flight. For example, the atmosphere was believed to be significantly denser during this period, with concentrations of oxygen as high as 35% about 300 million years ago compared to the current value of 21%. The density of the air is the major determinant of force production by an airfoil, be it biological or mechanical, and the increased density may have improved the chances that flight would evolve. Accompanying increased oxygen concentrations in the atmosphere were increases in tracheal diffusion and body size. Early flying insects were enormous compared to present-day insects; the largest known insect was an odonate ancestor living during the Carboniferous with a wingspan greater than 70 cm and an estimated mass of 200 g.

Purpose of Flight Behaviour

Taking to the air was probably the most important evolutionary step in the history of insects, conferring significant advantages in finding food, locating mates, colonizing new habitats, and escaping predation. Laying eggs in suitable position, maintain body temperatures, Long range dispersal and migration. This flight make the insects are most successful in the world to survive and reproduce in wide range of locations.

Evolution of Insect Wings

Two major hypotheses attempt to explain the evolution of wings from unwinged ancestors, but no transitional forms exist and there are none from the fossil record. The first hypothesis proposes that wings developed from thoracic winglets or *paranotal lobes* that might have been first used for thermoregulation, then as airfoils as they enlarged, and finally as flapping wings. The secondary wing articulation and musculature had to evolve accordingly. The small size of insects assures that they would have escaped harm from falling from any height, and the development of any new appendages would have been beneficial in gliding or in aiding their dispersal in the wind. The second hypothesis suggests that wings evolved from winglets that originated as gills. In this second case, protowings could have first evolved in aquatic larvae and enlarged to allow improvements in underwater navigation. Once the ancestors left the water, the significance of the wings could have shifted to a second function as locomotor devices. This *articulated gill theory* has support in the behaviour of some extant aquatic stoneflies that engage in surface skimming in which the wings are flapped but the insects remain in the water, a behaviour intermediate between swimming and flying. The aquatic gills might have been first used to "row" within the water, and they then became large enough for skimming and finally flight. The transitional use of abdominal gills that were in contact with both the air and water for rowing gave early winged insects a chance to exploit the increased concentration of oxygen in air compared to that dissolved in water. The reduced muscle power and wing movements used in skimming are sufficient to propel them through the water and explain the initial evolutionary benefits of wings before insects actually left the ground. Molecular data provide more evidence for the articulated gill theory. The ancestral arthropod limb segment is called a *podite*. Lobes along the inner (endite) and outer (exite) margins of the podite developed in some arthropod groups. The basal segment of the limb that is attached to the pleural wall is the *coxopodite*, and its outer lobe is known as the *epipodite*. In crustaceans, the epipodites are often modified into gills . Two ancient genes that have wing-specific functions in insects are also expressed in the epipodite gills of crustaceans. The expression of the same genes in the epipodites of crustaceans and the wings of insects suggest that insect wings evolved from these epipodites. The crustaceans consist of the only group that has been largely confined to the water or moist habitats. When terrestrialization occurred in the other groups, the epipodite gill was believed to have been modified into a wing in the line leading to pterygote insects, while it was lost in the other two groups.

Because insect wings arose not from walking legs as in birds and bats but as outgrowths of the body wall, they developed as a sandwich of two epicuticular layers with hemolymph, nerves, and trachea in between. Procuticle is absent, so chitin does not appear to be present in the membranous areas of the wings. Another difference between the wings of insects and those of other flying animals is that no intrinsic muscles are associated with the insect wing. Wing movement and changes in wing shape during flight must be controlled by muscles in the

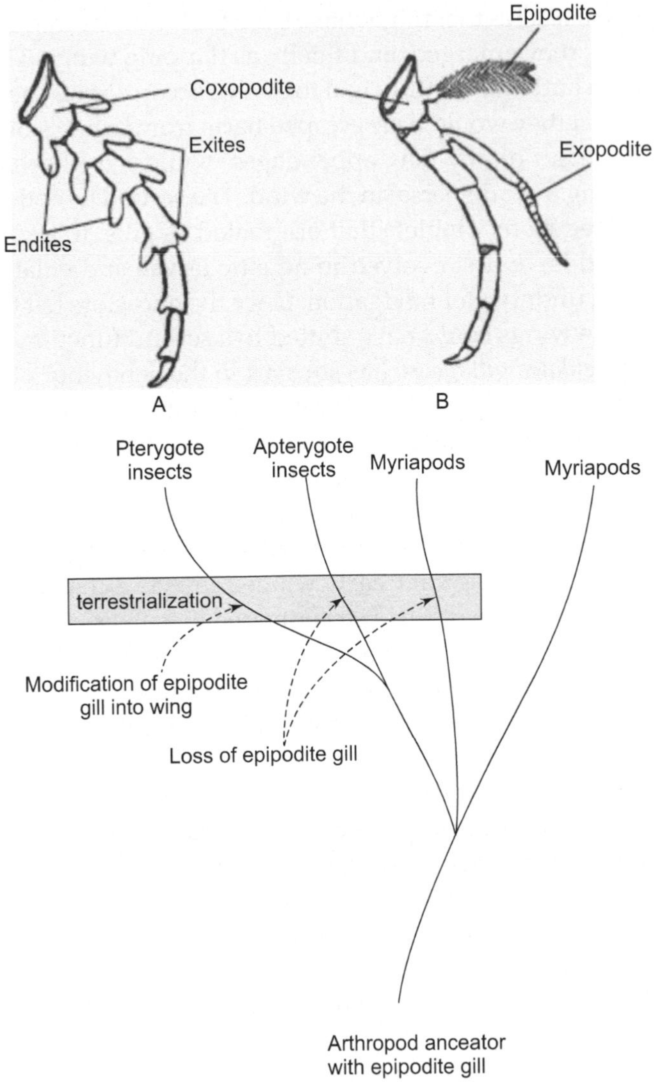

Generalised A. Trilobate limb B. Crustacean limb

thorax, with some deformations of the wing resulting from the wing structure itself as it responds to the aerodynamic forces. Most of the epidermal cells in the insect wing degenerate after adult emergence, leaving a largely a cellular membrane lined with veins, tracheae, and nerves. The loss of water as these cells degenerate makes the flapping movements of the wings more efficient. However, the absence of epidermal cells in the mature adult wing is also a reason that adult pterygotes no longer molt. Without functional epidermalcells, it is impossible to undergo the steps in molting and produce a new wing cuticle. Selection has favored the wing efficiency that comes with epidermal cell degeneration over the possible advantages of adult molting. The development of flight was accompanied by an increased capacity for information processing by the insect central nervous system. The flicker fusion frequency is the maximum rate that individual light impulses can be resolved and is a measure of the speed of optical processing. In humans, the flicker fusion frequency is less than 20 Hz, but it can reach as high as 200 to 300 Hz in flying insects.

Muscles Involved in Wing Movements

The flight muscles are usually the best developed of the muscles in the insect body and occupy most of the space in the thorax. Total flight muscle mass must be greater than 12% of body mass to support the weight of an insect in flight. The flight muscles of many insects undergo maturation during the adult stage. Some dragonflies may more than double their flight muscle size as the adults' age. The growth and maturation of the longitudinal skeletal muscles of the locust ovipositor are JH dependent, allowing these muscles to contribute to oviposition efficiency once the insect becomes reproductively competent. Flight muscles may also degenerate after adult emergence in order to reallocate nutrients for reproduction or diapause. This programmed cell death is triggered by environmental windows. Switching to a nondispersal morph diverts the investment in wing muscles to reproduction.

There are three general categories of muscles that power insect flight: *direct, indirect* and *accessory*. Direct flight muscles, consisting of the *basalar* and *subalar* muscles, insert directly at the base of the wing and provide the power for the downstroke in more primitive insects and also affect wing pronation and supination . Another direct muscle, the *third axillary* muscle, inserts on the third axillary sclerite. It affects wing supination and is also responsible for wing flexion against the body wall when the wings are at rest. In contrast, the indirect flight muscles indirectly move the wings not by moving them directly but by changing the conformation of the thorax. These muscles include the *dorsoventral* group that extends from the tergum to the sternum. Because of the structural relationships among the sclerites that make up the thorax, in all insects, when the muscles pull the tergum down they indirectly cause the wings to raise and produce the upstroke. Another indirect group, the *dorsal longitudinal* muscles, attach longitudinally between the two phragmata of each wing-bearing segment. When these contract, they shorten the segment and cause the tergum to elevate. In more advanced insects, this deformation of the notum by the dorsal longitudinal muscles produces the power stroke by depressing the wing. These muscles are reduced in more primitive insects that instead use the direct muscles for the downstroke. There are also accessory muscles that insert into the thorax and influence its mechanical conformation. For example, the *pleurosternal* and *pleurotergal* muscles modulate the power output and the nature of the wing-beat by changing the orientation of the thoracic plates and the resonance of the thorax.

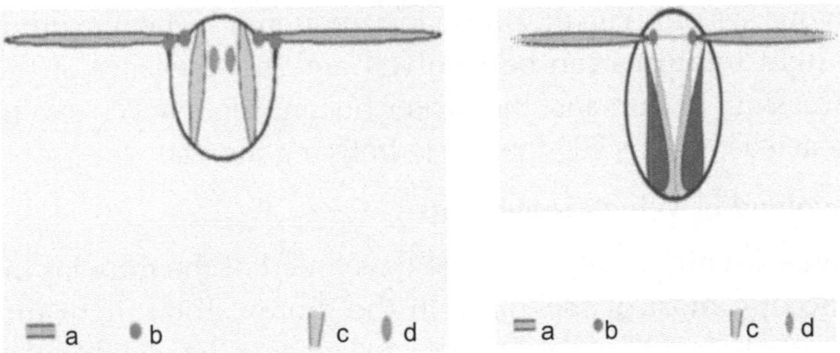

A. Indirect flight muscles B. Direct flight muscles

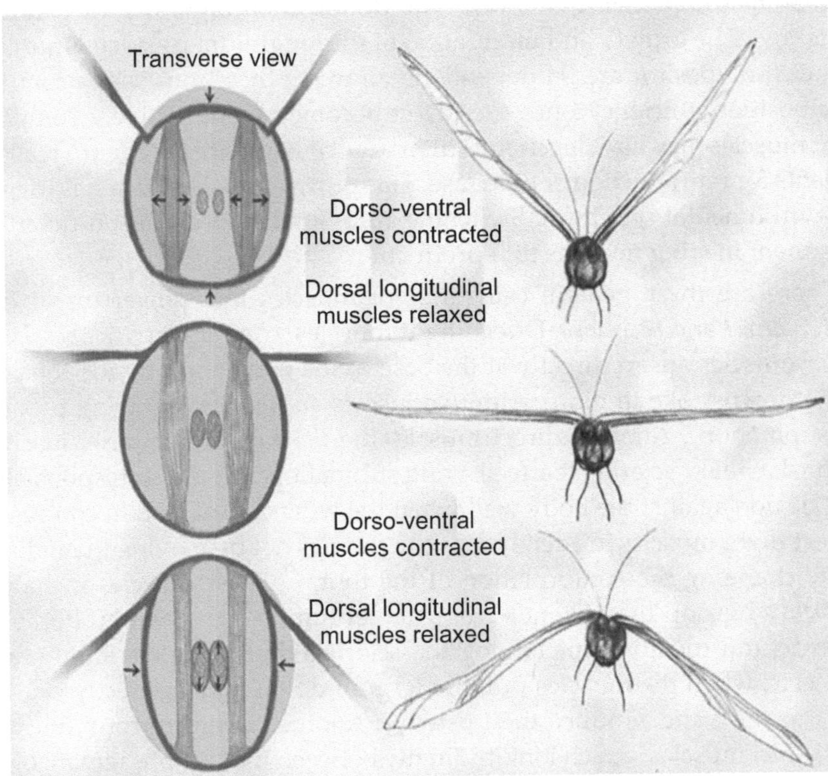

Dorsoventral and Dorso longitudinal muscles

Clap and Fling Mechanism

In aircraft, birds, and insects, a wing produces lift only when a pressure gradient is created between the upper and lower surfaces of the wing as low pressure air flows over the upper surface. In *Drosophila,* the rotation of the wing produces a circulation of air in the opposite rotational direction and a wake capture that uses the vortex from the previous stroke to generate airflow around the wing. By capturing this lingering vortex wake, a strong force-generating airflow is created that supports flight. The air is forced backward and downward, moving the insect forward, generating thrust, and upward, generating lift.

This mechanism of wing movement used by some small insects and also butterflies is called the *clap and fling*. The clap involves the raising of the wings so the tips touch dorsally with the leading edges touching before the trailing edges, forming a vertical plate. The wings are then quickly flung open so the gap between them is filled with entering air, and as they separate and twist, each carries a vortex of air that was formed during the fling. The bound vortex is added to the flow pattern of air that would be created by the simple wing movements. For insects that fly at a small Reynolds number, the viscosity of the air is important as air circulation becomes difficult and vortices created by the wings do not remain for long.

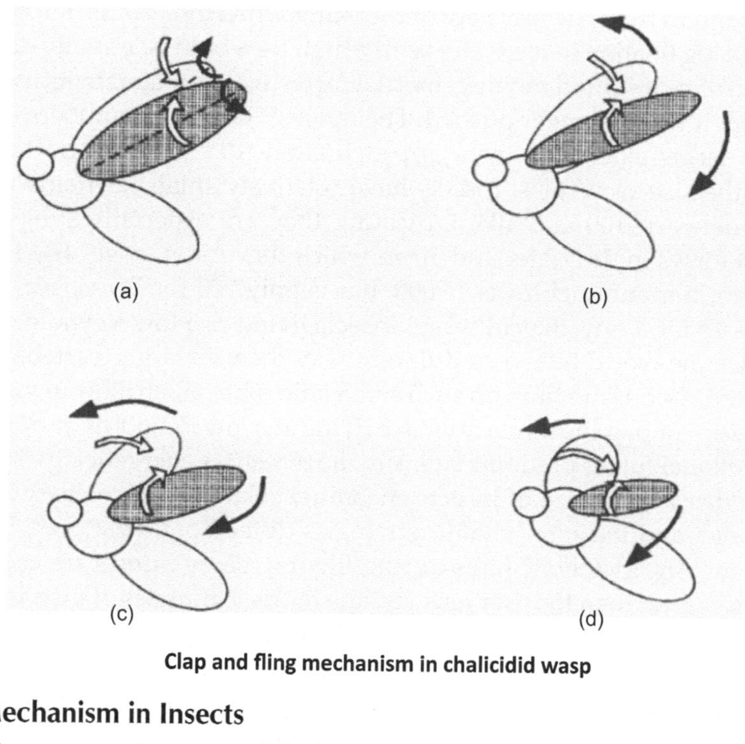

Clap and fling mechanism in chalicidid wasp

Click Mechanism in Insects

Insects have a another type of flight mechanism is called as click mechanism. Elastic energy stored as a result of distorations of the thorax. Lateral stiffness of the thorax is produced by the sterno pleural & tergopleural articulations of thorax.As a result of Lateral stiffness the position of the wings thought to be unstable and wings are thought to the stable in the extreme up and down positions.This arrangement is called click mechanism. Stretch activation of synchronous muscles still ocurrs as in the click mechanism but the mechanism and timing of strecting are different. The dorsoventral muscles cause up stroke this is occurred toward the end of the downstroke so that the muscles are activated at the appropriate time.But the stretch activation in bees does not depend on the click mechanism.

Reynolds Number

Whenever an object moves through a fluid medium such as air or water, forces are generated on the object by the elements of the fluid. The relationship between the viscous frictional forces from the fluid and the inertial force of the object can be quantified and expressed as the dimensionless *Reynolds number (Re)*. Re represents the ratio of the inertial and frictional forces. A low Re is produced by small size or low speed and indicates that frictional forces are large, whereas a high Re means that inertial forces are more important. For example, a toothpick with a low Re could be easily propelled in water but would be stopped by frictional forces from the viscosity of the water when the propulsion ceased. In contrast, a log floating in the water with a high Re would be initially difficult to move, but once it started moving, inertial forces would maintain its movement even when it was no longer pushed. The range of Reynolds numbers for living things is large, extending from approximately 10^{-6} for bacteria to 107 for animals the size of whales. Insects have relatively small Reynolds numbers ranging between 100 and 104, indicating they are especially subject to the frictional forces in the water and air in which they must move. The Reynolds number for a hummingbird is 15,000, but is only 200 for *Drosophila,* and it is as low as 15 for a tiny chalcid wasp. Insects living at a low Reynolds number experience the world in a very different way than do larger vertebrates. The effect of the viscous medium on such small animals is much like our swimming in molasses. Among the implications of living at a low Reynolds number is that when frictional forces predominate, any movement is energetically expensive. Animals that are the size of insects encounter relatively huge energy costs to move about, and the aerodynamic strategies differ from those used by larger animals that fly. Metabolic rates during flight in some insects are as much as 100 times greater than those at rest, and the thoracic muscles of insects in flight exhibit the highest metabolic rates of any tissue. As mentioned previously, the metabolic rate of a bumblebee in flight is about 65 ml of oxygen per gram of body mass per hour, compared to about 45 ml/g/h for a humming bird flying at the same speed. There is also a considerable inefficiency in the conversion of chemical energy to mechanical energy. As much as 80% or more of the energy used for insect flight is dissipated as heat. The one advantage of small size is the relative strength it confers, but the apparent strength of insects lies not in any differences in their muscles but in the relationship between the increase in body volume and muscle power that accompanies increases in body size.

The power of a muscle varies with its crosssectional area, which is a function of the square of its dimensions. The volume, and accompanying weight of an animal that is powered by the larger muscle, increases with the cube of its dimensions. As animals get larger, their relative strength diminishes because their weight increases at a faster rate, a cubic function, than their muscular strength, a square function. Smaller insects benefit from their reduced size and lightweight exoskeleton.

Muscles Contraction

The steps in the cycle of muscle contraction. A. The muscle fi ber at rest. Adenosine diphosphate (ADP) is bound to the myosin heads, and the troponin-tropomyosin complex has no bound calcium. B. The muscle fiber is activated when calcium is released from the sarcoplasmic reticulum and binds to the tropomyosin, causing them to expose actin binding sites. This allows the myosin heads to form cross-bridges between the thick and thin filaments. C. The attachment causes a conformational change in the myosin, and they exert forces that shorten the sarcomere by producing a greater overlap of the fi laments. D. When the power stroke is completed, ATP binds to the myosin head and causes it to detach from the actin. E. The energy contributed by the ATP reconforms the myosin head for attachment to another binding site. From Kandel *et al.,* (2000).

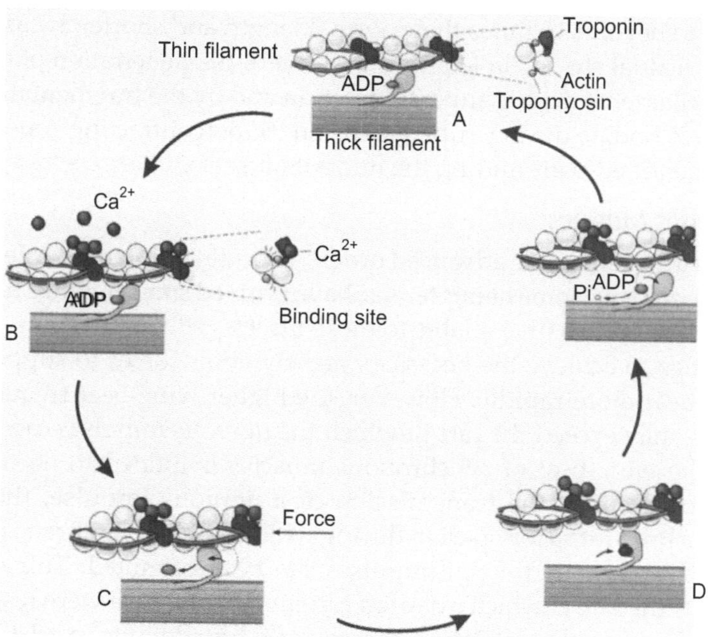

Synchronous and Asynchronous muscles

Synchronous Muscles

Most of the skeletal muscles in insects are called *synchronous* because they contract in synchrony with nervous signals from the motor neurons that innervate them. Each nervous signal is followed by a single contraction of the muscle, and in the case of wing muscles, with potential contraction frequencies of up to 550 Hz that commonly produce a wing-beat frequency in the range of 5 to 30 Hz. The abundant sarcoplasmic reticulum in synchronous muscle cells enables a large amount of calcium to be released when the muscles are stimulated, and the sarcomeres undergo a maximal degree of contraction. This extensive sarcoplasmic reticulum also allows the calcium to be efficiently resequestered for muscle relaxation. Synchronous muscles are found in what are considered to be the relatively primitive flight muscles of orthopterans, lepidopterans, and odonates. The sound-producing tymbal muscle in a cicada has the highest known frequency, 500 Hz, of contraction of any synchronous muscle, but the amount of sarcoplasmic reticulum that is necessary for this frequency occupies almost one third of the muscle cross section.

The contraction of most synchronous muscles is generally limited to a maximum shortening of about 50%, but there are special supercontracting and superextending muscles associated with structures that undergo an unusual degree of extension. For example, the intersegmental muscles that allow the elongation of the abdominal segments containing the ovipositor in some insects can stretch to beyond 10 times their normal length and shorten by as much as 90%. This unusual change in length is because of the penetration of the Z disc by the myofilaments during supercontraction and by the fragmentation of the Z disc into Z bodies during superextension. Supercontracting muscles have also been identif ed surrounding the midgut of tsetse.

Asynchronous Muscles

The insects in several more advanced orders, including dipterans, coleopterans, hymenopterans, and some hemipterans, have evolved smaller wings that enable them to occupy niches unavailable to those insects with large wings. For these smaller wings to achieve the necessary aerodynamic forces to support flight, they must beat more rapidly. However, the higher wing-beat frequency that is necessary may exceed the rate at which the nervous impulses can reach the muscles. The wing-beat of synchronous muscles is limited to no more than 550 Hz because after the transmission of a nervous impulse, the neuron undergoes a brief refractory period during which time its membrane potentials are restored and no additional impulses can be transmitted. This structural design limits the rate at which a neuron can fire. If wing-beat were restricted by the speed of nervous transmission, there would be a definite restriction on the lower size limit of flying insects, because flight by the smaller insects could only be possible if their smaller wings were able to beat faster. In the ceratopogonid midge, *Forcipomyia*, the wing-beat approximates 1000 per second, which is too fast for the control of flight muscles by individual nervous impulses. The rapid contraction of its flight muscles is only possible because another type of muscle is present that does not require individual nerve impulses to stimulate its contraction. These special muscles, found only in insects, are called either *fibrillar*, because of their relatively large myofibrils, or *asynchronous*, because they contract without the 1 : 1 synchrony with electrical events. The frequency at which nervous signals activate these muscles is considerably less than the frequency of contractions. In contrast to the one nervous impulse per contraction in synchronous muscles, asynchronous muscles generally oscillate through 5 to 25 contractions for each nervous impulse .

Fuels in Flight Muscles Metabolism

Flight requires a relatively enormous amount of energy both because of the high cost of flying at a low Reynolds number and the inefficiency of the conversion of energy. Yet insect flight muscles operate completely aerobically. Only about 10% of the chemical energy used for flight is translated into mechanical energy, with the rest being dissipated as heat. This heat can be used for thermoregulation in some insects to allow them to fly even when ambient temperatures are too low for optimal muscle activity. The energy for flight muscle contraction is drawn from several sources. Ideally, these substrates would be situated within the muscles themselves to be close to where they would be utilized, but the need to maintain high ratios of muscle power to weight limits the concentrations they can attain there, necessitating that the bulk of the components be stored elsewhere. Small amounts of substances are located in the flight muscles themselves to power the initiation of flight, but the initial store of ATP in muscle cells is only sufficient for a few seconds of fl ight. It is replenished by the transfer of a phosphate group to ADP from *arginine phosphate*, providing an additional brief period of flight. This system is similar to vertebrate muscle where creatine phosphate is instead used as a reservoir for high-energy phosphoryl groups. The muscle may also store small amounts of other fuels including proline, glycogen, and triacylglycerol that are drawn upon during flight, but these resources are similarly limited. Flight muscles draw the next most immediate source of energy from substrates in the hemolymph. The disaccharide trehalose is present in high concentrations as a circulating energy source that is used during the early phases of flight. Hemolymph diacylglycerol also bathes muscle cells, and the amino acid proline is utilized in some insects for flight. These are mobilized from fat body reserves to maintain their levels in the hemolymph, but upper limits on the osmotic pressure of the hemolymph prevent the concentrations of these substances from getting too high. The fuel for longer flights is stored in the fat body and transported to flight muscles through the hemolymph. This fuel use varies among insect orders. During long flights, dipterans and hymenopterans convert fat body glycogen into trehalose that is distributed to muscles through the hemolymph while migratory orthopterans utilize triacylglycerols in the fat body that are converted to diacylglycerols for transport.

Glycerophosphate Shuttle

Flight muscles completely oxidize carbohydrates to carbon dioxide and water in the absence of any anaerobic metabolism. Glycolysis in insect flight muscle occurs much like that in other animals, with a few additions. One is the presence of a glycerol phosphate shuttle. With the conversion of glyceraldehyde phosphate to 1,3 diphosphoglycerate during glycolysis, NAD^+ acts as a hydrogen acceptor and is converted to NADH. Because the NAD^+ is only present in catalytic amounts, the reduced NADH must be reoxidized to maintain the biochemical pathway. In vertebrate muscle and insect muscles not involved in flight, NADH is oxidized during the conversion of pyruvate to lactic acid and the liver or fat body rebuilds glucose as part of the oxygen debt. In insect flight muscle, no oxygen debt is incurred because the NADH is reoxidized by the enzyme glycerol phosphate dehydrogenase with dihydroxyacetone phosphate as a substrate to form glycerol-3-phosphate. Unlike NADH, the glycerol-3-phosphate can

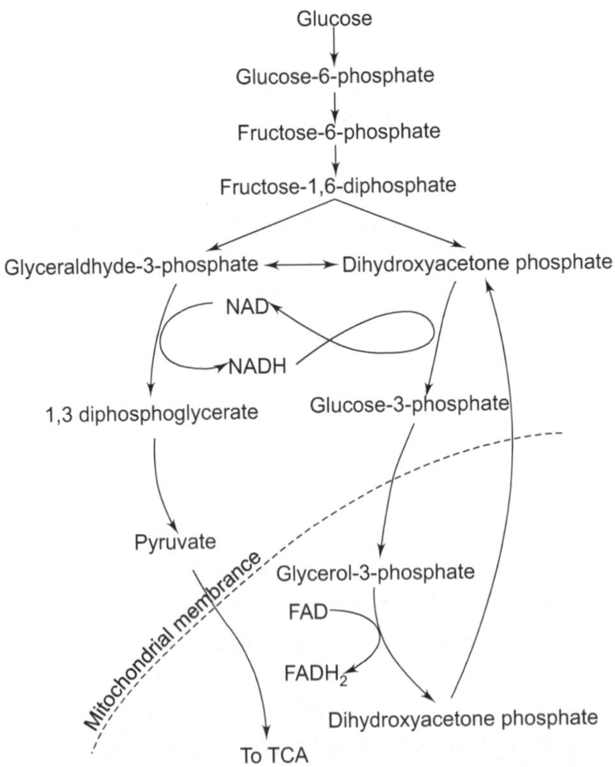

Glycerol phosphate shuttle operates in insect flight muscle

pass into the mitochondrion where it is reoxidized to form dihydroxyacetone phosphate. The dihydroxyacetone phosphate then leaves the mitochondrion to be oxidized by the NADH. Thus, the glycerol-3-phosphate shuttles the hydrogen into the mitochondrion where it can be harnessed for oxidative phosphorylation and also provide NAD^+ for glycolysis.

Proline Metabolism

Dipterans use proline as fuel for flight to different extents. The blow fly, *Phormia regina,* initially metabolizes proline to provide the tricarboxylic acid intermediates that are used for later flight. However, the tsetse fly, *Glossina,* also uses proline, but as the major fuel for flight. As tsetse initiate flight, hemolymph proline decreases in concentration along with a concomitant increase in alanine

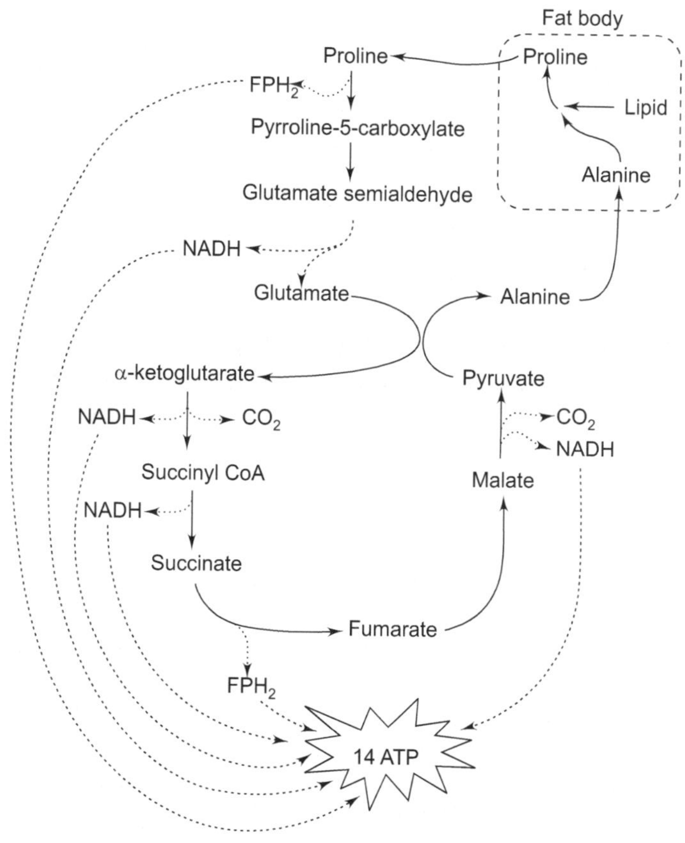

Proline metabolism in insect flight muscle.

concentrations and a brief increase in pyruvate during the first few seconds of flight. The pyruvate accumulates because it is produced faster than the rate of oxidation by mitochondria. These high levels of pyruvate initiate a series of biochemical steps beginning with the activation of the enzyme proline dehydrogenase that supplies tricarboxylic acid cycle intermediates to prime the cycle and speed up the rate of energy production. Glutamate is used to transaminate pyruvate so that proline enters the tricarboxylic acid cycle as á-ketoglutarate. The proline is not completely oxidized, losing two carbons to form alanine, which returns to the fat body and is reformed as proline by stored fatty acids. Thus the use of proline is actually a mechanism for shuttling two carbon units from the fat body to the flight muscles. Lepidopterans may employ either lipids or carbohydrates, regulating their choice of fuels based on their feeding history. In general, insects that engage in long-range flights oxidize lipid, whereas those that use carbohydrate fly for only short periods. Insects with high wing-beat frequencies and asynchronous muscles tend to utilize carbohydrates, whereas those with synchronous flight muscles are more likely to utilize lipid. Lipid is the most concentrated form of energy storage. To fly 10 h each day, a migratory locust may use 70 mg of stored lipid. If glycogen were utilized instead, 500 mg or 30% of the insect's weight would have to be oxidized. Glycogen is considerably more hydrated than lipid; as a result, it is also eight times heavier for the same caloric potential.

Flight Behaviour in Relation to Thermal Control

During flight, the flight muscles raise the thoracic temperature above ambient and, for many insects, the only way to avoid overheating at high air temperature is to stop flying. Some species, however, have the ability to regulate thoracic temperature physiologically. For example, in flight, *Manduca* keeps its thoracic temperature between 38 and 42°C over a range of ambient temperatures from 12 to 36°C. Some other moths, bees, beetles and dragonflies are known to have a similar capacity. The large dragonfly, *Anax*, reduces its wing beat frequency from about 35 Hz at an air temperature of 20°C to 25 Hz at 35°C, at the same time reducing its flight speed (May, 1995). Dragonflies also make more intermittent flights and spend more time gliding at higher temperatures. In honeybees, reduction of wing beat frequency at high temperatures is also known to contribute to regulation of thoracic temperature (Harrison *et al.*, 1996).

Heat Exchanger

In general, however, flying insects control their body temperature by regulating heat loss. Moths and bumblebees do this by varying the heat transfer to the abdomen which acts as a radiator of heat as it is less well insulated than the thorax. As the thorax warms up, the heart beats more rapidly and with greater amplitude. The effect of this is to increase the rate of circulation to the abdomen and reduce the efficiency of the heat exchanger. In bumblebees, the efficiency of the heat exchanger may be greatly reduced at high ambient temperatures by the hemolymph being pushed back into the gaster in discrete slugs. Consequently, the difference in temperature between the gaster and the air is greater at high temperatures. In honeybees, however, this is not true. The temperature of the gaster is always very similar to ambient probably because the efficiency of the heat exchanger is so high that little or no thoracic heat reaches the gaster.

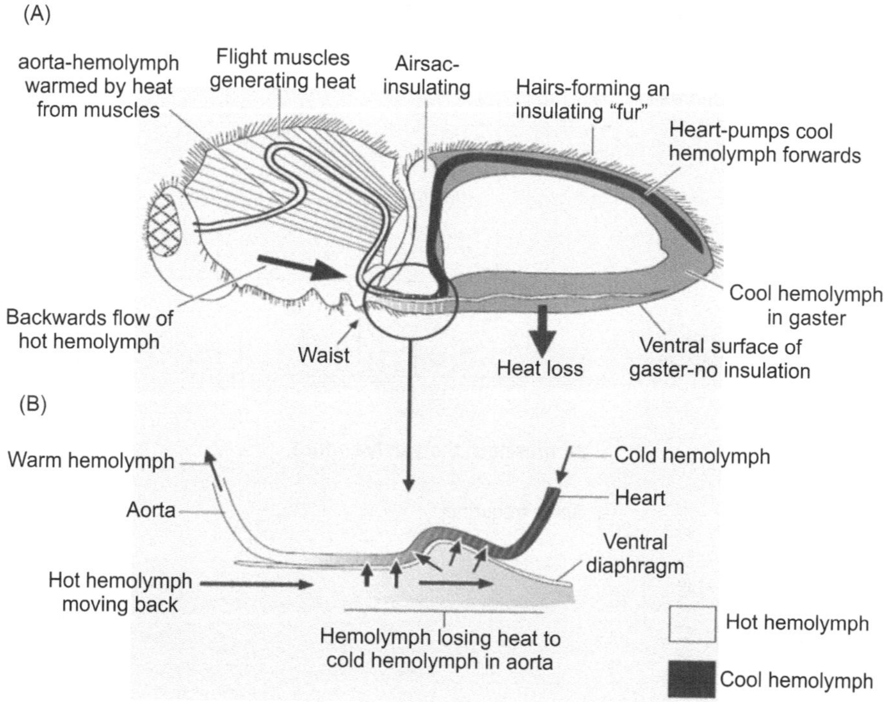

Warming up Behaviour

During warm-up, the depressor and levator muscles of the wings contract together, instead of in antiphase as they do in flight. This difference results from a change in the pattern of firing of the motor neurons. In the Lepidoptera, with synchronous flight muscles, the motor neurons fire in phase instead of in antiphase. Dipterans and Hymenoptera, however, have asynchronous flight muscles in which muscle contractions are not determined by the rate of firing of the motor neurons, but depend on stretch activation of one set of muscles by its antagonists. During warm up, however, the muscles function as synchronous muscles.

Flight at Low Temperature

Numbers of moths fly habitually when air temperature is close to 0°C. Some moths like *Eupsilia* sps raising thoracic temperature to 30°C above even at an ambient temperature is 0°C. Winter moth like *Operophtera* can fly without having to raise thoracic temperature. Some moths having low wing beat frequency i.e. 4 HZ enough power to keep insects air borne. Dipterans also fly at low temperature.

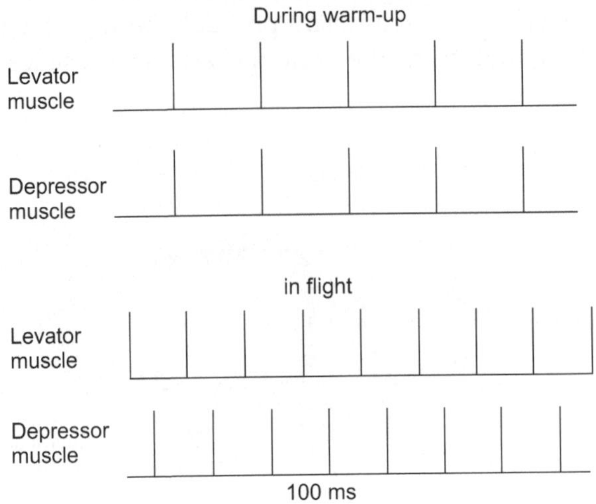

(a) muscle activity in Manduca

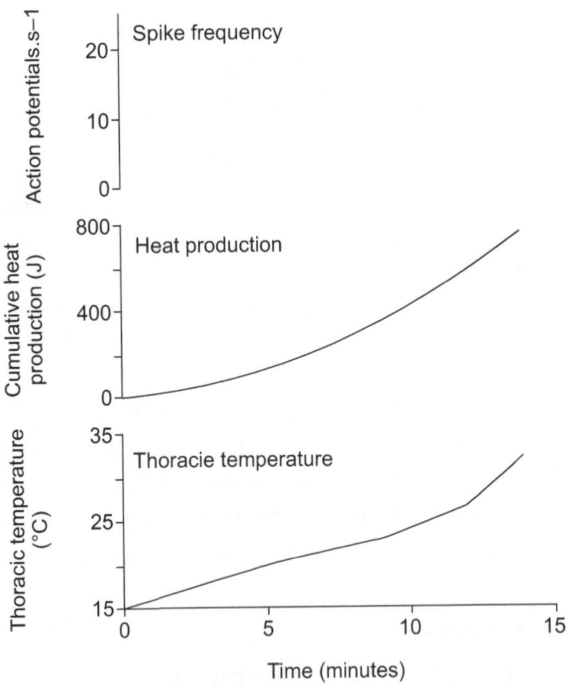

(b) warm-up in Bombus

Flight Behaviour in Relation to Reproduction

Wing dimorphic female crickets of *Eobiana engelhardti*. Short winged females (SWF) produces eggs more intensively in an early period compare to long winged females (LWF). As incase of males long winged males (LWM) developed significantly lower accessory glands compare to short winged males (SWM). (SWM) produces significantly heavier spermatophore in single copulation compare to (LWM). The development & maintainance of flight muscles have a cost in (LWM). Prolonged flight behavior in females of the grasshopper, *Melanoplus sanguinipes* decreases as ovarian tract. Flight activity influences age at 1st oviposition to over all reproductive behaviour. Flight or possession of wings slower nymphal development, increased time to first oviposition, decreased numbers of developed ovarioles, decreased overall fecundity. Species in which an oogenesis-flight syndrome exists, but females are capable of inter-oviposition flight. Females in which ovaries comprised at least 15% of the body weight never made long flights and were near oviposition as indicated by the frequent appearance of mature oocytes in the lateral oviducts. The alate morphs of some species of aphids also delay larviposition. Prolonged flight itself has been shown to have no deleterious effects on reproduction in some species. In oncopeltus the mean number of eggs produced in flown bugs tended to be greater compared to unflown bugs. Flight greatly accelerates the rate of oocyte growth in laboratory cultures of the locusts. *Oncopeltus fasciatus, Hippodamia convergens and Danaus plexippus,* while females with fully mature oocytes make few if any long flights, migration and oogenesis in these species proceed simultaneously.

Flight Behaviour in Relation to Predation Escape

Insects when engaged in flight behavior, respond to ultrasound by suddenly altering their flight, showing acoustic startle or negative phonotaxis, which serve as bat-avoidance behaviour. Noctuids, arctiids, geometrids and pyralids show phonotactic avoidance behavior during flapping flight: they fly away from directional sources. Green lacewings fold their wings when stimulated by actual or synthetic bat bio sonar signals and simply drop to the ground. Praying mantises having a pair of scolopophorous hearing organs on the midline of metathoracic wings. Flight activity enhances auditory responsiveness.

Effects of Age

Flying makes flies more vulnerable to oxidative damage than not flying, and lipid peroxidation causes damage to the cell membrane and its end-products may cause damage to DNA in the form of DNA adducts. Early onset foraging or extended daily flight duration while foraging decrease lifespan in honey bee workers. In bumblebees, the suppression of foraging activity slightly increases body mass and the immune response later in life. Wing kinematics and the frequency of foraging trips decrease in old honey bee foragers, although age has no effect on the flight performance of nurse bees.

Effects of Temperature

Insects from cold environments could also increase wing area relative to body mass which should reduce induced power requirements and increase lift production. Wing area was larger in cold-reared flies and more than compensated for the minor increase in body size. As a result, flies developing at cold temperatures had the lowest wing loading. For their size; males had relatively higher wing loading than female's. Males had relatively shorter wings than females. Flying insects could also increase their flight muscle ratio to generate more power for flight. Larger flies had faster WBFs whereas flies with larger wing areas had slower *WBFs*. Cold-reared fruit flies do not compensate for colder flight temperatures by increasing wing-beat frequency. Decreased wing loading in *Drosophila spp.* in response to cold developmental temperatures .Insects that developed in cold temperatures had significantly lower WBF than flies that developed at warm temperatures at all test temperatures. Insects that developed in cold temperatures were heavier and had larger wings and larger insects tend to have reduced wing-beat frequencies.

CONCLUSIONS

Flying insects are co – evolved with flowering plants. Flight behaviour in insects genetically determined. Wings are arose once in insect evolution. By using of olfactory cues we can alter the flight of an insects. Better understanding of flight behaviour one of the new cultural technique in IPM programmes. Models flight behaviour are constructed that helps in predicting Dispersal and Migration. Flight makes insects most successful in the world survive and reproduce in wide range of locations. By using aerodynamics of insect flight, air crafts and micro air vehicles are developed.

REFERENCES

Boettiger, E.G.1960. Insect Flight Muscles and Their Basic Physiology. *Annu. Rev. Entomol.* **5**: 1–16.

Dickinson, M., G. Farman, M. Frye, T. Bekyarova, D. Gore, D. Maughan, T. Irving. 2005. Molecular Dynamics of Cyclically Contracting Insect Flight Muscle *in vivo*. *Nature* **433**: 330–334.

Dickinson, M. 1994. The Effects of Wing Rotation on Unsteady Aerodynamic Performance at Low Reynolds Numbers. *J. Exp. Biol.* **192**: 179–206.

Dickinson, M. 2001. Solving the Mystery of Insect Flight. *Sci. Am.* **284**: 48–57.

Dickinson, M. 2006. Insect Flight. *Curr. Biol.* **16:** R309–R314.

Dickinson, M.H. 1999. Haltere-mediated Equilibrium Reflexes of the Fruit Fly, *Drosophila Melanogaster*. *Phil. Trans. R. Soc. Lond.* B **354**: 903–916.

Dickinson, M.H., C.T. Farley, R.J. Full, M.A. Koehl, R. Kram, S. Lehman. 2000. How Animals Move: An Integrative View. *Science* **288**: 100–106.

Dickinson, M.H., K.G. Gotz. 1996. The Wake Dynamics and Flight Forces of the Fruit Fly *Drosophila melanogaster*. *J. Exp. Biol.* **199**: 2085–2104.

Dickinson, M.H., S. Hannaford, J. Palka. 1997. The Evolution of Insect Wings and their Sensory Apparatus. *Brain Behav. Evol.* **50**: 13–24.

Dickinson, M.H., F.O. Lehmann, S.P. Sane. 1999. Wing Rotation and the Aerodynamic Basis of Insect Flight. *Science* **284:** 1954–1960.

Dudley, R. 1998. Atmospheric Oxygen, Giant Paleozoic Insects and the Evolution of Aerial Locomotor Performance. *J. Exp. Biol.* **201**: 1043–1050.

Dudley, R. 2000. The Evolutionary Physiology of Animal Flight: Paleobiological and Present Perspectives. *Annu. Rev. Physiol.* **62**: 135–155.

Dudley, R., R. Srygley. 1994. Flight Physiology of Neotropical Butterflies: Allometry of Airspeeds During Natural Free Flight. *J. Exp. Biol.* **191**: 125–139.

Eisenberg, E., T.L. Hill. 1985. Muscle Contraction and Free Energy Transduction in Biological Systems. *Science* **227**: 999–1006.

Harrison, J.F., S.P. Roberts. 2000. Flight Respiration and Energetics. *Annu. Rev. Physiol.* **62**: 179–205.

Hesselberg, T., Lehmann, F.O., 2009. The Role of Experience in Flight Behaviour of Drosophila. *J. Exp. Biol.* **212**: 3377-3386.

Lehmann, F.O., S.P. Sane, M. Dickinson. 2005. The Aerodynamic Effects of Wing-wing Interaction in Flapping Insect Wings. *J. Exp. Biol.* **208:** 3075–3092.

Schaefer, C.W., J.P. Vanderberg, J. Rhodin. 1967. The Fine Structure of Mosquito Midgut Muscle. *J. Cell Biol.* **34**: 905–910.

Suarez, R.K. 1998. Oxygen and the Upper Limits to Animal Design and Performance. *J. Exp. Biol.* **201**: 1065–1072.

Suarez, R.K. 2000. Energy Metabolism During Insect Flight: Biochemical Design and Physiological Performance. *Physiol. Biochem. Zool.* **73**: 765–771.

Truong, T.V., Byun, D., 2012. Flight Behavior of the Rhinoceros Beetle *Trypoxylus Dichotomus* During Electrical Nerve Stimulation. *Bioinspir. Biomim.* **7:** 1 -11.

Wigglesworth, V.B. 1990. The Direct Transport of Oxygen in Insects by Large Tracheae. *Tiss. Cell* **22:** 239–243.

Wigglesworth, V.B. 1990. The Properties of the Lining Membrane of the Insect Tracheal System. *Tiss. Cell* 22: 231–238.

Analytical Techniques in Chemical and Biological Sciences **Page: 158-166**
Edited by: Dr. Deep Mala and Dr. Pawan Kumar 'Bharti'
ISBN: 978-93-86841-59-9
Edition: 2018
Published by: Discovery Publishing House Pvt. Ltd., New Delhi (India)

12

A Study on Biotic Community of Umaim River in East Khasi Hills, Meghalaya

Pawan K. Bharti[1] and Vijender Singh[1, 2]

ABSTRACT

Umaim river is a major river of East Khasi Hills district in Meghalaya along with many small tributaries near Bangladesh Border. It has a great importance as a natural habitat among the various ecosystems of the region, whereas there is a large scale limestone mining area and no more industrial and agricultural pollution. Anthropogenic factors mainly activities of local people and catchments runoff may influence the index of nutrients in river water and may alter the physico-chemical characteristics and also the whole water quality and the structure of biotic community. Physico-chemical parameters play an important role into niche restoration maintenance, self-regulation of water quality. Location variation in nutrients concentration of the river was studied with special reference to physico-chemical parameters and heavy metals in the river water.

Calcium and Magnesium were observed in very low range in Umaim river water at upstream as well as downstream in comparison to rivers and hill-streams of North India. Dissolved oxygen was found 9.2 to 11.0 mg/l at upstream and downstream during the study period. Heavy Metals were found almost nil or in very low concentrations at both selected site. The present study deals with the preliminary physico-chemical characteristics of the river water and exhibits the natural quality of water with minimum anthropogenic activities, which contribute in pollution load of an ecosystem.

Key words: Water quality, Pollution status, biotic community, Heavy Metals

INTRODUCTION

Water is a resource circulated throughout all ecosystems and is one of the most important factors of them (Odum 1971). From the point of view of ecohydrology, for the main elements of an ecosystem including inorganic and organic compound, producers and consumers both the quantity and the

[1] Shriram Institute for Industrial Research, Delhi-7, India.
[2] Green Environmental Consultancy and Services, 3263, Urban Estate, Safido Bypass, Jind (Haryana), India.

chemistry of water have a decisive impact on its biomass and biotic composition. Information obtained form current hydro-chemical analyses of water specimens is very important but it is sometimes difficult to Gauge the overall situation especially the occurrence of nutrient, which may be very important to an ecosystem (Malik and Bharti, 2005a). Ecological, geo-chemical and hydrological research has been carried out in various ecosystems to understand the factors controlling the chemistry of natural water (Baron & Bricker, 1990; Malik and Bharti, 2005a). Many of such studies have been under taken during the last two decades to understand the processes that control the hydrochemistry of alpine and sub-alpine systems of North America and Europe (William *et al.* 1993 and Psenner, 1989). Similar studies were also done in China and central Asia (Xue & Schnoor, 1994).

Indian mountains are the cradle of a large number of streams and mighty rivers. In North-East region and very close to Bangladesh border, a hill-stream Umaim, 90 Km. far away from Shillong city is the study site for the accounting of physico-chemical parameters and Heavy Metals in natural water and fluctuations at the different locations along with the stream. Adequate understanding of the North-East regional streams is extremely important for the development of a realistic program for utilizing the potential of water that exist in the form of hidden water resource in the area. The impact of anthropogenic pollution from industrial, agricultural, sources, quarrying and tourists activity on water quality has concerned environmentalists and scientists for the past three decades.

The present study reveals to characteristics the water nutrient chemistry, influenced by anthropogenic activity & quarrying of the geologically sedimental environments and to determine the nature and degree of anthropogenic impacts on qualitative and quantitative variations occurred in nutrients in relation to physico-chemical parameters and Heavy Metals of stream water.

Study Area

The seven states of North East India are quite famous as Seven Sisters, and Meghalaya is very well known for the record of rainfall, the state consists of the two places namely Cherrepunjee and Mawsinram for maximum rainfall throughout the year. So, the maximum water resources are depending chiefly on total precipitations of the region. The Meghalaya has been surrounded by the natural beauties with lovely trees and cool climate, which is not only a pleasant place to live in but relaxing for holiday also. This is not only a popular state but also valuable or important place for tourism, Shillong is the capital of Meghalaya state. Mowlong Cherra Cement Ltd and Lafarge Umaim Mining Ltd are the major industries of the region.

Umaim river originated from the hills of Assam-Meghalaya basically. Upstream of Umaim is near village Dissong and Downstream near Village

Pyrkan. The water of Umaim is very useful for the local people. Population of the region is completely depending upon the river water for drinking, bathing, and other activities. *Geologically,* North-east hills are enriched with various

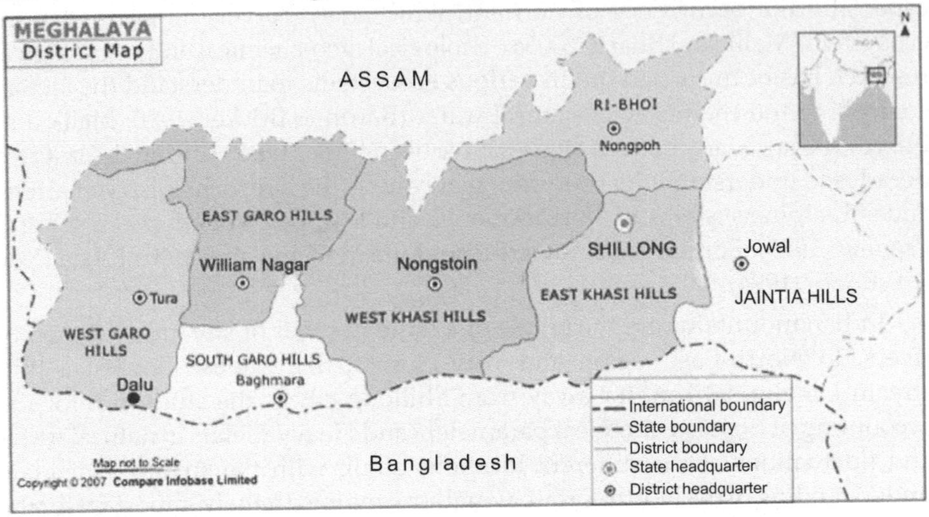

Fig. 12.1: District map of Meghalaya

Fig. 12.2: Map of district East Khasi Hills

minerals and the hills near Bangladesh are rich in limestone. *Geographically*, the study area is situated in the globe on a Latitude 25° 11′ 40.8″ N & Longitude 91° 38′ 16.4″ E for Upstream site and Latitude 25° 10′ 43.8″ N & Longitude 91° 38′ 19.2″ E for Downstream site. *Meteorologically*, region has a cool & pleasant climate.

MATERIALS AND METHODS

The water samples were collected from Umaim River upstream (U/S sampling site A) Near Disong village and downstream (D/S sampling site B) near Shella Bazar according to the analytical requirement in morning period 9:00 Hrs. to 10:00 Hrs.

The samples for physico-chemical parameters and Heavy Metals were collected by using rinsed Borosil glassware and analyzed with the help of the procedure described by APHA (1995) and Trivedi and Goel (1984). Colour, odour, turbidity, velocity, temperature and Dissolved oxygen were analyzed on sampling sites. Samples were collected from selected sites and immediately preserved in ice boxes and transfer to the lab for further analysis. Water samples were digested and Heavy Metals were detected using Atomic absorption spectrophotometer. The study of biotic community of Umaim river was carried out with the help of Schwoerbel (1991), Santhanam, *et al.*, (1989). The macro-benthic biota and Plankton were identified with the help of Edmondson (1959).

RESULTS AND DISCUSSION

Umaim river is flowing throughout a valley of North-east hills chain near the Bangladesh Border, enriched with limestone and lignite rocks, which affect the water quality of stream according to the locations. Nutrients concentration, Heavy Metals and related physico-chemical parameters from selected sites are depicted in tables.

Umaim river has the spatio-temporal variations of water temperature, which plays a vital role in all physico-biochemical reactions and self-purification power of aquatic system (Badola & Singh, 1981). Higher value of temperature was found 18-°C in summer at downstream and minimum 12 °C in winter season at downstream. Turbidity is striking characteristic of the physical status of the water bodies. Although in Umaim river water is clear because there is no more pollution, siltation was the main source of turbidity in tributaries. Detritus and other non-organic material being added to water mass due to rainfall and anthropogenic activities (Camron, 1996). Maximum turbidity was recorded 8 NTU during rainy season at upstream and minimum 1 NTU in summer season at downstream. The maximum depth of photic zone provides the better biological production for all aquatic organisms especially phytoplankton (Malik and Bharti, 2005b).

Total dissolved solids were found in the range of 41 mg/l in to 55 mg/l in monsoon season, due to the gradual increases in velocity of river which favoured effective sedimentation (Subramanian, 1979). Chemical oxygen demand (3-6 mg/l) represents chemically oxidizable organic matter load in water, while biochemical oxygen demand is only biodegradable materials (Malik and Bharti, 2005c). In the present study the values observed during monsoon months may be attributed maximum biological activities and high temperature, stimulate the growth of microorganisms (William *et al.*, 1993).

The pH of natural water was controlled in a great extent by the interaction of hydroxyl ions arising from the hydrolysis of bicarbonate (Sharma, 1986). The pH of Umaim river was recorded slightly alkaline (6.8 – 7.5). Total hardness is mainly due to percentage of calcium and magnesium salts of bicarbonates, carbonates, sulphates and chlorides, while the value of alkalinity occured due to presence of bicarbonates. The highest concentration of hardness was analyzed 22-32 mg/l during the study. Alkalinity was also found 22-42 mg/l with a small fluctuation. A positive relationship between hardness and alkalinity was recorded in river Ganga at Rishikesh (Chopra and Patric, 1994).

Maximum chloride concentration was recorded (10 mg/l) in winter and minimum in summer (5 mg/l). Chloride and hardness showed a positive relationship to one another (Chopra and Patric, 1994). Chloride was found in the form of chloride ion, and one of the major inorganic anion present in natural water (Malik and Bharti, 2009).

Calcium and magnesium the dominant cations, and these represent the main weathering products, but significant hydro-chemical differences between the two sampling sites associated with the bedrock geology exist (Jenkins *et al.*, 1995) Calcium is one of the essential nutrients, which plays an important role in biological system. Maximum calcium concentration was recorded (14 mg/l) in summer and minimum in monsoon (8 mg/l). Positive relationship between, calcium and temperature was also reported by Khanna and Singh (2000) in river Suswa, Dehradun. Magnesium is also an essential element but it is toxic at higher concentration. The concentration of magnesium in Umaim river was found maximum (4 mg/l) and minimum (1 mg/l) and it was very low in comparison to Hill-streams of Uttarakhand (Bharti, 2004).

During the summer season nutrients concentration in rivers and hill-streams became more. Miller *et al.,* (1997) described the nutrients availability in selected environmental settings of the Potomac River and Cameron (1996) showed the similar type of fluctuation in Fraser river of British Columbia. Bond (1979) described similar nutrients concentration pattern in a stream draining a mountain ecosystem in Utah.

Heavy Metals like Cadmium, copper, iron, manganese, lead and zinc were not found in high concentration at both sites during any season. Cadmium was absolutely absent in all seasons, while copper, lead and manganese concentrations were also found below detection limit in maximum samples. The concentration of iron was maximum observed 0.09 mg/l during monsoon season. Manganese was found maximum 0.03 mg/l in summer and zinc concentration was 0.07 mg/l in monsoon season. Malik *et al.*, (2009) described the role of Heavy Metals in the surface water of north India. The results of Bharti *et al.*, (2010) were also indicated the relation of Heavy Metals and phytoplankton in a north Indian water body.

The concentrations of Calcium and Magnesium were observed in very low range in Umaim river water at upstream as well as downstream in comparison to rivers and hill-streams of North India. Dissolved oxygen was found 9.2 to 11.0 mg/l at upstream and downstream during the study period. Heavy Metals were found almost nil or in very low concentrations at both selected site. The present study deals with the preliminary physico-chemical characteristics of the river water and exhibits the natural quality of water with minimum anthropogenic activities, which contribute in pollution load of an ecosystem.

Table 12.1: Physical Characteristics of Umaim River Water

S.No.	Parameters	Unit	Umaim Upstream			Umaim Downstream			Desirable Limit
			Winter	Summer	Mon-soon	Winter	Summer	Mon-soon	
1.	Temperature	°C	13	17	16	12	18	15	-
2.	Colour	-	Clear	Clear	Clear	Clear	Clear	Clear	-
3.	Odour	-	Nil	Nil	Nil	Nil	Nil	Nil	-
4.	Turbidity	NTU	2	3	8	3	1	5	5
5.	Velocity	m/s	0.2	0.2	0.3	0.1	0.1	0.3	-
6.	TDS	Mg/l	41	43	48	46	48	55	500

Table 10.2: Chemical Characteristics of Umaim River Water

S.No.	Parameters	Unit	Umaim Upstream			Umaim Downstream			Desirable Limit
			Winter	Summer	Mon-soon	Winter	Summer	Mon-soon	
1.	pH	-	7.1	6.9	7.4	6.8	7.5	7.3	6.5-8.5
2.	Alkalinity	Mg/l	22	25	30	28	32	28	200
3.	Total Hardness	Mg/l	22	34	26	42	32	24	300
4.	Calcium	Mg/l	8	10	8	12	14	8	75
5.	Magnesium	Mg/l	1	3	4	1	3	2	30
6.	Chlorides	Mg/l	7	6	6	10	5	7	250
7.	DO	Mg/l	10.4	11.0	9.5	10.5	10.6	9.2	-
8.	BOD	Mg/l	Nil	Nil	Nil	Nil	Nil	Nil	-
9.	COD	Mg/l	4	3	5	6	5	6	-

Table 10.3: Heavy Metals in Umaim River Water

S.No.	Parameters	Unit	Umaim Upstream			Umaim Downstream			Desirable Limit
			Winter	Summer	Mon-soon	Winter	Summer	Mon-soon	
1.	Cadmium	Mg/l	BDL	BDL	BDL	BDL	BDL	BDL	0.01
2.	Copper	Mg/l	BDL	BDL	BDL	0.01	BDL	0.01	0.05
3.	Iron	Mg/l	0.06	0.08	0.09	0.06	0.02	BDL	0.3
4.	Lead	Mg/l	0.01	0.02	BDL	BDL	BDL	BDL	0.05
5.	Manganese	Mg/l	BDL	0.03	0.01	BDL	BDL	BDL	0.1
6.	Zinc	Mg/l	BDL	0.03	0.03	0.07	0.05	BDL	5.0

The present results conclude that significant differences in river water nutrient concentrations exist among different environmental settings within the two subunits. The environmental setting with the highest potential by more soluble nutrients, fluctuations in nutrient concentrations were the land use and carbonate bedrock that was predominated in the North East valley. The spatial variations in TDS are attributed to climatic and lithological control over the ionic concentrations. Absence or low concentration of Heavy Metals shows that the water is still industrial pollution free. However, the Indian standards are not so strict (Bharti, 2007), but Heavy Metals never cross the limits during the study period. On the basis of nutrients and Heavy Metals, the water may be considered for drinking and other purposes.

Table 10.4: Preliminary Study of Biotic Communities in Umaim River

Category	Family/Phylum	Genus/Species
Neuston	**Arthopods**	*Mayfly nymph, Water spider*
Plankton	**Phytoplankton :** Chorophyceae-Bacillariophyceae- Rhodophyceae-Cyanophyceae- **Zooplankton:** Protozoans-Coelentrata	*Volvox, Chlorella, Ulothrix, Vaucheria, Zygnema, Diatoms Batrachospermun Rivularia, Nostoc Vorticalla, Paramoecium, Amoeba, Chrysamocha, Volvox, Cyclopes, Hydra, Ceratella*
Necton	Amphebia-Piscies	*Rana Schizothorax richardsonii (Gray)- Asella Barilius barila (Ham.)*
Benthos	Macroinvertibrate-Annelida-	*Snails, Beetles, SepiaPheretima, Leeches, Flatworms,*
Aquatic macrophytes	Bryophyta -Rannunculaceae -	*Moss , Fern , Weedy rooted aquatic herbs Rannunculus*

The preliminary study of biotic community of Umaim ecosystem was also carried out in a lengthy stretch of Umaim basin. The genera, species and their related category are given in Table 12.4 with the scientific names. Rundle, *et al.*, (1993) also observed the similar species of biota in the river of Nepal. Plankton

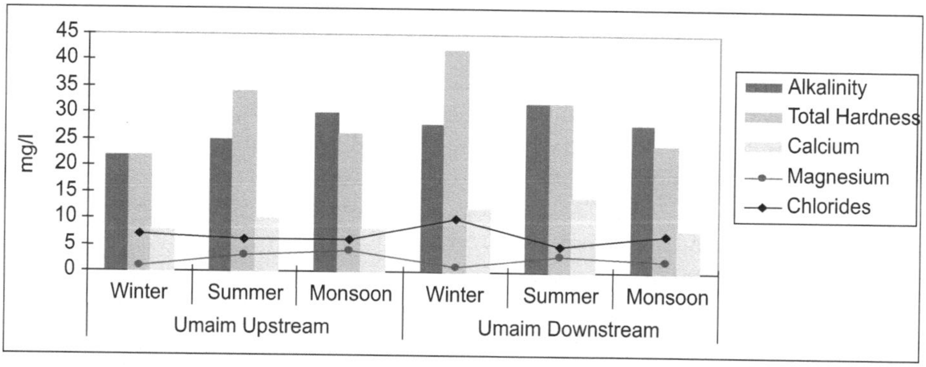

Fig. 12.1: Showing the nutrients concentration in Umaim river during the study period.

of chlorophyceae family was found dominantly in Umaim river ecosystem. Planktons are the primary producers of and aquatic ecosystem (Hynes, 1970). So, ecosystem always balanced by the presence of each and every necessary species of flora and fauna.

REFERENCE

APHA (1995): Standard Methods for Examination of Water and Waste Water. *American Public Health Association, 19th edition. Inc, New York.* pp. 1970.

Badola, S.P. and Singh, H.R. (1981) Hydrobiology of the River Alaknanda of Garhwal Himalaya. *Indian J. Ecol.*, 8(2): 269-276.

Baron, J. & Bricker, O.P. (1990) Hydrological and Chemical Flux in Loch Vale Watershed, Rocky Mountain National Park. In: Biogeochemistry of Major Rivers. SCOPE 42. Wiley and Sons, New York, USA.

Bharti, P.K. (2004): Limnobiological Study of Sahastradhara Hill-stream at Dehradun, *M.Sc. Dissertation*, Submitted to Gurukula Kangri University, Hardwar, pp. 102.

Bharti, P.K. (2007): Why Indian Standards are not so Strict?, *Current Science*, 93(9): 1202.

Bharti, P.K., Malik, D.S. and Rashmi Yadav (2010): Influence of Heavy Metals on Abundance of Cyanophyceae Members in Three Spring-fed Lake in Kempty, Dehradun, In: 'Advances in Aquatic Ecology, Vol. III' ed. by V.B. Sakhare, *Daya Publishing House, New Delhi*, pp. 107-111.

Bond, H. B. (1979): Nutrient Concentrations Patterns in a Stream Draining a Montane Ecosystem in Utah. *Ecology*. 60(6): 1184-1196.

Cameron, E. M. (1996): Hydrogeo-chemistry of the Fraser River British Columbia: Seasonal Variation in Major and Minor Components. *J. Hydrol.* 182(1-4): 209-255.

Chopra, A. K. and Patrick, N. J. (1994): Effect of Domestic Sewage on Self-purification of Ganga Water at Rishikesh. *A. Bio. Science.* 13(11): 75-82.

Edmondson, W.T. (1959): Fresh Water Biology - Rotifera, 2nd edition, *Wiley & Sons, New York*, pp. 420-484.

Hynes, H.B.N. (1970). The Ecology of Running Waters. *Liverpool University Press, Liverpool, 4th Impression*: 1-555.

Jenkins, A., Sloan W.T. & Cosby, B.J. (1995) Stream Chemistry is the Middle Hills and High Mountain of the Himalaya, Nepal. *Journal of Hydrology.* Vol. 166, No. 1-4: 61-79.

Khanna, D.R. and Singh. R.K. (2000). Seasonal Fluctuations in the Plankton of Suswa River at Raiwala Dehradun. *Env. Conservations J.* 1(2 & 3): 89-92.

Malik, D. S. and Bharti, P. K. (2005b): Fluctuation in Planktonic Population of Sahastradhara Hill-Stream at Dehradun (Uttaranchal), *Aquacult.* 6 (2): 191-198.

Malik, D. S. and Bharti, P. K. (2005c): Primary Production Efficiency of Sahstradhara Hill-stream, Dehradun, *Env. Cons. J.* 6 (3): 117-121.

Malik, D. S. and Bharti, P. K. (2009): Ecology of Sahastradhara Hill-stream at Dehradun (Uttaranchal), In: 'Advances in Aquatic Ecology, Vol. I' ed. by V.B. Sakhare, *Daya Publishing House, New Delhi,* pp. 1-11.

Malik, D. S. and Bharti, P. K., Negi, K.S. and Rashmi Yadav (2009): Distribution of Metals in Water of an Artificial Lake at Mussoorie, Uttarakhand, In: 'Aquatic Biology and Aquaculture' edited by V.B. Sakhare, Ambajoagi, MS, *Manglam Publication, New Delhi,* pp. 77-95.

Malik, D. S. and Bharti, Pawan K. (2005a): Nutrient Dynamics in Rhithron Zone of Shivalik Himalayan Stream Sahastradhara, Dehradun (Uttaranchal), *Env. Cons. J.* 6 (2): 63-68.

Miller, C. V.; Denis, J. M.; Ator, S. W. and Brakebill, J. W. (1997): Nutrients in Stream during Baseflow in Selected Environmental Settings of the Potomac River Basin. *J. American Wat. Resources Association.* 33(6): 1155-1171.

Odum, E. P. (1971): Fundamentals of Ecology. New York. W. B. *Saunders and Co.* pp. 1-344.

Psenner, R. (1989). Chemistry of High Mountain Lakes in Siliceous Catchments of Central Alps. *Aquatic Sci.* 51: 108-128.

Rundle, S.D., Jenkins, A. and Ormerod, S.J., (1993) Macroinvertebrate Communities in Streams in the Himalyas, Nepal. *Freshwater Biol.* 30: 169-180.

Santhanam, R.; Velayntham, p. and Jegatheesan, G; (1989) A Manual of Freshwater Ecology. *Daya Publishing House Delhi,* 3-17, 53-92.

Schwoerbel, J. (1991) "Handbook of Limnology", *Ellis Horwood Limited, Chichester, England:* pp. 95-114.

Shrama, R.C. (1986). Effect of Physico-chemical Factors on Benthic Fauna of Bhagirathi River Garhwal Himalaya. *Indian. J.Ecol.* 13(1): 133-137.

Subramanian, V. (1979) Chemical and Suspended Sediment Characteristics of River of India. *J. Hydrol,* 44: 37-55.

Trivedi, R. K. and Goel, P. K. (1984): Chemical and Biological Methods for Water Pollution Studies. Karad. Environmental Publication, pp. 1-25.

William, M.W., Brown, A. & Melack, J.M. (1993). Geochemical and Hydrologic Controls on the Composition of Surface Water in the High Elevation Basin, *Sierra Navada. Limnol. Oceanogr,* 38: 775-797.

Xue, H.B. and Schooner, J.L. (1994) Acid Deposition and Lake Chemistry in Southwest China. *Wat. Air, Soil Pollut.* 75: 61-78.

Analytical Techniques in Chemical and Biological Sciences
Edited by: Dr. Deep Mala and Dr. Pawan Kumar 'Bharti'
ISBN: 978-93-86841-59-9
Edition: 2018
Published by: Discovery Publishing House Pvt. Ltd., New Delhi (India)

Page: 167-176

13 Micronuclei and Associated Instabilities: Origin, Mechanism, Fate and Relevance in Geno-toxicological Studies

Dr. Shraddha Dwivedi[1]

INTRODUCTION

Micronuclei (MN) or Howell-Justin body is an additional nuclei in a cell. It was first observed and identified in nineteenth century by hematologist William Howell and Justin Jolly in erythrocytes, and they considered it as a nuclear remnant (Sears and Udden, 2012). Later in a mid-twentieth century Dawson and Bury (1961) demonstrating the association between formation of MN with the pathological state like deficiency of folic acid and vitamin B. Since then among a number of toxicological testing parameters *viz.*, Chromosomal aberration test and Single cell gel electrophoresis, micronuclei assay came out as one of the most acceptable indicators, because of its sensitivity, simplicity, and reliability (Anbumani and Mohankumar, 2012; Dwivedi *et al.*, 2015; Liu *et al.*, 2001; Mussali-Galante *et al.*, 2013; Sangle *et al.*, 2016; Serpeloni *et al.*, 2010; Yadav and Trivedi, 2009). Apart from MN other cellular instabilities like nuclear bud, disintegrated nucleus; microcyte (MC), erythrocytes less than one-third of the normal erythrocytes and nucleoplasmic bridges (NpBs), bridge like formation between two cells are also commonly observed in cytogenetically unstable cells (Anbumani and Mohankumar, 2015; Brassesco *et al.*, 2009; Fenech *et al.*, 2011). These instabilities were closely associated with the mechanism, by which MN forms. Thus their quantification is equally important as it can provide additional information related to genomic instabilities (Fenech *et al.*, 2011; Lindberg *et al.*, 2007; Stello *et al.*, 2003).

The increasing interest and importance of the micronucleus assay from last few decades in the field of toxicological studies was well demonstrated by Bolt *et al.*,(2011), when he entered the terms "micronucleus or micronuclei" into ISI Web of Knowledge. For the term "micronucleus or micronuclei" he found less than 2000 hits in 1992, the numbers were increased in 2004 over 6,000 hits and more than 13,000 in 2010, which is remarkably high compared to other toxicity tests. Thus it's completely worthwhile to review the mechanistic and practical aspects of micronuclei and other cellular instabilities at a glance.

[1] M.Sc. (Zoology), Ph.D, Ad-hoc Faculty, Department of Zoology, Isabella Thoburn Girls Degree College Lucknow-226007, UP, India

Sources and Origin of MN and Associated Instabilities

Exposure of several exogenous (Ionizing radiation and Chemical mutagens) and endogenous (Reactive Oxygen Species) genotoxic agents results in either direct or indirect DNA damages (Single strand break or Double strand breaks). The action of genotoxic chemicals has been found dependent on different stages of cell cycle (Fenech *et al.*, 2016). On the basis of their actions these chemicals are called S-independent (Damage repaired/mis-repaired independently of DNA synthesis) or S-dependent (Damage is not repaired before the DNA synthesis leading to mis-replications/replication stress that may result in the formation of chromatid-type or chromosome-type aberrations).

Unrepaired DNA damage that causes replication stress, will ultimately results in acentric or whole chromosome fragments during mitosis. These chromatin fragments (Acentric or whole chromosomes) are left behind in the cell cytoplasm during anaphase and are not included in the daughter nuclei at telophase. These left out fragments after encapsulation by nuclear membrane are considered as micronuclei (Kirsch-Volders *et al.*, 2011). Lindberg *et al.*, (2007) also demonstrated that nuclear fragment, which are much smaller in size; left in cell cytoplasm during telophase is either encapsulated by nuclear membrane to form MN directly or encapsulated later in S phase by forming nuclear buds. Sometimes DNA breaks leads into dicentric chromosomes which form NpBs, cells with unbroken anaphase bridges, which eventually breaks and initiate recurring breakage-fusion-bridge cycles (Fenech *et al.*, 2016). Breakage-fusion-bridge (BFB) cycles results in gene amplification and elimination of amplified DNA as nuclear buds which is either undergo apoptosis directly or by forming MN (Fenech *et al.*, 2011; Mansilla *et al.*, 2009). Micronuclei can also be eliminated by the cell, giving rise to a microcyte which further undergoes apoptosis (Souza and Fontanetti, 2006). Overall mechanism involved is represented in Figure 13.1. Thus, amplified genetic material is either expelled from the cell by formation of cellular instabilities or by the formation of MN to maintain the integrity of cell.

Table 13.1: Different Type of Chemicals Produces Chromosomal Aberrations at Different Cell Cycle Stages on Treatment.

Compounds producing gaps and deletions in late S and G2 cells
• Inhibitors of DNA synthesis (e.g. Hydroxyurea, Methotrexate)
• Inhibitors of DNA repair (e.g. Cytosine arabinoside, 3-aminobenzamide)
Compounds producing chromatid-type aberrations in late S and G2 cells
• May also induce chromosome aberrations in G0 or G1
• Induce DNA strand breaks as well as base lesions directly
• Radiomimetic (e.g. Bleomycin) or oxidative radical generators (e.g. H_2O_2)
Compounds producing chromatid-type aberrations, but only in cells treated in G1 and early S phase

• Most are known to react with DNA or its precursors directly • Cause excision-repairable DNA lesions • If unrepaired may cause replication stress leading to gaps in daughter strand • Most compounds that cause chromatid/chromosome aberrations are in this class • Compounds that cause all types of chromatid aberrations at all stages of the cell cycle • Probably many compounds because of indirect effects on DNA metabolism

*The table is taken from Fenech *et al.*, (2016)

Table 13.2: Molecular Events Associated with Expression of and Associated Instabilities

Cellular instabilities	Molecular events associated with biomarker
MN	Lagging acentric chromosome or chromatid fragment at anaphase. Misrepair of DNA breaks Unrepaired DNA breaks Lagging whole chromosomes at anaphase Hypomethylation of repeat sequences in centromeric and pericentromeric DNA Defects in kinetochore proteins or assembly Dysfunctional spindle Defective anaphase checkpoint genes nresolved replication stress intermediates
NpBs	Dicentric or multicentric chromosomes with centromeres pulled to opposite poles of the cell at anaphase Misrepair of DNA breaks Telomere end fusions due to excessively short telomeres dysfunctional telomeres or lack of telomeres Defective separation of sister chromatids at anaphase due to failure of decatenation Unresolved replication stress intermediates
Nuclear Bud	Active process of elimination of nuclear material from nucleus Elimination of DNA repair DNA-protein complexes Elimination of excess chromosomes—may occur in polyploid cells to facilitate aneuploidy rescue.

*The table is taken from Fenech *et al.*, (2011)

Fate of Micronucleated Cells

The post mitotic fate of micronucleated cell after their formation is still unclear. One possibility is that MN re-incorporates again into the main nucleus during repeated cell cycles (Leach and Jackson-Cook 2004; for review Mateuca *et. al.*, 2006; Decordier *et. al.*, 2002; for review Terradas *et.al.*, 2010). Secondly micronucleated cell can retain MN in the cytoplasm as an extra cellular entity which will lead to production of many more micronucleated cell by

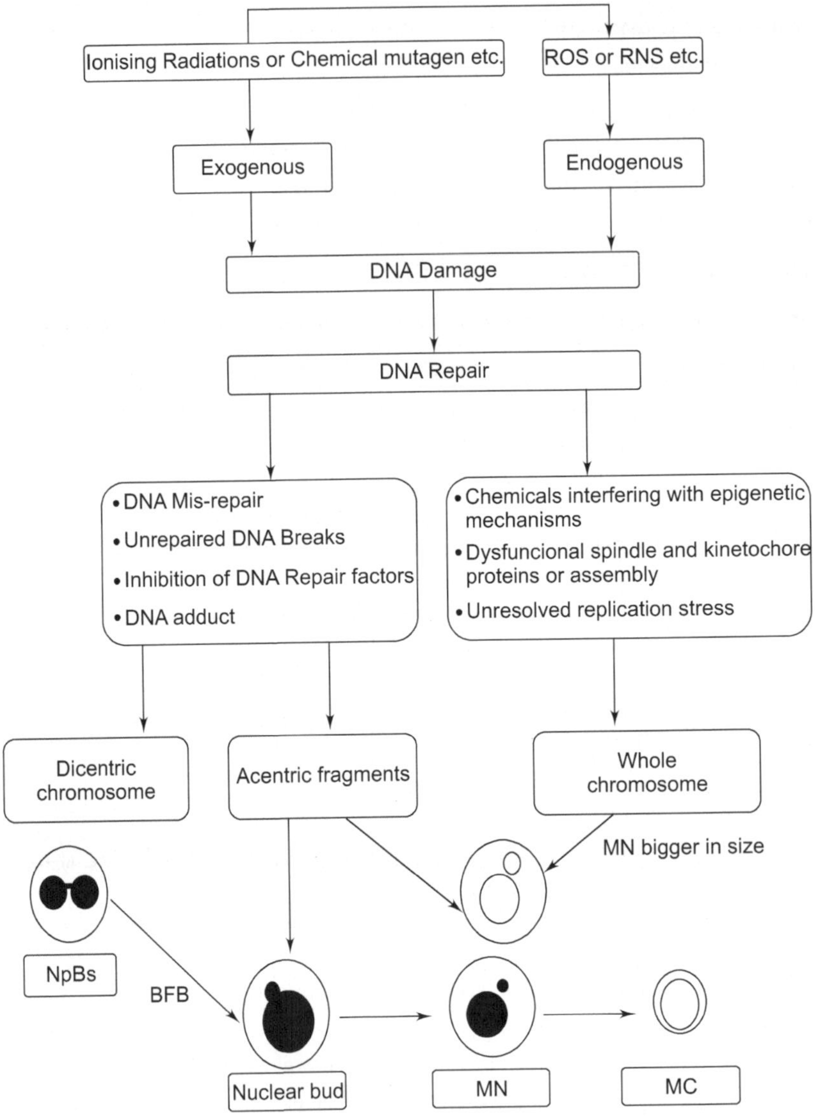

Fig. 13.1: Mechanism involved in formation of MN and associated instabilities. BFB; Breakage-fusion-bridge, MN; micronuclei, NpBs; nucleoplasmic bridges, MC; microcyte.

every rounds of cell cycle. The presence of micronuclei was also found to be frequently associated with apoptosis. Utani *et. al.*, (2010) reported that frequency of apoptotic cell death is more frequent in micronucleated cell (16/5 = 30%) in comparison to normal cells (38/321 = 12%) and even the frequency is more (3/5 = 60%) in cells having both MN and nuclear bud. Decordier *et. al.*, (2005) in his study suggest that caspase-3, besides its function as an effecter caspase in the apoptotic pathway, it also involved in the formation of MN.

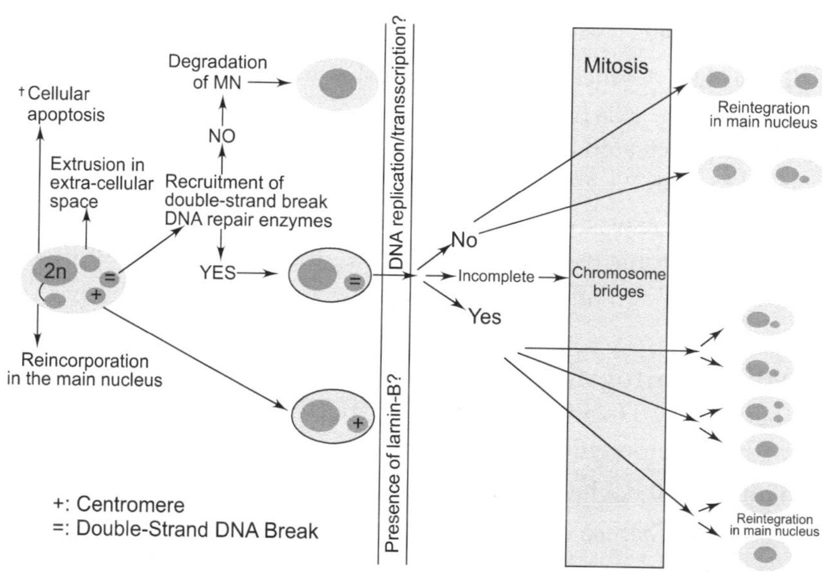

Fig. 13.2. Overview of the possible post-mitotic fates of MN (The figure is taken from Kirsch-Volders et al. (2011).

Details Protocols for Micronucleus Assay and Its Evaluation

MN in Human Lymphocytes:

Lymphocyte Isolation

- Lymphocytes were isolated using Ficoll-Paque density gradients.
- Blood was diluted 1:1 with phosphate buffered saline (PBS).
- PBS diluted blood was layered onto Ficoll-Paque with ratio of 4:3 (Blood + PBS: Ficoll).
- The blood was centrifugated at 1800 rpm for 35 min at room temperature.
- The lymphocyte layer (buffy coat) was removed and washed twice in PBS at 1200 rpm for 10 min each, following the same wash with media RPMI 1640.

Culture Conditions

- Lymphocytes were cultured at 37° in a humidified, 5% CO_2 incubator in 15 ml conical polystyrene centrifuge tubes. Typically, each culture consisted of an initial density of 1×10^6 cells in 2 ml of culture medium.
- Culture medium consisted of RPMI 1640 supplemented with 10% fetal bovine serum 2 mM L-glutamine, 100 units/ml penicillin, 100 ug/ml streptomycin and 1.5% phytohemagglutinin.

Micronucleus Assay

- **Time: 44 h, Cytochalasin B** was added to the cultures. Cytochalasin B prevents the cells from completing cytokinesis resulting in the formation of multinucleated cells. Final concentration of cytochalasin B in the cell cultures was 3 μg/ml.
- **Time: 72 h**, 2 washing steps (RPMI + 2% Fetal Calf Serum (FCS)) and a mild hypotonic treatment (RPMI/H_2O, 4:1), followed by smearing and fixation in Methanol/Acetic acid = 3/1.

Or

Mild centrifugation-mild hypotonic treatment with the cold KCl, followed by 3 fixation steps in Methanol/Acetic acid=3/1, supplemented with formaldehyde at 1st fixation.

Time: 80-90 h, Harvesting, with or without hypotonic treatment.

Staining: Giemsa or fluorescent DNA-specific dyes.

MN from Fish Blood

Collection of Blood from Fish

- Rinsed syringe with heparin solution (75 U/ ml) and left approx. 2 mm gap at top of syringe column.
- Pricked the needle at middle of the ventral side of caudle peduncle reaching up to the vertebral column.
- As blood started flowing in to syringe started pulling the dispenser very gently outwards to collect the blood.

Micronucleus assay

- Made a thin smear on pre-cleaned slide with the help of blood smear slide.
- Air-dried the slides over night in dust & moisture free environment at room temperature.
- Fix the slides by dipping them into absolute methanol for 5-10 min allow the slides for air drying at least for 1 hour.
- Stained the slides with May-Grunnwald's Solution 1 for 2-3 min and May-Grunnwald's Solution 2 for 3-6 min. Followed by washing with double distilled water and allow it to dry.
- Stained the slides in 6-10 % Giemsa stain in phosphate buffer (working solution) for 30 min.
- Washed the slides with DDW to remove all the Giemsa particles carefully by washing. Allow the slide to air-dry overnight.
- Made the slides permanent with DPX-mount and dried them over hot plate at 60°C overnight.

Scoring Criteria Were as Follows (Yadav and Trivedi, 2009)

1. Cells should have a round or oval appearance with an intact cytoplasm.
2. Nuclei should similarly be round or oval with an intact nuclear membrane.
3. Only cells having undergone one nuclear division should be scored for the presence of micronuclei.
4. Micronuclei should be counted only if they are one third or less the size of the main nuclei.
5. Micronuclei should be stained similar to the main nuclei.
6. Micronuclei should be clearly separated from the main nuclei. Scoring was performed by.

The frequency of MN was established by estimating the number of MN in at least 1000 cells.

The cells or nuclei that are not as micronuclei (Fenech *et al.,* 1999)

1. Degenerated or degenerating cells.
2. Apoptotic cells.
3. Cell that is not well recognized or morphology unclear.
4. Cytoplasm fragmented.
5. Cells that are overlapping cells.
6. Hazy background, full of debris, obscuring the details.
7. Main nuclear morphology distorted or having no distinct nuclear perimeter.

MN as Biomarker

From last 15-20 years micronuclei has been broadly used as a biomarker, as their detection offers a great opportunity to monitor the cytogenotoxic status of individuals or populations exposed to variety of mutagenic and carcinogenic chemicals. Several prior studies demonstrated genotoxicity in association with environmental/job risk. They observed an significant higher frequency of MN in exfoliated buccal cells from people exposed to organic solvents, anti-neoplastic agents, diesel derivatives, polycyclic aromatic hydrocarbons, lead containing paints and solvents, and drinking water contaminated with arsenic (Afshari *et al.,* 1994; Fenech *et al.,* 2004; Migliore *et al.,* 1999, 1996). Furthermore, these biomarkers offer additional endpoints for evaluation of levels or degree of genotoxicity by detection of chromosomal instability and gene amplification via nuclear buds, cytokinesis arrest due to aneuploidy via binucleated cells, and different cell death events (*e.g.,* karyorrhectic and pyknotic cells). MN frequencies can be used to detect some specific diseases like Xeroderma pigmentosum,

Down syndrome (73.3% increased MN from the younger controls and 78.5% increased MN older controls) and Diabetes mellitus (doubled genetic damage than the controls) (Dev *et al.,* 2016). MN detection can also be used to describe beneficial effects against genotoxicity produced herbal plant extracts (Dwivedi *et al.,* 2017). MN is also simple, cheap, minimally invasive, and painless and it is performed through visualization of cells morphology with a microscope after they are collected, fixed, and stained. MN is thus a potential biomarker to screen mutagencity, genotoxicity and bio-monitoring various diseases.

Knowledge Gap

Despite decades have passes since MN assay were introduced, it is reasonable to say that there is gap of knowledge between our understanding and the exact mechanisms that lead to the formation of MN and other cellular instabilities. Still there are number of important questions that need to be answered like (Fenech *et al.,* 2011):

- Can we use MN scoring on routine smears in cancer screening?
- Can MN frequency predict the progression of a pre-neoplastic condition?
- Which of the MN, NpBs and nuclear buds biomarkers is most predictive of cancer and other degenerative diseases and what is the underlying molecular basis.
- Which genetic defects and their interactions are likely to increase the incidence of these DNA damage biomarkers and under which environmental conditions are these genetic effects most evident?
- Which exposure, dietary and lifestyle factors and their combinations substantially affect these biomarkers and what are the molecular mechanisms?
- Is it technically feasible to study the multiple mechanisms leading to MN, NPB and NBUD formation using multiple molecular probes simultaneously?
- Are there specific gene expression patterns that are highly correlated with the formation of MN, NPB and NBUD in cells?

SUMMARY

In this article author have discussed about micronuclei and associated instabilities, their origin and possible fates. Author has given an overview of detailed protocols for human lymphocytes and fish blood. Since MN is a manifestation of day to day exposure to environmental pollutants, infections, nutrition, radiation, foods, life style etc which makes it a potential biomarker for cyto-geno-toxicological studies. This will helpful for policy makers for making policies for waste management.

REFERENCES

Afshari, A.J., McGregor, P.W., Allen, J.W., Fuscoe, J.C., 1994. Centromere Analysis of Micronuclei Induced by 2-aminoanthraquinone in Cultured Mouse Splenocytes Using Both a Gamma-satellite DNA Probe and Anti-kinetochore Antibody. Environ. Mol. Mutagen. 24, 96–102.

Anbumani, S., Mohankumar, M.N., 2015. Cytogenotoxicity Assessment of Monocrotophos and Butachlor at Single and Combined Chronic Exposures in the Fish Catla Catla (Hamilton). Environ. Sci. Pollut. Res. 22, 4964–4976. doi:10.1007/s11356-014-3782-y.

Anbumani, S., Mohankumar, M.N., 2012. Gamma Radiation Induced Micronuclei and Erythrocyte Cellular Abnormalities in the Fish Catla Catla. Aquat. Toxicol. 122–123, 125–32. doi:10.1016/j.aquatox.2012.06.001.

Bolt, H.M., Stewart, J.D., Hengstler, J.G., 2011. A Comprehensive Review About Micronuclei: Mechanisms of Formation and Practical Aspects in Genotoxicity Testing. Arch. Toxicol. 85, 861–862. doi:10.1007/s00204-011-0738-6.

Brassesco, M.S., Valera, E.T., Neder, L., Castro-Gamero, A.M., Arruda, D., Machado, H.R., Sakamoto-Hojo, E.T., Tone, L.G., 2009. Polyploidy in Atypical Grade II Choroid Plexus Papilloma of the Posterior Fossa. Neuropathology 29, 293–8. doi:10.1111/j.1440-1789.2008.00949.x.

Dawson, D.W., Bury, H.P.R., 1961. The Significance of Howell-Jolly Bodies and Giant Metamyelocytes in Marrow Smears. J. Clin. Pathol. 14, 374–380. doi:10.1136/jcp.14.4.374

Decordier, I., Cundari, E., Kirsch-Volders, M., 2005. Influence of Caspase Activity on Micronuclei Detection: A Possible Role for Caspase-3 in Micronucleation. Mutagenesis 20, 173–179. doi:10.1093/mutage/gei025.

Dev, M.S., Grover, S., Batra, J., Talathi, R., Jaiswal, M., Patil, R.S., 2016. Micronucleus as a Non-invasive Biomarker – A\nReview. J. Adv. Med. Pharm. Sci. 6, 1–9. doi:10.9734/JAMPS/2016/24136.

Dwivedi, S., Kumar, M., Trivedi, S.P., 2017. Mitigating Potential of Melissa Officinale Against As^{3+}-induced Cytotoxicity and Transcriptional Alterations of Hsp70 and Hsp27 in fish, Channa Punctatus (Bloch). Environ. Monit. Assess. 189, 306. doi:10.1007/s10661-017-6002-7.

Dwivedi, S., Tiwari, V., Trivedi, S.P., 2015. Arsenite Induced Genotoxic Effect and Its Phytoremediation by Acacia Catechu Leaf Extract in Freshwater Fish, Channa Punctatus (Bloch). Int. J. Fish. Aquat. Stud. 2, 163–165.

Fenech, M., Baghurst, P., Luderer, W., Turner, J., Record, S., Ceppi, M., Bonassi, S., 2004. Low Intake of Calcium, Folate, Nicotinic Acid, Vitamin E, Retinol, Carotene and High Intake of Pantothenic Acid, Biotin and Riboflavin are Significantly Associated with Increased Genome Instability—Results from a Dietary Intake and Micronucleus Index Survey in South Australia. Carcinogenesis 26, 991–999. doi:10.1093/carcin/bgi042

Fenech, M., Holland, N., Chang, W.P., Zeiger, E., Bonassi, S., 1999. The Human Micro Nucleus Project—An International Collaborative Study on the Use of the Micronucleus Technique for Measuring DNA Damage in Humans. Mutat. Res. Mol. Mech. Mutagen. 428, 271–283. doi:10.1016/S1383-5742(99)00053-8

Fenech, M., Kirsch-Volders, M., Natarajan, A.T., Surralles, J., Crott, J.W., Parry, J., Norppa, H., Eastmond, D.A., Tucker, J.D., Thomas, P., 2011. Molecular Mechanisms of Micronucleus, Nucleoplasmic Bridge and Nuclear Bud Formation in Mammalian and Human Cells. Mutagenesis 26, 125–132. doi:10.1093/mutage/geq052.

Fenech, M., Knasmueller, S., Bolognesi, C., Bonassi, S., Holland, N., Migliore, L., Palitti, F., Natarajan, A.T., Kirsch-Volders, M., 2016. Molecular Mechanisms by Which in vivo Exposure to Exogenous Chemical Genotoxic Agents Can Lead to Micronucleus Formation in Lymphocytes in Vivo and Ex Vivo in Humans. Mutat. Res. - Rev. Mutat. Res. 770, 12–25. doi:10.1016/j.mrrev.2016.04.008.

Kirsch-Volders, M., Plas, G., Elhajouji, A., Lukamowicz, M., Gonzalez, L., Vande Loock, K., Decordier, I., 2011. The in vitro MN assay in 2011: Origin and Fate, Biological Significance, Protocols, High Throughput Methodologies and Toxicological Relevance. Arch. Toxicol. 85, 873–899. doi:10.1007/s00204-011-0691-4.

Lindberg, H.K., Wang, X., Järventaus, H., Falck, G.C.-M., Norppa, H., Fenech, M., 2007. Origin of Nuclear Buds and Micronuclei in Normal and Folate-deprived Human Lymphocytes. Mutat. Res. 617, 33–45. doi:10.1016/j.mrfmmm.2006.12.002.

Liu, J., Kadiiska, M.B., Liu, Y., Lu, T., Qu, W., Waalkes, M.P., 2001. Stress-Related Gene Expression in Mice Treated with Inorganic Arsenicals. Toxicol. Sci. 61, 314–320. doi:10. 1093/toxsci/61.2.314.

Mansilla, S., Bataller, M., Portugal, J., 2009. A Nuclear Budding Mechanism in Transiently Arrested Cells Generates Drug-sensitive and Drug-resistant Cells. Biochem. Pharmacol. 78, 123–132. doi:10.1016/j.bcp.2009.03.027

Migliore, L., Bevilacqua, C., Scarpato, R., 1999. Cytogenetic Study and FISH Analysis in Lymphocytes of Systemic Lupus Erythematosus (SLE) and Systemic Sclerosis (SS) Patients. Mutagenesis 14, 227–31.

Migliore, L., Cocchi, L., Scarpato, R., 1996. Detection of the Centromere in Micronuclei by Fluorescence in situ Hybridization: Its Application to the Human Lymphocyte Micronucleus Assay After Treatment with Four Suspected Aneugens. Mutagenesis 11, 285–90.

Mussali-Galante, P., Tovar-Sánchez, E., Valverde, M., Rojas, E., Castillo, D., 2013. Biomarkers of Exposure for Assessing Environmental Metal Pollution: From Molecules to Ecosystems. Rev. Int. Contam. Ambie 29, 117–140.

Sangle, V.A., Bijjaragi, S., Shah, N., Kangane, S., Ghule, H.M., Rani, S.A., 2016. Comparative Study of Frequency of Micronuclei in Normal, Potentially Malignant Diseases and Oral Squamous Cell Carcinoma. J. Nat. Sci. Biol. Med. 7, 33–8. doi:10.4103/0976-9668.175049

Sears, D.A., Udden, M.M., 2012. Howell-Jolly Bodies: A Brief Historical Review. Am. J. Med. Sci. 343, 407–409. doi:10.1097/MAJ.0b013e31823020d1

Serpeloni, J.M., Grotto, D., Mercadante, A.Z., de Lourdes Pires Bianchi, M., Antunes, L.M.G., 2010. Lutein Improves Antioxidant Defense in vivo and Protects Against DNA Damage and Chromosome Instability Induced by Cisplatin. Arch. Toxicol. 84, 811–822. doi:10.1007/ s00204-010-0576-y.

Souza, da S., Fontanetti, C.S., 2006. Micronucleus Test and Observation of Nuclear Alterations in Erythrocytes of Nile Tilapia Exposed to Waters Affected by Refinery Effluent. Mutat. Res. Toxicol. Environ. Mutagen. 605, 87–93. doi:10.1016/j.mrgentox.2006.02.010.

Stello, S.L., Latimer, K.S., Bain, P.J., Krimer, P.M., 2003. The Significance of Echinocytosis in Blood Smears. Athens, GA 30602- 7388.

Utani, K.I., Kohno, Y., Okamoto, A., Shimizu, N., 2010. Emergence of Micronuclei and their Effects on the Fate of Cells Under Replication Stress. PLoS One 5. doi:10.1371/journal. pone.0010089.

Yadav, K.K., Trivedi, S.P., 2009. Sublethal Exposure of Heavy Metals Induces Micronuclei in Fish, Channa Punctata. Chemosphere 77, 1495–1500. doi:10.1016/j.chemosphere. 2009.10.022.

Index